Colorado

FODOR'S TRAVEL PUBLICATIONS, INC.
New York & London

ISBN 0-679-01616-3

Fodor's Colorado

Editor: Andrew E. Beresky
Area Editors: Curtis W. Casewit, Diana Hunt
Contributing Editors: Kereen M. Allord, Don Long
Maps: Jon Bauch Designs, Pictograph
Drawings: David Canright, Sandra Lang
Cover Photograph: Nicholas DeVore III/Photographers Aspen

Cover Design: Vignelli Associates

MANUFACTURED IN THE UNITED STATES OF AMERICA
10 9 8 7 6 5 4 3 2 1

CONTENTS

CONTENTS

FOREWORD

Whether you're looking for world-class skiing, magnificent wilderness areas in which to hike and camp, the chance to rub elbows with the "beautiful people" at resorts like Aspen and Beaver Creek, or simply mountain lakes to relax beside, Colorado is the place to be. *Fodor's Colorado* is designed to help you plan your own trip to this majestic state, based on your time, your interests, your budget—your idea of what this trip should be.

While every care has been taken to assure the accuracy of the information in this guide, the passage of time will always bring change, and consequently the publisher cannot accept responsibility for errors that may occur.

All prices and opening times quoted in this guide are based on information available to us at press time. Hours and admission fees may change, however, and the prudent traveler will avoid inconvenience by calling ahead.

Fodor's wants to hear about your travel experiences, both pleasant and unpleasant. When a hotel or restaurant fails to live up to its billing, let us know and we will investigate the complaint and revise our entries where the facts warrant it.

Send your letters to the editors at Fodor's Travel Publications, 201 E. 50th Street, New York, NY 10022, or 30–32 Bedford Square, London WC1B 3SG, England.

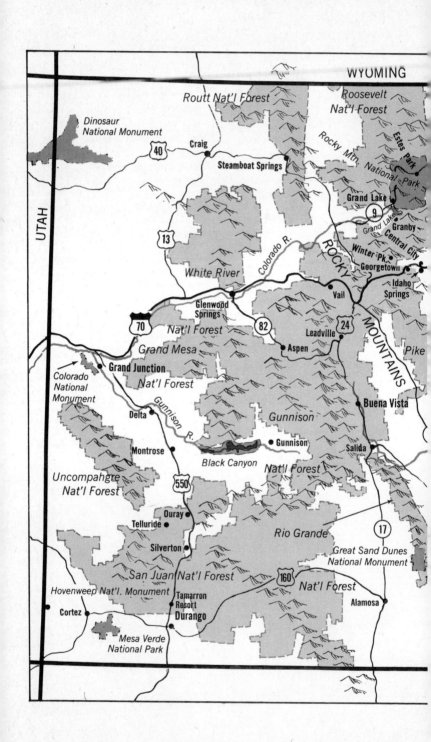

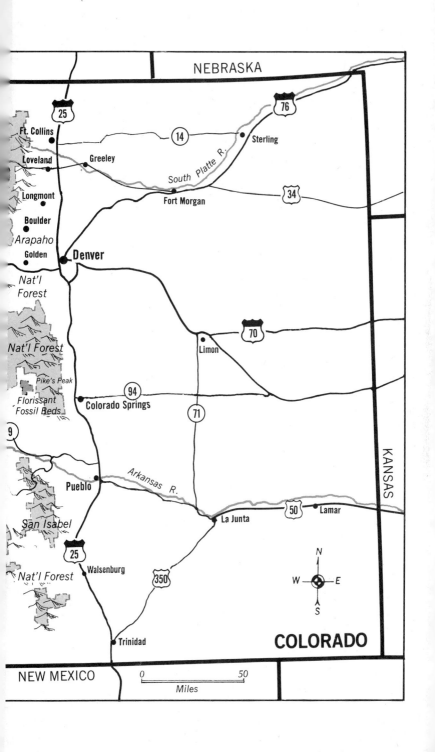

FACTS AT YOUR FINGERTIPS

FACTS AT YOUR FINGERTIPS

FACTS AND FIGURES. Colorado got its name from the Spanish for "red" or "muddy," referring to the Colorado River. Colorado's nicknames are *Centennial State* (because it entered the Union on August 1, 1876) and *Silver State.* The state flower is the Rocky Mountain columbine; state tree: the Colorado blue spruce; state bird: the lark bunting; state animal: the Rocky Mountain bighorn sheep; the state motto: *Nil sine numine* ("Nothing without Providence"); the state song: "Where the Columbines Grow." Its area is 104,247 square miles; altitude, 3,350–14,431 feet. The state population at last estimate was over 3,000,000. Denver, Colorado's largest city, is the state capital.

The Continental Divide and the Rocky Mountains cut a north-south path down the center of the state, forming the headwaters of six great rivers and dividing the state into the flat eastern region of the Great Plains and the high plateaus and deep gorges of the west. The mountainous western area contains some of the highest mountain peaks in the country as well as some of America's finest resort areas. Mining remains an important industry. The state is a leading source of molybdenum, oil shale, and uranium.

VISITOR INFORMATION. The official *Visitor's Guide,* which includes a map, listings of attractions, an events calendar, and shopping and dining information, is available from the *Denver Metro Convention & Visitor's Bureau,* 225 W. Colfax, Denver 80202; 303–892–1112. Check also at the many chambers of commerce throughout the state.

TIPS FOR BRITISH VISITORS. Passports. You will need a valid passport and a U.S. Visa (which can only be put in a passport of the ten-year kind). You can obtain the visa either through your travel agent or directly from the *United States Embassy,* Visa and Immigration Department, 5 Upper Grosvenor St., London W1A 2JB (01–499–3443). Note that you can only apply for your visa by post; the American Embassy no longer accepts applications made in person.

No vaccinations are required for entry into the U.S.

Customs. If you are 21 or over, you can take into the U.S.: 200 cigarettes, or 50 cigars, or 3 lbs. of tobacco; 1 U.S. quart of alcohol; duty-free gifts to a value of $100. Be careful not to try to take in meat or meat products, seeds, plants, fruits, etc. And avoid narcotics like the plague. Keep all matches in a closed container if carrying them in your luggage.

Returning from Colorado you may bring home: (1) 200 cigarettes or 100 cigars or 250g of tobacco; (2) two liters of still table wine and one liter of alcohol over 22° proof (most spirits) or two liters of alcohol under 22° proof (fortified or sparkling wine) or an additional two liters of still table wine; (3) 50g of perfume and ¼ liter of toilet water; (4) other articles up to a value of £32.

Insurance. We heartily recommend that you insure yourself to cover health and motoring mishaps, with *Europe Assistance,* 252 High St., Croydon CRO 1NF (tel. 01–680 1234). Their excellent service is all the more

valuable when you consider the possible costs of health care in the U.S.
It is wise to take out insurance to cover loss of luggage (though check that
this isn't already covered in any existing homeowner's policies you may
have) and trip cancellation. The *Association of British Insurers,* Aldermary
House, Queen St., London EC4N 1TT (01 248–4477), will give compre-
hensive advice on all aspects of vacation insurance.

Airfares. We suggest that you explore the current scene for budget flight
possibilities. Unfortunately there is no longer standby service on any of
the major airlines; but do check their Apex and other fares which may
be a considerable saving over the full price. Quite frankly, only business
travelers who don't have to watch the price of their tickets fly full-price
these days—and find themselves sitting right beside an Apex passenger!
Check out the small ads in Sunday newspapers or magazines such as *Time
Out* as there are often cheap, round-trip, seat-only fares available. Start
looking well in advance and be prepared to be flexible about the day and
time you travel—you'll be extremely lucky to get a flight on the exact day
and time you want to go. But your perseverance may be rewarded with
an affordable ticket. As we went to press round-trip fares to Denver cost
around £300 compared to between £458 and £565 on an Apex ticket.

Tour Operators. *Albany Travel* (Manchester) Ltd., 190 Deansgate,
Manchester M3 3WD (061–833–020), offers hotel vacations in Denver
ranging in price from £541 to £783 depending on grade of hotel and season. They also offer an eight-day sightseeing tour of the Colorado Rockies
starting from £591, and taking in the Colorado Springs, Durango, Grand
Junction, and the Rio Grande Railway.

American Airplan, Marlborough House, Churchfield Rd., Walton-on-
Thames, Surrey KT12 2TJ (0932–246166).

Jetways, 93 Newman St., London W1P 3LE (01–637–5444), is worth
trying for independent travel. A roundtrip flight to Denver will cost about
£390 and you can hire a motor home also through this company. A stan-
dard-sized motorhome, which sleeps four to five people, costs between £48
to £76 per day depending on season.

Kuoni Travel Ltd., Kuoni House, Dorking, Surrey RH5 4AZ
(0306–885044).

Trek America Ltd., Trek House, The Bullring, Deddington, Oxford,
Oxon 0X5 4TT (0869–38777).

WHEN TO GO. From **November to early April** there is some of the
best skiing in the country at some thirty Colorado areas and resorts. As
the weather warms up, many of the ski resorts become **summer** playgrounds, with summer sports readily available. From **spring to fall,** backpackers, campers, drivers, dude ranch fanciers, and water-sport enthusiasts can enjoy the magnificent wilderness: mountains, woods, lakes,
streams. Most hunting seasons open in the fall.

PACKING. Dress is fairly casual, although Colorado has its share of
elegant hotels and restaurants, particularly in Denver and the resort areas.

Be sure to check what temperatures will be like along the route. Traveling in mountains can mean cool evenings, even in summer—and so can
traveling through the desert. Certainly, in winter warm ski clothes are in
order, but skiing in March, April, and May is often more comfortable in
a light windbreaker, short sleeves, even shorts for some hardy folks. In
summer bring a sweater, warm jacket, hat, and gloves to put over your

light shirts and shorts; rain gear and comfortable walking or hiking shoes are important, too, as are bathing suits.

Don't forget to carry sun protection (sunglasses, sunscreens, hats), summer and winter. Colorado's ultraviolet rays can wreak havoc with most skin types, especially if the rays are being reflected off a river or a mountainside of snow.

CLIMATE. At work or at play, the high, dry, sunny climate of Colorado is most certainly one of the Top-of-the-Nation State's outstanding assests. The climate allows a choice of activity in any season. While summer temperatures are quite high on Colorado's eastern prairies, the front-range cities are cooler, and the weather seldom reaches the sweltering discomfort of America's more humid regions. Colorado's dry air seems lighter, and one can stroll, jog, or play tennis in relative comfort even as the mercury hits the 80s. Rains can be expected on some summer afternoons. Throughout the state, evenings are cool.

Winters are as moderate as summers. The average January temperature is in the 30s and the occasional snows melt in a day or two in the cities. Cold is tolerated easily in the dry air; in fact, many tennis resorts and outdoor swimming pools remain open all year. Unseasonably warm and sunny winter days are always a pleasant surprise. Still, snows—light or heavy—are unpredictable. They may come well before Thanksgiving or not until Christmas. Plan your late fall or spring visits as though snowfalls could be a part of it.

Month	Temperature Chart (F) Max.	Min.	Avg.	Average Daily Average Sunshiny Days	Average Precipitation (in inches)	Average Humidity 11:30 A.M. (percent)
January	42.5	17.6	30.7	25	.47	.44
February	44.7	21	32.8	21	.85	.40
March	51.3	27.2	39.3	24	1.15	.35
April	60	35.6	47.7	23	1.61	.32
May	68.9	44.5	56.7	25	1.76	.30
June	80.5	53.5	66.8	26	1.46	.26
July	85.7	59.5	72.7	27	1.90	.27
August	84.3	58.3	71.3	26	1.77	.29
September	77	49.3	62.9	25	1.29	.29
October	64.6	38.4	51.5	26	1.12	.31
November	52.6	27.8	40.3	23	.76	.35
December	44.5	20.5	32.5	25	.78	.42
Yearly Averages and Totals	63.1	37.8	50.4	296	14.92	.33

ALTITUDE. Be sure to ease into Colorado's higher elevations. There is no doubt that a sudden stay at 7,000 to 13,000 feet above sea level will have an effect on the flatlander. At first you may tire a little and perhaps even feel light-headed. Your skin may become dry and require supplementary moisture. And if you cook in the Colorado mountains, you'll notice that the 3-minute soft-boiled egg may take 4 to 5 minutes and that foods usually requiring 15 minutes' cooking need 20 or more.

In the sports world it is said that it takes one full day to get accustomed to every 1,000 feet of altitude if you arrive from sea level. Certainly you should not engage in strenuous exercise on your first day here. Families might want to restrict their exertion during the first few days.

The same caveat applies to skiers, despite all the temptations of the high country: Take a day to get used to the high, thin air.

Remember, too, that the air in the mountains is pure—no dust or other airborne matter is there to filter the sun. On a bright day, unprotected skin and lips can blister quickly. Bring sunscreen; sunglasses are also helpful.

WHAT WILL IT COST? This is obviously a crucial question and one of the most difficult. A couple can travel comfortably in this section of the U.S. for about $115 a day (not counting gasoline or other transportation costs), as you can see in the table below.

Typical Expenses for Two People

Room at *moderate* hotel or motel	$45
Breakfast, including tip	8
Lunch at *inexpensive* restaurant, including tip	12
Dinner at *moderate* restaurant, including tip	33
Sightseeing bus tour	16
An evening drink	7
Admission to museum or historic site	7
	$128

In some areas you can cut expenses by traveling in the off-season, when hotel rates are usually lower. The budget-minded traveler can find bargain accommodations at tourist homes or family-style YMCA's and YWCA's. Some state and federal parks also provide inexpensive lodging. And in this area some colleges offer dormitory accommodations to tourists during the summer vacations at single-room rates of $5–$25 per night with meals from $1–$5. A directory of about 500 such bargains all over the world is the *Travel and Accommodations Guide* available from Campus Travel Service, 1303 E. Balboa Blvd., Newport Beach, CA 92661.

Another way to cut down on the cost of your trip is to look for out-of-the-way resorts. Travelers are frequently rewarded by discovering very attractive areas that haven't yet begun to draw quantities of people.

If you are budgeting your trip, don't forget to set aside a realistic amount for the possible rental of sports equipment (perhaps a boat, canoe, or skis), entrance fees to amusement and historical sites, etc.

After lodging, your next biggest expense will be food, and here you can make very substantial economies if you are willing to get along with only one meal a day (or less) in a restaurant. Plan to eat simply and to picnic. It will save you time and money, and it will help you enjoy your trip more. Sooner or later, however, you will wind up eating in a restaurant, and restaurants range from the elegant Denver establishments to simple, hearty cafeterias.

HINTS TO THE MOTORIST. The speed limit on Colorado's highways is 55 or 65 miles per hour unless marked otherwise. In most cities the limit is 25, although this varies. Turns are permitted on a red light after full-stops, unless a sign prohibits them. Children under four and weighing less than 40 pounds must, by law, be strapped into an approved child-safety seat.

A tightly closed automobile can be a hazard at high altitudes. The lack of oxygen causes vehicles to emit more carbon monoxide than at sea level, yet the human body can tolerate much less carbon monoxide at high altitudes just because there is less oxygen than at sea level. An air vent should be kept slightly open at all times. If you get a headache or become drowsy, open the windows and breathe fresh air for several minutes. If your automobile's carburetor is set for sea level, expect the car to be sluggish climbing the hills.

You may encounter signs reading "Four-wheel drive vehicles only beyond this point." In this wild, rugged country, you follow routes, not roads, through shifting sand and up trickling stream beds that can turn into raging torrents during a sudden storm. The wheels of even four-wheel drive vehicles can sink hopelessly into the sand if they don't move along briskly, and you may have to climb a 27-degree face of sheer rock. This is an area where, off the well-traveled, well-kept main roads, the motorist can have virtually any driving experience he or she cares to meet.

DESERT DRIVING

You will encounter long stretches of desert driving in the southern portions of Colorado. Better cars, better roads, and more service facilities make desert driving less hazardous than it once was. A principal point to check before crossing the hot desert is your tires. Put them at normal driving pressure or slightly below. Heat builds pressure. If your car seems to be bouncing too readily, stop to let your tires cool. If you have a good radiator, don't worry about extra water, but keep an eye on the water gauge. Be alert for sudden sandstorms and rainstorms. If you have a car radio, keep it tuned to local stations for information about unusual road conditions. In spite of its dryness, the desert, in a flash flood, can become a death trap. In sandstorms, pull off the road and wait it out.

MOUNTAIN DRIVING

Unless you venture onto more rugged mountain roads, you should have little trouble with mountain driving. Today's mountain highways are engineered for the ordinary driver. They are of normal width, well graded, and safe. Be especially wary of exceeding the speed limits posted for curves. Keep to the right. If your normal driving is at low altitudes, have a garage mechanic check your carburetor. It may need adjusting for mountain driving. Use your motor for downhill runs, putting it into second or low gear to save your brakes. If your car stalls and your temperature gauge is high, it could mean a vapor lock. Cover the fuel pump with a damp cloth for a few minutes.

WINTER DRIVING

In winter, control is the key. If you find yourself driving on ice, don't brake or turn suddenly; make smooth, careful changes. In a snowstorm, use the dim setting of your car's lights; brights intensify the falling flakes and obscure your vision. Chains or snow tires are occasionally required during bad storms on mountain highways. Pack a shovel, blankets, and a flashlight for emergencies.

PULLING A TRAILER

If you plan to pull a trailer (boat or house) on your holiday trip, and have never done so before, don't just hook up and set out. You need a whole new set of driving skills—starting, stopping, cornering, passing, *being* passed, and, most tricky of all, backing up. Try to practice in an open field or empty parking lot, but if this is not possible, take your maiden trip in light traffic. A few useful hints: In starting and stopping, do everything a little more slowly and gradually than is normal; in cornering, swing wider than usual, remembering the trailer won't follow exactly the rear wheels of the towing car. Too sharp a right turn will put your trailer wheels on the curb. In passing, remember you're longer than usual. Allow more safe distance ahead to pull back into the right lane. A slight bit of extra steering will help if you're *being* passed by a large truck or bus. In this situation, the trailer is inclined to sway from air currents. Don't worsen it by slowing down. It's better to speed up slightly. For backing up, the basic technique is to turn the steering wheel opposite to the way you would want the car to go if you were driving it alone. From there on, it's practice, practice, practice. Most states have special safety regulations for trailers, and these change frequently. If you plan to operate your trailer in several states, check with your motor club, the police, or the state motor vehicle department about the rules. Also talk it over with the dealer from whom you buy or lease your trailer. Generally, speed limits for cars hauling trailers are lower, parking of trailers (and automobiles) is prohibited on expressways, and tunnels bar trailers equipped with cooking units that use propane gas.

ACCOMMODATIONS. Hotel and motel chains. In addition to the hundreds of excellent independent motels and hotels throughout Colorado, there are also many that belong to national or regional chains. A major advantage of the chains, to many travelers, is the ease of making reservations en route, or at one fell swoop in advance. If you are a guest at a member hotel or motel, the management will be delighted to secure you a sure booking at one of its affiliated hotels for the coming evening at no cost to you. Chains also usually have toll-free WATS (800) lines to assist you in making reservations on your own. This, of course, saves you time, worry, and money. Check a telephone directory or call 800–555–1212 for the toll-free number of the chains that interest you.

The main national motel chains are *Holiday Inn, Howard Johnson, Quality Inns, Ramada Inns, Sheraton Motor Inns,* and *TraveLodge.* Prices vary widely by region, location, and season. *Hilton* and *Marriott* are among the most expensive of these nonbudget chains.

Alongside the style that these places represent, however, are other less luxurious and less costly chains. Some that operate in Colorado are: *Budget Host Inns,* Box 10656, Fort Worth, TX 76114, call 817–626–7064; *Days Inns of America,* 2751 Buford Hwy., NE, Atlanta, GA 30324, call 800–325–2525; *Econo Lodge,* Box 240066, Charlotte, NC 28224, call 800–446–6900; *Friendship Inns International,* 739 S. Fourth West, Salt Lake City, Utah 84101, call 800–453–4511; *Imperial 400 Inc.,* 1000 Wilson Blvd., Suite 820, Arlington, VA 22209, call 800–368–4400; *LaQuinta Motor Inns,* Box 32064, San Antonio, TX 78216, call 800–531–5900; *Motel*

6 Inc., 51 Hitchcock Way, Santa Barbara, CA 93105, call 805–682–6666; *Regal 8 Inns,* Box 1268, Mount Vernon, IL 62864, call 800–851–8888; *Super 8 Motels,* Box 4090, Aberdeen, SD 57401, call 800–282–0711.

HOTEL AND MOTEL CATEGORIES

Hotels and motels are divided into categories arranged primarily by price, but also taking into consideration the degree of comfort, the amount of service, and the atmosphere that will surround you in the establishment of your choice. Categories are *Deluxe, Expensive, Moderate,* and *Inexpensive.* Our ratings are flexible and subject to change. We should also point out that many fine hotels and motels have to be omitted for lack of space.

Although the names of the various hotel and motel categories are standard, the prices listed under each category may vary from area to area. This variance is meant to reflect local price standards and take into account that what might be considered a *moderate* price in a large urban area might be quite *expensive* in a rural region. In every case, however, the dollar ranges for each category are clearly indicated.

In some instances, prices reflect the inclusion of a certain number of meals. *Full American Plan (FAP)* includes three meals daily. *Modified American Plan (MAP)* automatically means breakfast and dinner. *Continental Plan (CP)* offers European-style breakfast (roll or croissant and tea or coffee). *European Plan (EP)* means no meals are included in the price quoted.

Free parking is assumed at all motels and motor hotels; you must pay for parking at most city hotels, though certain establishments have free parking, frequently for occupants of higher-than-minimum-rate rooms. *Baby sitter* lists are always available in good hotels and motels, and *cribs* for the children are always on hand—subject to availability—often at no charge, or at a cost of $1 or $2 per night. The cost of a *cot* in your room, to supplement the beds, is around $5 per night, but moving an *extra single bed* into a room costs around $10 in better hotels and motels.

Hotel chains in general are becoming more cognizant of the requirements of **women guests.** Inquire at reservation time if interested in "female" amenities such as skirt hangers or "women only" floors, which may require a special key. If security is a concern, it's often wise to take rooms above the first floor and to be sure that hotel personnel do not announce your room number at the front desk. Many women when traveling alone prefer to stay only in rooms that do not have direct access from the outside.

America is quickly catching on to Europe's **Bed and Breakfast.** These guest houses are often large, still fairly elegant old homes in quiet residential or semiresidential parts of larger towns or along secondary roads and the main streets of small towns and resorts. Styles and standards vary widely, of course; generally, private baths are less common and rates are pleasingly low. In many small towns such guest houses are excellent examples of the best a region has to offer of its own special atmosphere. Each one will be different, so that their advantage is precisely the opposite of that "no surprise" uniformity that motel chains pride themselves on. Few, if any, guest houses have heated pools, wall-to-wall carpeting, or exposed styrofoam-wooden beams in the bar. Few if any even have bars. What you do get, in addition to economy, is the personal flavor of a family atmosphere in a private home. In popular tourist areas, state or local tourist information offices or chambers of commerce usually have lists of homes that let out spare rooms to paying guests, and such a listing usually means that the places on it have been inspected and meet some reliable standard of cleanliness, comfort, and reasonable pricing. A helpful book, *Bed and Breakfast U.S.A.: A Guide to Guest Houses and Tourist Homes,* is available from Tourist House Associates of America, Inc., Box 355-A, Greentown, PA 18426.

While bed and breakfasts are still more common in the eastern U.S. than in the Rockies and plains area, new B and B's are opening all the time. For a directory of state guest homes write *Bed and Breakfast Colorado, Ltd.,* Box 6061, Dept. V, Boulder, CO 80306, or *Bed & Breakfast Rocky Mtns.,* Dept. A, Box 804, Colorado Springs, CO 80901.

Colorado's wilderness can also be enjoyed by vacationing at four dozen **dude ranches.** All of them emphasize horseback riding, but some ranches also feature swimming pools and tennis courts. Fishing in nearby mountain streams is popular as well.

All dude ranches offer a comfortable lodge or cabins, cookouts, and horseback riding aplenty—from guided rides for beginners to breakfast rides, steak cookouts at night to six-day pack trips through the wilderness. Children have their own supervised programs. Dude ranches are popular, so reservations should be made as far in advance as possible (never less than two months ahead). Costs range from $280 to $800 per person per week.

Beaver Village Guest Ranch at Winter Park (Box 43, 80482, 303–726–5741 or 800–525–3561) on US 40, is a well-known retreat ranch. Tennis, pool swimming, lake and stream fishing are available with condo accommodations. On Colorado State Highway 7, directly under Long's Peak, there beckons *The Long's Peak Inn and Guest Ranch* (not far from Estes Park, 303–586–2110), which has some of the state's most exciting scenery.

The *C Lazy U Ranch* (80446, 303–807–3344), near Granby has a reputation for luxurious facilities, tennis, swimming, and all-year-round programs, including cross-country skiing in winter. Also located in the mountains, the *Peaceful Valley Ranch,* Lyons (Star Route, 80540, 303–747–2582), made a name for itself as a riding center. It is the only such Colorado ranch that also specializes in square dancing. The location, not far from Boulder, is convenient and easy to reach.

In south-central Colorado, west of Pueblo, the *Don K Ranch* (2677 S. Siloam Rd., 81005, 303–784–6600), boasts its own small ghost town. With the San Isabel Forest and the Sangre de Cristo Range to prowl, its good food, heated pool, cocktail lounge, and children's counselors, this may be the place for your Colorado vacation. *The Tumbling River Ranch* (Grant, 80448, 303–838–5981), is a wildly romantic retreat southwest of Denver. It can be reached in an hour via Highway 285. Guests find magnificent scenery, seclusion, outdoor barbecues, lots of family rides, and hikes along one of Colorado's more dramatic rivers. *The Lazy H Ranch* (in Allenspark, 80510, 303–747–2532) doubles as a cross-country ski center in winter. It has been operating for some five decades. Year-round there is excellent food and a pleasant atmosphere. The *Vista Verde Ranch* (in Steamboat Springs 80477, 303–879–3858), has hunting in fall and sleigh rides in winter. Every ranch has its own character and diversions, but all feature horses. For more information, write *Colorado Guest and Dude Ranch Association,* Box 300, Tabernash, CO 80478, 303–887–3128.

In larger towns and cities, a good bet for clean, plain, reliable lodging is a **YMCA** or **YWCA.** These buildings are usually centrally located, and their rates tend to run to less than half of those of hotels. Nonmembers are welcome, but may pay slightly more than members. Sexes are usually segregated, decor is spartan, and the cafeteria fare plain, but a definite advantage is the use of the building's pool, gym, reading room, information services, and other facilities. **YMCA of the Rockies,** near Estes Park, offers rustic lodges and cabins on 1,400 scenic acres. For a directory, write to *National Council of the YMCA,* 101 N. Wacker Drive, Chicago, IL 60606, and the *National Board of the YWCA,* 135 W. 50th St., New York, NY 10020.

American Youth Hostels provide inexpensive dormitory-type accommodations. For details write *American Youth Hostel Association, Inc.,* National Campus, Delaplane, VA 22025.

DINING OUT. Colorado's restaurants are as diverse as its landscape. In the major cities and resort areas, virtually every type of dining is available—from authentic Japanese *sushi* with pickled ginger and *wasabi* to duck à l'orange presented on antique china.

For evening dining, the best advice is to make reservations whenever possible. Most hotels and farm-vacation places have set dining hours. For motel stayers, life is simpler if the motel has a restaurant. If it hasn't, try to stay at one that is near a restaurant. If in doubt about accepted dress at a particular establishment, call ahead.

When figuring the tip on your check, base it on the total charge for the meal, not on the grand total, if that total includes a sales tax. Don't tip on tax.

RESTAURANT CATEGORIES

The restaurants mentioned in this volume that are located in large metropolitan areas are categorized by type of cuisine: French, Chinese, German, etc., with restaurants of a general nature listed as American-International. Restaurants are divided into price categories as follows: *deluxe, expensive, moderate,* and *inexpensive,* with an exceptionally expensive restaurant listed as *super deluxe.* As a general rule, expect restaurants in metropolitan areas to be higher in price, but many restaurants that feature foreign cuisine are surprisingly inexpensive. We should also point out that limitations of space make it impossible to include every establishment. We have, therefore, listed those that we recommend as the best within each price range.

Although the names of the various restaurant categories are standard, the prices listed under each category may vary from area to area. This variation is meant to reflect local price standards and take into account that what might be considered a *moderate* price in a large urban area might be quite *expensive* in a rural region. In every case, however, the dollar ranges for each category are clearly stated before each listing of establishments.

SENIOR CITIZEN AND STUDENT DISCOUNTS. Seniors ride public buses for a dime during off-peak hours in Denver. Many theaters, movie houses, museums, public pools, and motels offer discounts; ages and requirements vary. Sometimes, you need to present some form of ID with proof of age.

Senior citizens may in some cases receive special discounts on lodgings. The Days Inn chain offers various discounts to anyone 55 or older. Holiday Inns give a 10 percent discount year-round to members of the NRTA (write to *National Retired Teachers Association,* Membership Division, 215 Long Beach Blvd., Long Beach, CA 90802; 213–432–5781) and the AARP (write to *American Association of Retired Persons,* Membership Division, 215 Long Beach Blvd., Long Beach, CA 90802). Members of the AARP, the NRTA, the *National Association of Retired Persons,* the *Catholic Golden Age of United Societies of U.S.A.,* and the *Old Age Security Pensioners of Canada,* and similar organizations benefit increasingly from a number of discounts, but the amounts, sources, and availability of these change, so it is best to check with either your own organization or with the hotel, motel, or restaurant chain you plan to use when you make reservations. The *National Council of Senior Citizens,* 925 15th St. N.W., Washington, DC 20005; 202–347–8800, works especially to develop low-cost travel possibilities for its members.

DRINKING LAWS. Colorado Law requires that anyone purchasing hard liquor, wine, or "6 percent" beer must be *21 years of age.* Persons over 18 may purchase so-called "3.2" beer. Drinks must be off the table at closing hour. Packaged goods are not sold in bars, but may be obtained in package stores, open until midnight, Mon.–Sat. Children may sit at a table if they are accompanied by an adult. In recent years, the state has introduced stiff drunk-driving laws. Supermarkets and convenience stores sell 3.2 beer seven days a week.

LOCAL TIME. Colorado is on Mountain Standard Time: this is two hours behind Eastern Standard Time; one hour behind Central; one hour ahead of Pacific. Daylight Savings Time extends from May–October.

SUMMER SPORTS. *Swimming* is invigorating in many of the lakes and reservoirs and relaxing in the hot spring pools of Colorado. *Water skiing* and *sailing* are popular on the larger lakes, from the world's highest anchorage at Grand Lake to Bonny Reservoir on the plains.

The many rivers and streams offer exciting possibilities for *canoeing, kayaking,* and *rafting.* For more information write to Colorado Division of Parks and Recreation, 1313 Sherman St., #618, Denver, 80203.

Colorado has 1,143 mountains that rise to 10,000 feet or more above sea level. Fifty-three snow-capped peaks tower to more than 14,000 feet to give the state more than six times the mountain area of Switzerland. The Rocky Mountains offer ample opportunity for *hiking, backpacking,* and *mountain climbing* or *horseback riding.* Many areas are accessible only on foot or by horse. (See "Hiking, Backpacking, and Rafting," below.)

Bicycling has become increasingly popular in Colorado, and it's not unusual to see a loaded-up bike whizzing down one of the mountain passes. For routes and rules write to Colorado Department of Highways, 4201 E. Arkansas, Denver 80222.

In light of this area's western frontier heritage, it's not surprising that *rodeo* is the most pervasive of the spectator sports throughout this region. In general, the season runs from late spring into early fall.

There are many fine *golf* courses throughout the area. *Tennis* is also a popular sport, and courts are found at virtually every major resort or urban area. Many winter play areas become summer play areas. Among the best are *Keystone*—elegant, classy, and diverse; and *Vail* and *Aspen,* where visitors can hike through glorious mountain scenery, window-shop along the mall to the sounds of string quartets, and attend performances by world-renowned musicians.

HUNTING AND FISHING. Colorado is one of America's most popular *hunting* regions. Big-game animals include the deer (mule and whitetail), elk, bear, mountain lion, bighorn sheep, and the Rocky Mountain goat.

Regular elk and deer seasons open in October. The antelope season starts in September, and bighorn sheep and mountain goat seasons begin in late August. Special archery, muzzleloading, and high-country deer and elk periods usually start prior to the regular deer and elk rifle seasons. Black bear may be hunted during the spring and summer and again during the state's regular big game seasons. The period for hunting mountain lion runs concurrently with the regular big-game dates.

Residents and nonresidents may bag all species of big-game animals except bighorn sheep and Rocky Mountain goat. The shooting of these two species is limited to Colorado residents only.

All regular big-game licenses may be bought from authorized license agents, i.e., most of the state's hardware and sporting goods stores. However, the Colorado Wildlife Commission may insist that you get your deer and elk licenses at Division of Wildlife offices after the opening of the regular rifle seasons. Licenses for some areas, for specified and antlerless deer and elk hunting, for bighorn sheep, mountain goat, and antelope hunting are issued by application and drawing. The latter are usually available after May 1 each year. The passage of a hunter safety course or proof of completion of such a course is required for hunting. A license from another state is not sufficient.

Printed regulations on deer, elk, bear, and mountain lion seasons may be obtained after August 1 each year. Contact the division for information on waterfowl, pheasant, quail, partridge, and grouse seasons. Archery regulations are available in late May.

Guides are not required by law for big game hunting. But hunters unfamiliar with Colorado's more rugged mountains would be wise to use guide services, especially for elk hunting. A list of licensed guides and outfitters is published in July of each year by the State Board of Outfitters, 1525 Sherman St., Suite 606, Denver, CO 80203; phone 303–866–3898.

Fishing, equally popular, extends to some 11,300 miles of mountain streams and most of Colorado's 2,400 lakes. Each spring and early summer the state stocks the lakes and many rivers with more than a million pounds of trout. Colorado's fishing season runs almost the year round with varying exceptions. Nonresident licenses are good for the balance of the calendar year in which they're purchased. Nonresident licenses for ten days are available, as are two-day permits. Licenses are sold through many hardware and outdoor-equipment shops. For a booklet on fishing regulations, contact the Colorado Division of Wildlife, 6060 Broadway, Denver, CO 80216; 303–291–7227.

Among Colorado's most widely known trout streams are the Gunnison, down to the Blue Mesa Reservoir; the Rio Grande, through the San Luis Valley and above it; the Arkansas, from below Leadville to Pueblo; the Roaring Fork River, near Aspen; and the entire stretch of the Colorado, White, Yampa, and North Platte rivers.

Some of the more popular trout lakes are Grand Lake at the town of Grand Lake; Granby and Shadow Mountain reservoirs near Granby; Trappers Lake east of Meeker; Sweetwater Lake near Glenwood Springs; Twin Lakes near Leadville; Monument Lake near Trinidad; Vallecito Reservoir near Durango; lakes of the Grand Mesa near Grand Junction.

Other popular trout lakes are Delaney Butte Lakes and Lake John near Walden; the Red Feather Lakes northwest of Fort Collins; Eleven Mile and Antero reservoirs in South Park; Taylor Reservoir near Gunnison; Williams Creek Reservoir near Pagosa Springs; Williams Fork Reservoir near Parshall; and Lon Hagler Reservoir near Loveland.

The relatively crowded waters of Dillon Reservoir at Dillon; Vega Reservoir near Colbran; Navajo Reservoir southwest of Pagosa Springs; and North Michigan Lake near Walden can all be of interest to trout anglers; ditto for the Blue Mesa Reservoir near Gunnison.

Near Denver, try the South Platte River from below the city to the town of Deckers; Bear Creek Lake, east of Morrison on US 285; or Cherry Creek Reservoir on the edge of southeast Denver.

HIKING, BACKPACKING, RAFTING. Seasoned outdoorspeople may want to try the *hiking* trails that honeycomb the high country. The Colorado Mountain Club is located at 2530 W. Alameda Ave., Denver, CO 80219; 303–922–8315. The club also sponsors easy hikes and rock-climbing adventures for beginners. Guests are welcome for a small daily fee. Maps can be obtained from the *U.S. Geological Survey,* Federal Center, W. Sixth Ave., Denver 80225; 303–234–3832.

Backpackers should have both warm and cool clothing, crepe- or Vibram-soled shoes (impervious to sharp-edged rocks), a frame pack that centers its weight on the hips instead of shoulders, and a first-aid kit. When trekking through government-supervised areas, you are required to sign in and out and let rangers know the general direction you're heading and roughly when you expect to return.

Those who tire of walking can go *rafting.* Guided river trips are available, lasting from a half-day to three weeks. River adventures vary in intensity, depending on whether you go along for the ride or grab an oar and wrestle the current yourself. Reservations, often a month or more ahead, are essential during the summer months. If you are experienced and prefer to go on your own, several outfitters rent rafts. Some stretches of river are open to raft-riders by permit only. Check locally.

WINTER SPORTS. The state that brings you Aspen and Vail, Winter Park and Steamboat Springs is renowned for its *skiing.* Justly so: Colorado has a greater number of major ski resorts and areas than any other U.S. state or Canadian province. In all, you can ski at nearly three dozen places that vary in size from giants like the Aspen complex to smaller areas such as Ski Copper. All these places appeal to nonskiers as well.

Colorado has attained an international reputation for its reliable snow conditions, sunshine aplenty, resorts en masse, good ski lodgings, restaurants, night life. Both eastern and western skiers enjoy the long descents and the variety of ski centers on mountains of every kind. Colorado serves the total novice, intermediate, and expert, with ski schools ready to teach all ages in record time. The aficionados arrive from all over the world, spanning all economic levels.

Ski passions show up in places like Winter Park, an area owned by the City of Denver. The mountain is constantly polished by a motorized army of snowcats, graders, rollers, packers. Yet by Saturday or Sunday noon, the major runs are dotted with people. On holidays, thousands of Denverites come here in their own automobiles, in car pools, in chartered buses, and via special weekend ski trains.

High-speed buses leave regularly from Stapleton International Airport, taking the traveler directly to the resorts. Large ski meccas such as Aspen or Vail have their own shuttle buses from lodges and condos to the lifts. And major complexes like Summit County, which includes Breckenridge, Copper Mountain, Keystone, among others, are interconnected by shuttles. Likewise, air carriers cater to skiers. Continental and United Airlines, for instance, plan their flights with the winter sports crowd in mind, with scheduled flights to many mountain communities.

Which ski center should you pick? That depends on what you want. A traveler may opt for the prestige and urban big-city qualities of Vail, which nestles in a valley 100 miles, or two hours, west of the Mile High City. An economy skier with a family may be drawn to Ski Estes Park, which is operated by the Rocky Mountain National Park about 76 miles from Denver. A half-dozen major areas can be reached more quickly; each of these spots is different. Indeed, the flavor of Colorado's ski stations varies enormously. There are the former mining towns like Crested Butte, for example, and there are the sleek contemporary spas like Beaver Creek. Your choice will be influenced by many factors that include costs, types of slopes (from the gentlest to the steepest), and the kind of clientele you want to mix with. Some places—Winter Park, for instance—attract budget-conscious families more than the single jetsetter who favors the Aspen region. The chapter "Ski and Summer Resorts" provides information on the major resort areas.

Colorado Ski Country USA publishes an 80-page guide to the state's ski centers. Write to Colorado Ski Country USA, 1560 Broadway, # 1440, Denver, CO 80202. The guide is free if picked up at their office, or at the Denver Airport booth, located near doors 3 and 10 on the baggage level. *The Skier's Companion* (Viking Press) also gives much data on Colorado's snow sports.

Downhill skiing is by no means the only winter activity you'll find in Colorado. *Cross-country skiing,* or *ski touring,* is becoming increasingly popular, as both a means of escape from the cost of lift tickets and the ever-longer lift lines and as a means of enjoying the breathtaking scenery.

Each year, *snowmobiling* attracts more and more people who enjoy the thrill of speeding along snow-covered mountain trails or over open meadows. Many areas have organized rallies and races.

Ice skating on frozen lakes and ponds, or in year-round rinks, also has its share of enthusiasts.

ROUGHING IT. Some six million people stay in Colorado's hundreds of campgrounds each summer. You can buy a pass to gain entrance to campsites at the many state-supervised outdoor areas; otherwise, there are also per-night fees. The same prices are found in the national parks. At both, check with rangers for camping regulations. For complete listings of summer camps contact *American Camping Association,* 400 S. Broadway, Denver, CO 80211; 303–778–8774.

At *Rocky Mountain National Park,* camping sites are scarce during the high summer season. Most are available on a first-come, first-served basis. At Glacier Basin Campground or Moraine Park Campground, reservations may be made up to eight weeks in advance for the peak summer season. Write Ticketron Reservation Office, Box 2715, San Francisco, CA 94126. For information on Colorado's National Parks contact National Park Service, 12795 W. Alameda Pkwy., Box 25287, Denver, CO 80225; 303–969–2000.

Reservations may be made for campsites in State Parks. Call or write the Division of Parks, 1313 Sherman, Denver, CO 80203 (303–866–3437), for reservations and information. Reservations can also be made through Mistix; 303–671–4500. A fee is charged.

On lands controlled by the U.S. Forest Service, only group campsites may be reserved; individual sites are on a first-come, first-served basis. For reservations and a list of sites in the area of your interest write: U.S. Forest Service, Recreation, 11177 W. Eighth Ave., Lakewood, CO 80225; 303–236–9520.

The *Bureau of Land Management,* Building 50, Denver Federal Center, Denver, CO 80225; 303–236–6485, can give information on hiking, hunting, camping, and fishing.

Many of Colorado's privately owned campgrounds offer thousands of vehicle and tent sites in the state. Commercial camping organizations include *KOA (Kampgrounds of America),* Box 30558, Billings, MT 59114. Or check your bookstore for one of several books listing commercial campgrounds around the country.

STATE PARKS. The great outdoors is what Colorado's all about, and some of its most impressive scenery can be found in the state's 27 parks and recreation areas. From *Golden Gate State Park,* with its 100-mile panoramas of the Continental Divide to the towering red sandstone monoliths at *Roxborough State Park,* these parks offer every type of outdoor recreation. Hike, camp, fish, sail, or just enjoy that spectacular scenery. For a list of the state's parks write Colorado Division of Parks, Dept. of Natural Resources, 1313 Sherman, Denver, CO 80203. Annual parks passes are available for $25. A daily pass costs $3–$7, depending on the park. The Aspen Leaf Passport, for those 62 and over, is good for a lifetime admission to all state parks and is free.

NATIONAL PARKS AND MONUMENTS. The Black Canyon of the *Gunnison National Monument* has to be seen to be believed. The Gunnison River has cut a narrow gorge, at times only 40 feet wide, through nearly solid granite to depths ranging from 1,730 to 2,425 feet. Some of the best fishing in Colorado is to be found on the Gunnison. The North Rim of the canyon is reached by gravel road east of Crawford on State 92. The South Rim, closed winters, is reached by US 50 to Montrose and then State 347 six miles east.

State 340 west from Grand Junction or US 70 from Fruita lead into Rim Rock Drive of the *Colorado National Monument.* Amazing rock formations, plants, and animals abound. Nearby, the largest flat-topped peak in the United States, Grand Mesa, sprinkled with lakes and two miles high, may be reached on State 64.

Dinosaur National Monument in the northwestern corner of Colorado, off Hwy. 64, has park headquarters two miles east of the town of Dinosaur, on US 40. Much of the scenic beauty is a result of erosion by the Yampa and Green rivers. Steamboat Rock, carved out of layers of sandstone by the confluence of the Yampa and Green, is now 700 feet above the river surface that once flowed over it. Its broad slab sides act as a sounding board for nearby Echo Park. Pictographs estimated to be 1,000 years old may be seen. Archeologists removed the delicate bones of dinosaurs from their sedimentary storehouses; more than 20 skeletons dating back some 100,000 years have been reconstructed here. The skeletons are housed in a museum reached through Jensen, Utah, 20 miles west of Dinosaur on US 40. Roads into the monument may be closed in winter due to snow.

Mesa Verde National Park contains ruins of cliff dwellings of a prehistoric civilization that lived nearly 1,000 years before the American Revolution. The park may be reached by car on US 160, ten miles east of Cortez.

Hovenweep National Monument is a series of long-abandoned Pueblo settlements. The prehistoric buildings, evidently built by a people similar to those who built Mesa Verde, are open for inspection. Located west of Pleasant View, off State 666.

Rocky Mountain National Park, with headquarters at Estes Park, is scenically stunning. Trail Ridge Road (US 34), the highway that runs through part of the Park, has been called "breathtaking." The highest paved highway in the US, its 15 miles of road above timberline, some times at altitudes of 12,000 feet, look down on great sloping meadows of wildflowers. Slowly melting glaciers provide the water supply for a host of waterfalls, streams, and deep mountain lakes. At the western end of Trail Ridge Road is Grand Lake, which covers an area of 515 acres, and at 8,400 feet is the home of what may be the highest yacht club in the world. Water sports are popular here, but be prepared for the icy waters of a lake whose depths have never been completely sounded.

Great Sand Dunes National Monument, located on State 150, 31 miles northeast of Alamosa, contains the highest naturally formed sand piles in the U.S., some exceeding a height of 800 feet above the valley floor.

A Golden Eagle passport allows you and anyone in your vehicle to enter many national parks and recreational areas during a full calendar year. The passport doesn't cover all areas, nor does it include special fees. A Golden Age passport provides free park access to anyone 62 years of age or older. Blind or handicapped persons can use the Golden Access passport. Information and applications for these passports are available from any office of the National Park Service, Forest Service, Bureau of Land Management, and at most ranger stations. Or you may write to National Park Service Headquarters, U.S. Department of the Interior, 18th and C streets N.W., Washington, D.C. 20240.

HOT SPRINGS. Colorado has a number of hot springs, among them *Glenwood Springs, Idaho Springs, Pagosa Springs, Hot Sulphur Springs,* and *Steamboat Springs,* most with facilities for enjoying the waters. Of these, Glenwood Springs is the most extensive, with two outdoor pools, one of them two blocks long. Open all year, these are fed by natural warm mineral waters. *Hot mineral baths* are available at the Vapor Cave Baths and Health Spa.

INDIANS. Colorado's history is inextricably bound to Indian culture and lore. Today the state has two reservations, the *Ute Mountain Ute* and *The Southern Ute* reservations, in southwestern Colorado. The mountain

Utes maintain many ancestral traditions. Each year the tribes hold cere-
monial dances and powwows throughout the state. The ceremonies are
religious, and often visitors are not allowed; when attending such a dance,
respect the participants' wishes regarding the use of cameras, tape record-
ers, and even pen and paper. The southern Utes hold their traditional Bear
Dance near Ignacio in May. Powwows also feature dances, and have contests as well. In late March, an all-tribe powwow is held in Denver. Fort
Lewis College in Durango hosts a powwow the second week in March.
The Lone Feather Council three-day powwow is held the third weekend
in June in Colorado Springs. The Southern Ute Fair is held each September in Ignacio. For further information contact the Indian Commission
of Colorado, 144 State Capitol, Denver, 80203; 303–866–3027.

POSTAGE. Rates for domestic mail are as follows: 22 cents for one
ounce or under, 17 cents per ounce thereafter; postcards are 14 cents. Surface letters to Canada and Mexico are the same price. Surface letters to
other foreign destinations are 37 cents for the first ounce. Airmail letters
to most international destinations (excluding Mexico, Canada, and Central America) are: 44 cents per half-ounce for the first two ounces; 39 cents
for each ounce thereafter. Postcards to foreign countries are 25 cents for
surface mail, 33 cents for airmail, except to Mexico and Canada, which
go at the domestic rate of 14 cents. Aerogram letters cost 36 cents.

TELEPHONES. The area codes for Colorado are 303 (Northern Region) and 719 (Southern Region). There is no need to dial the area code
when calling between cities in the state. Directory assistance in Denver
is 1–411; from outside the city dial 303–555–1212. For information on toll-
free numbers call 800–555–1212. Dial 0 and the number you wish to reach
for operator assisted (collect, person-to-person, etc.) calls. Pay phones require 20 or 25 cents.

PHOTOGRAPHY. In the high altitude and low humidity of Colorado,
the air is clear and thin and there is an abundance of ultra-violet light
which, though invisible, is picked up as a blue haze by color film. The use
of a skylight filter cuts out these rays, and your pictures will appear normal. The light at these high altitudes is very bright, and pictures of sunlit
scenes require a half to one full stop less exposure than you would ordinari-
ly use. If you can afford the extra cost in film, expose at the stops both
over and under in addition to what seems to be the correct exposure, to
be nearly certain of getting a perfectly exposed photograph.
   If your camera has interchangeable lenses, a wide-angle lens can capture
not only the broad panoramic shots from the high peaks, but also ensure
that both the river and sky will appear in photos of the deep canyons.

HINTS TO HANDICAPPED TRAVELERS. Colorado is becoming
aware of the special needs of the handicapped, and public facilities are
more accessible. An excellent guide titled *Access Denver* describes the facilities of motels, restaurants, banks, churches, museums, stores, and theaters
of that city. Write The Sewall Rehabilitation Center, 1360 Vine St., Denver, CO 80206, to receive a copy. A $2.50 donation is appreciated but not
required. For information on wheelchair lifts on public buses call
303–778–6000. Other important sources of information in this field are
the books: *Travel Ability,* by Lois Reamy, published by Macmillan Pub-

lishing Co., Inc., 101K Brown St., Riverside, NJ 08370, and *Access to the World: A Travel Guide for the Handicapped,* by Louise Weiss, available from Facts on File, 460 Park Avenue South, New York, NY 10016, and *The Wheelchair Traveler,* by D. R. Annand, Ball Hill Road, Milford, NH 03055, which gives valuable information about motels, hotels, and restaurants (rating them, telling about steps, table heights, door widths, etc.); the *Travel Information Center,* Moss Rehabilitation Hospital, 12th Street and Tabor Road, Philadelphia, PA 19141; *Easter Seal Society,* Director of Education and Information Service, 2023 West Ogden Avenue, Chicago, IL 60612. Many of the nation's national parks have special facilities for the handicapped. These are described in *National Park Guide for the Handicapped,* available from the U.S. Government Printing Office, Washington, DC 20402.

Access Tours, a travel agency specializing in travel arrangements for the handicapped, can plan tours for groups of four or more with any disability. They can be reached at Suite 1801, 123-33 83d Ave., Kew Gardens, NY 11415 (718–263–3835 or 800–533–5343) and are most helpful. Also useful for assessment of travel destinations and reference tips is the *LTD Travel* newsletter. You can get a subscription to this quarterly by writing to 116 Harbor Seal Court, San Mateo, CA 94404.

METRIC CONVERSION. Although there is always talk about the U.S. going metric, it has yet to take hold in most areas of American life. The following charts may prove helpful to foreign visitors in Colorado.

CONVERTING METRIC TO U.S. MEASUREMENTS

Multiply:	by:	to find:
Length		
millimeters (mm)	.039	inches (in)
meters (m)	3.28	feet (ft)
meters	1.09	yards (yd)
kilometers (km)	.62	miles (mi)
Area		
hectares (ha)	2.47	acres
Capacity		
liters (L)	1.06	quarts (qt)
liters	.26	gallons (gal)
liters	2.11	pints (pt)
Weight		
grams (g)	.04	ounce (oz)
kilograms (kg)	2.20	pounds (lb)
metric tons (MT)	.98	tons (t)
Power		
kilowatts (kw)	1.34	horsepower (hp)
Temperature		
degrees Celsius	9/5 (then add 32)	degrees Fahrenheit

CONVERTING U.S. TO METRIC
MEASUREMENTS

Multiply:	by:	to find:
Length		
inches (in)	25.40	millimeters (mm)
feet (ft)	.30	meters (m)
yards (yd)	.91	meters
miles (mi)	1.61	kilometers (km)
Area		
acres	.40	hectares (ha)
Capacity		
pints (pt)	.47	liters (L)
quarts (qt)	.95	liters
gallons (gal)	3.79	liters
Weight		
ounces (oz)	28.35	grams (g)
pounds (lb)	.45	kilograms (kg)
tons (t)	1.11	metric tons (MT)
Power		
horsepower (hp)	.75	kilowatts
Temperature		
degrees Fahrenheit	5/9 (after subtracting 32)	degrees Celsius

AN INTRODUCTION TO
COLORADO

The Mountainous Land

by
DON LONG

Don Long is completing a career with The Denver Post *that spans more than 30 years, having served from 1977 to 1985 as the newspaper's travel editor. He grew up in northern Colorado and graduated from the University of Colorado. As a member of the Society of American Travel Writers, he traveled on assignment in Australia, South America, China, Europe, Japan, Africa, the Soviet Union, and Yugoslavia.*

What is it that sets Colorado apart, that makes it clearly different from the other 49 pieces of the U.S. jigsaw?

Only a half-dozen of our 50 states have a quick answer to such a question: Rhode Island because it's so small, Texas because it's so big, Florida because it has two coasts, Maine because it holds down such a blustery corner, Alaska because it's so cold and remote, Hawaii because it's so warm and water-bound.

Any flatlander who comes here from the east can give you Colorado's answer in a hurry. It's the mountains, and in particular the Rocky Mountains.

19

Those of us who grew up here tend to take the mountains for granted. But others, especially those from the Midwest where Colorado draws so many of its newcomers, are likely to remember the exact time they first sighted the snowcapped range that serves as such a dramatic backdrop to the eastern half of the state.

Think of Colorado and you're certain to think of the Rocky Mountains. Think of the Rockies and you'll think of Colorado. The two are inseparable, each an inextricable part of the other—even though the Rockies, of course, run through states other than Colorado, and Colorado covers a lot more land than merely its share of the Rockies.

The Geography

Look at a map of the lower 48 and you'll see Colorado as a nice even rectangle some 375 miles wide and 275 miles deep, bordered on the south by New Mexico, on the west by Utah, on the north by Wyoming, and on the east by Kansas.

If it's a topographical map you'll also see that the spine of the Rockies, a rugged north-south ridge commonly called the Continental Divide, effectively splits the state into two broad north-south strips—one in the west that is half mountains and half plateaus (the plateau half bordering Utah), and one in the east that is one-third mountains and two-thirds plains (the two-thirds next to Kansas).

Thus we have a state consisting of plateaus, mountains, and plains; no one driving east or west can cross Colorado without crossing all three.

Most of Colorado's three million inhabitants live on the plains but within eyesight of the mountains, in a north-south urban belt along the east flank of the Front Range of the Rockies that includes all three of the state's largest cities—Denver, Colorado Springs, and Pueblo—and five of its smaller ones: Boulder, Fort Collins, Greeley, Longmont, and Loveland (whose aggregate population exceeds 300,000).

The Capital

Denver, the capital, lies astride the South Platte River some 90 miles south of the Wyoming line. Known as the Mile High City because of its altitude, it is 50 miles east of a point in the Continental Divide that is more than twice as high: Loveland Pass at 11,902 feet. And Loveland Pass is a piker when it comes to height. Colorado has 54 peaks higher than 14,000 feet; Mount Elbert is the highest at 14,433.

Denver suffers from its founding fathers' failure to spread its city limits far enough. The result is that the city proper has become hemmed in by vigilant suburbs insistent on their own territorial integrity. Unable to broaden its boundaries, Denver has a constant 500,000 inhabitants while its environs have more than twice that many. And while Denver itself can't grow, its suburbs can't seem to quit growing, especially Aurora on the mushrooming east side where growth threatens to leapfrog halfway to the Kansas border 130 miles away.

Still, Denver stands for much more than you might expect from a city of 500,000 souls. A great manufacturing, distribution, and transportation center, it has become the West's energy capital as well, with dozens of oil and gas firms maintaining regional headquarters here along with other energy companies and hundreds of major business firms. Federal and state government installations add to the mix, as do five institutions of higher learning and an impressive array of cultural organizations.

Reflecting all this, Stapleton International Airport, sixth busiest in the world—yes, the world—is on the threshold of a $3 billion relocation to a site ten miles from its impacted perch on the city's northeast corner. The project is expected to begin soon and be completed by the middle 1990s.

Other Cities

Colorado Springs, the state's second city, neighbor to Pike's Peak and the U.S. Air Force Academy 70 miles south of Denver, has expanded almost as rapidly as Denver's suburbs. Twenty years ago its population scarcely topped 100,000. Today it is home for 230,000 people and growing. Pueblo, some 40 miles farther south, is a distant third. Its steel industry declining, Pueblo's population is a mere 99,000 and shrinking.

On the other side of the mountains, which Coloradans call the western slope, Grand Junction is the only sizable city, at 30,000. Durango and Montrose are next, with 12,000 and 9,000, respectively.

Colorado History

Colorado's recorded history begins in the cliffs and canyons of Mesa Verde (now a national park), where Indians later known as the Basketmakers left evidence of a civilization that originated in the eighth century A.D. and flourished until the 13th century when it died mysteriously, the apparent victim of drought. Other Indians roamed the state's eastern plains for centuries thereafter, until the buffalo hunters arrived to take away much of their sustenance in the early 1800s.

Only the Utes have reservation land in Colorado—in its extreme southwestern corner, not far from Mesa Verde—although both the Comanches and the Pawnees have National Grasslands, in southeast and northeast sectors of the state.

The U.S. government acquired much of what is now Colorado in 1803 as part of the Louisiana Purchase from France (at a mere 3½ cents an acre). This set the stage for exploration by Col. Zebulon Pike in 1806, Maj. Stephen Long in 1820, and Lt. John C. Fremont from 1842 to 1852. Fur trappers and frontiersmen made sketchy contributions to Colorado history during this time, but little effort was made toward harnessing the mountainous state till gold and silver were discovered not long after midcentury.

That's when Colorado got one of its nicknames, the Silver State. The other came in 1876, some 15 years after Colorado was declared a U.S. territory. Statehood was granted exactly 100 years after the signing of the Declaration of Independence; thus the more popular nickname, the Centennial State.

Spanish and Indian names alternate with those of frontiersmen and early settlers as place names in Colorado: such names as Alamosa, Bowie, Buena Vista, Cheraw, Durango, Gunnison, Kiowa, Kit Carson, Manzanola, Meeker, Ouray, and Saguache. The mining boom contributed such monickers as Gold Hill, Gypsum, Leadville, Silverton, and Telluride.

The name Colorado itself, of course, came from the Spanish word for "ruddy," a choice influenced perhaps by the terrain of what is now Red Rocks Park near Denver, Redcliff near Vail, and the Garden of the Gods near Colorado Springs.

Colorado's first census, in 1860, showed a population of 342,770, which by 1910 had increased to 800,000, and by 1950 to 1,325,000. By 1980 it was 2,889,000, and the estimates for 1990 put it close to 3.5 million. Colorado is the nation's eighth largest state in area, with 104,247 square miles, but only the 27th largest in terms of population.

Attractions of the Climate

If the mountains divide Colorado into western slope and eastern slope, the weather divides it less distinctly into pleasant summers, brisk autumns, uneven winters, and balmy springs that never quite live up to their promise.

Thirty years ago, winter in Colorado's high country was simply a season to be endured. Then began the development of recreational skiing, brought on by the growing realization that this was the magnet destined to draw (most of) the rest of the nation to visit the Centennial State.

The summer months had always brought vacationers to Colorado, from the time highway construction began to catch up with the zooming number of automobiles, but only the very foresighted could see what skiing would do. From a handful of ski centers in 1950—such places as Aspen, Steamboat Springs, and Winter Park—the number of ski areas has soared to more than thirty, most of them served by great clusters of condominiums with facilities enough to serve all who can afford to go. Vail and nearby Beaver Creek, Keystone, and Copper Mountain, none of which existed 30 years ago, have developed international reputations close to that of Aspen, while Snowmass, Breckenridge, Crested Butte, and Steamboat attract their full share of attention.

Until recent years the attraction was pretty much limited to downhill skiers, but now cross-country skiing is booming as well. Nearly half the state's 50-some dude ranches, previously operated in summers only, now offer their facilities for cross-country ski vacations for a weekend, a week, or longer.

Tourism has become a strong second to light manufacturing among Colorado's leading revenue producers. Third is agriculture and livestock production, both centered on the eastern plains although ranches can be found throughout the mountains and, in particular, on the western plateaus.

Mining, once the kingpin, is a poor fourth, but only if you include oil production. Gold and silver have never made the comeback expected of them, and specialized metals have filled part of the gap. One such, molybdenum, used to toughen steel, is found in larger quantities in Colorado than in any other state. The state's shale-oil industry, so promising a decade ago, has been on hold ever since Exxon cut back its operations to the bone in a move announced May 2, 1982, referred to on the western slope as "Black Sunday." Since then, industry hopefuls have been biding their time till strong crude-oil demand reappears. Like molybdenum, shale-oil occurs more extensively in Colorado than in any other state. Because of the decline in the oil industry, Colorado's unemployment rate is slightly higher than the national average, and its economy is suffering.

More than Skiing

What is there for Colorado's many visitors to see and do if it's not winter or they don't ski?

First and foremost, the state is a bit like Alaska—it must be seen to be believed, and driving is the only way to go. East of the Front Range it's not much different from Kansas and Nebraska, but from Denver, Colorado Springs, and Pueblo on west, there's no end of tourist attractions, beginning with the gold-domed Capitol in Denver and the Air Force Academy at Colorado Springs. The state has two national parks, six national monuments, and 11 national forests, each containing natural beauty that lends suspense to every bend in the highway. Deer and elk won't be seen very often, but just the possibility they'll be grazing within view adds to the enjoyment. Eleven major rivers and countless streams and lakes add another dimension to the scenery.

Mesa Verde National Park, with the incredible cliff dwellings of the Indians who once lived there, is an education in itself, as is Rocky Mountain National Park, 250 miles away. Trail Ridge Road in Rocky Mountain Park is the highest route over the Continental Divide in the United States and is closed by snow eight months of the year.

Dinosaur National Monument in the baked plateau land of northwestern Colorado stands in marked contrast to the shifting terrain of the Great Sand Dunes National Monument in south central Colorado, near Alamosa. Other national monuments open to visitors include the Black Canyon of the Gunnison River, a gorge of amazing depth—some 2,500 feet; Colorado National Monument near Grand Junction, where 1,000 feet above the Grand Valley breathtaking views, wildlife, and wildflowers abound; Florissant Fossil Beds west of Colorado Springs, a 6,000-acre site once covered by a prehistoric lake; and Hovenweep National Monument on the Colorado-Utah border, site of prehistoric Indian ruins (Hovenweep being the Ute word for "deserted valley").

Interstate 25 spans the state from north to south, almost in the shadows of the Front Range, while Interstate 70 crosses it from east to west, ducking under the Continental Divide through 1.7-mile Eisenhower Tunnel. Feeding the two interstates is an 8,200-mile network of state highways that reach nearly every scenic sector of the state.

Coloradoans

As for the people, you can characterize Coloradoans by their love for the mountains, but beyond that they don't seem to share many traits, unless it be a consuming interest in the Denver Broncos football team, whose games attract a prodigious TV audience around the state, especially with their Super Bowl appearances in 1987 and 1988.

Those living out on the eastern plains are more Kansan than Coloradoan in their outlook, and those living along the Front Range or in its foothills are more urban than mountain in theirs. Those living in the mountains are more outdoor-oriented, interested in such pursuits as fishing, hunting, horsemanship, and skiing. In general they are the bluff, hearty, helpful type whose livelihood is often tied to the number of visitors Colorado can attract.

DENVER AND ENVIRONS

Growing by Leaps and Bounds

by
CURTIS W. CASEWIT

Curtis W. Casewit has lived in the Denver area for almost 40 years. He has written a number of travel guides and writes travel features for some 40 international newspapers, garnered several Best Book awards from the Colorado Author's League; he teaches journalism at the University of Colorado/Denver Center.

Anyone who knew Denver in the early 1970s wouldn't recognize it today. The growing city with a small-town ambience has become a full-fledged metropolis.

Denver is the center of finance and commerce for the Southwest, the center of a thriving region. The city's population swells with arrivals from New York, Dallas, San Francisco, and other capitals. The new families have reclaimed dilapidated downtown neighborhoods, such as historic Capitol Hill, restored the old brick and frame homes, and made the area thrive again.

The new Denverites have brought with them their favorite shopping, dining, and entertainment from around the world. City stores offer wares from antique clothing to Oriental jade, computers, even Greek and Thai groceries. Lovers of haute cuisine will find their pleasure in scores of restaurants, such as the award-winning Chateau Pyrennees or the chic Rattlesnake Grill, which rival standards set by prestigious restaurants of both U.S. coasts.

Indeed, the visitor to the Mile-High City can now find any ethnic dining experience: there are restaurants with authentic French, German, Swiss, Italian, Spanish, Greek, Mexican, and assorted oriental cooking. You even find Afghan and Moroccan places. Denver's ethnic cuisine reflects its varied populace.

Thanks to a more and more sophisticated public, the Colorado state capital also excels in its cultural life. The Denver Symphony and the Denver Center Theater Company are at home in ultramodern performance halls in the heart of downtown. The Denver Art Museum regularly hosts top international exhibits. Foreign motion pictures garner large audiences. Denver is now rated among the more sophisticated cities in the United States.

EXPLORING DENVER

You will understand Denver's layout best by keeping in mind that there are two major thoroughfares: Broadway, which runs north and south and Colfax, which runs east and west. To the east of Broadway, you find East Colfax, which leads all the way to Aurora, a suburb. Conversely, West Colfax travels west to Lakewood and Golden. South Broadway, meanwhile, allows you to reach the suburb of Englewood. Street names fall in alphabetical order west of South Broadway and east of Colorado Boulevard.

In the heart of downtown Denver, thoroughfares run diagonally to the normal grid. Numbered streets are in this section; the balance of the city has numbered avenues. (17th St., for instance, is immediately downtown—17th Ave. is not).

You can pick up assorted pamphlets from the city's Visitors' Bureau at 225 W. Colfax, just off the main business section and at the edge of the Civic Center complex. The center is directly across the street from City Hall (distinguishable by the clock tower and chimes), which Denverites call the City and County Building.

The Civic Center Area

The U.S. Mint, 320 West Colfax, is across from the Visitors' Bureau. A Denver branch of the U.S. Treasury opened at 16th and Market streets in 1862, but, due to "the hostilities of the Indian tribes along the routes," coinage didn't begin here until the present building was finished in 1906.

More than five billion coins are stamped here each year. The mint is open for weekday tours all year, except the last two weeks in June (usually until July 5) when it closes for inventory. The second largest cache of gold bullion is on display, too, and souvenir coin sets and other collectors' items may be purchased.

The mint stands on the west side of Denver's Civic Center, a three-block stretch of lawns and gardens. It's the inner-city oasis where office workers and tourists picnic, stroll, or just rest. The Greek-style amphitheater on the center's south edge was built in 1919 and was once used for concerts, religious services, and public meetings. The curved walkways on each side

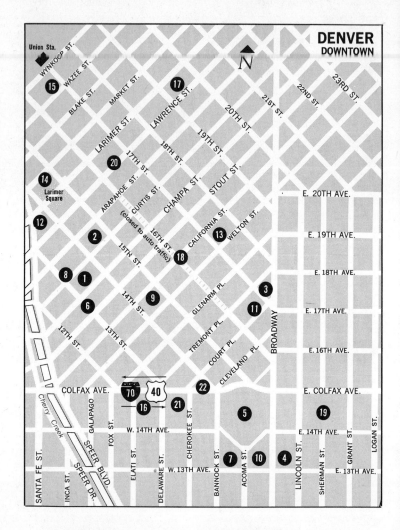

Points of Interest

1) Auditorium Arena & Theater
2) Brooks Tower
3) Brown Palace Hotel
4) Colorado Historical Society
5) Civic Center
6) Convention Center, Currigan Hall
7) Denver Art Museum
8) Denver Center for the Performing Arts
9) Denver Post Building
10) Denver Public Library
11) Denver Radisson Hotel
12) The Tivoli
13) Hyatt Regency Denver
14) Larimer Square
15) The Oxford–Alexis Hotel
16) Rocky Mountain News Building
17) Sakura Square
18) Sixteenth St. Mall
19) State Capitol
20) Tabor Center Shopping Mall and Westin Hotel Complex
21) U.S. Mint
22) Visitor's Bureau

display the Colonnades of Civic Benefactors, listing in bronze letters the prominent folks who donated toward the center's construction. The area is rich in statuary.

The Civic Center was inspired by the famous mall in Washington, D.C., and leads visitors to the Capitol Building (modeled after the nation's Capitol).

The 160-room building was completed in 1894, with gold leaf hammered from Colorado ore covering the dome. From the balcony just below, visitors can see a 150-mile panorama of the Rockies to the west.

The interior wainscoting is in an exotic ochre marble found in a single deposit in southern Colorado. Capitol construction used the entire deposit; the paneling can never be duplicated or replaced. Other highlights include murals by famed Colorado artist Allen True that are accompanied by verses of Thomas Hornsby Ferril, the state's poet laureate. The 13th step at the entrance marks a point exactly one mile above sea level.

Two blocks away at 13th and Broadway is the Heritage Center, which houses treasures collected by the Colorado Historical Society. Artifacts and photos from Denver's early life, ancient Mesa Verde Indian pieces, and a fascinating diorama of Denver as it was in 1860 are among the exhibits.

The Denver Public Library is at 1357 Broadway, across from the Heritage Center. Of special interest: the fourth floor Western History Department. There's plenty of information here on the old and new West, and Denver in particular, for travelers and history buffs. (James Michener researched some of *Centennial* at these tables.)

The Denver Art Museum towers behind the library. You can't overlook the angular gray-tiled building with windows in seemingly random sizes and shapes. Italian architect Gio Ponti designed the edifice to house the museum's collection in style. The items span cultures as well as time: African, Oriental, pre-Columbian, and early American, with one or two masterpieces by Rembrandt, Picasso, Matisse, Renoir, Rubens, and others. There's also a good collection of contemporary art, textiles, costumes, pottery, jewelry, period rooms, and antique furniture. The Native American exhibit is excellent.

More of Downtown

The Buckhorn Exchange at 1000 Osage Street, close to downtown, is worth a visit just before lunchtime. Several generations have enriched this museum and dining emporium. The contents include hundreds of historic photos (some of the mining family the Tabors, for instance, whose rags-to-riches story is a favorite part of local lore), ancient western guns, trophies, and antlers of every description, stuffed animals, Indian mementos, paintings. Admission is free.

One block behind the Visitors' Bureau, you'll discover the Denver Firefighters Museum at 1326 Tremont Place. Old hand pumpers, uniforms, photos, and other items are housed in Fire House No. 1, built in 1909. Nearby Currigan Exhibition Hall, 14th and Champa, hosts many shows, conventions, and festivals.

The highlight of downtown Denver sightseeing is Larimer Square, on Larimer Street between 14th and 15th. This is the city's original business block. Denver had abandoned lower Larimer Street in the early 1900's, leaving it to vagrants and disrepair until a local preservation group rescued

the buildings and restored them to become Denver's first officially desig-
nated Historic District. Here there are all manner of shops and exotica:
bistros, fine restaurants, silversmiths, and leatherworkers' studios. Consider lunching at the nearby Oxford-Alexis Hotel in the charming old dining
room.

Another outstanding downtown shopping and strolling spot is the 16th
Street Mall, a brick-lined section closed to traffic. Browse, listen to the
street musicians, try one of the excellent restaurants, or visit the ultramodern Tabor Center, which features over 70 retailers and restaurants.

Dynasty

The heart of Denver's phenomenal boom is 17th Street, the city's financial district. Here, amid more than a dozen imposing office towers of glass,
chrome, and steel, many of the Fortune 500 companies occupy sleek new
offices. The Anaconda Corporation, an international mining and minerals
conglomerate, constructed a 40-story office tower next to the gleaming
Hyatt Regency Denver Hotel.

The nation's leaders in finance, industry, and engineering are flocking
here to pursue their careers and business deals in the progressive milieu.
As you walk along 17th Street you will overhear conversations about new
petroleum finds, multimillion dollar stock transactions, and new technical
advances in computer design. And you may find yourself on the lookout
for Blake Carrington or Alexis Colby.

A brief walk west, just across Speer Boulevard, is the sleek Auraria
Higher Education Center. Metro State College, Denver Community College, and University of Colorado all use the ultramodern educational village. Don't miss Ninth Street Historic Park, tucked behind the classroom
building. It's a block of restored Victorian working-class houses from one
of the earliest settlements of Denver, now used as offices for the colleges.
The ornate white building with the blue roof at the foot of the campus
is the old Tivoli Brewery, now transformed into trendy shops, restaurants,
and a 12-screen cinema.

Across the Platte River on 15th Street is the Forney Transportation Museum, filled with vintage vehicles, "pufferbellies" and historic railroad
cars, old-time airplanes, and more.

East of Downtown

The Denver Botanic Gardens, at 909 York Street, offer seasonal displays, herbal acreage, and a two-acre classic Japanese garden. The conservatory, looking like a quilted bubble, shelters an authentic tropi-
cal/subtropical forest with streams, paths, foot bridges.

City Park, northeast of the Botanic Gardens along 17th Avenue between York Street and Colorado Boulevard, yields 640 acres for recreation
and learning. Start at the Museum of Natural History, which has many
floors of dinosaurs, Indian artifacts, insects, birds, and animals from
around the world. Don't miss the moose and elk displays and the whale
exhibit. Headphones can be rented that plug into outlets at each display
for brief talks. The Gates Planetarium, attached to the museum, offers
laser light concerts and trips through time and space projected onto an
overhead 50-foot dome while the audience watches from reclining chairs.
The complex is also home to the Imax Theater, with its 4½-story-tall,
6½-story-wide screen.

A short walk west takes you to the Denver Zoological Gardens. Several thousand animals are housed in native habitats. The Children's Zoo sports a monkey island and cavorting seals. There are also several walk-through bird houses. The well-groomed, flowered, and landscaped expanse of City Park is the centerpiece of Denver's 25,000-acre municipal park system.

PRACTICAL INFORMATION FOR DENVER

HOW TO GET THERE. Because of its central location, Denver has always been a major transportation hub. Most airlines, bus companies, and trains serve this western metropolis, offering a large number of choices and price ranges. Generally, if you arrive from far away, flying is the least expensive way to go. For shorter trips and for travel within the state, buses have the edge.

By air. Denver's Stapleton Airport is the eighth busiest in the world and is served by most major carriers. Among these are: *American, Delta, Continental, Eastern, TWA, United,* and *US Air.* Currently, *America West* Airlines has expanded its Denver hub with frequent flights throughout the western U.S. Regional lines include *Air Midwest, Northwest, Chicago Air,* and *Midway.* Among the Commuter Carriers are *Centennial, Continental Express,* and *United Express. Skyworld* can provide worldwide charter service. Most international air carriers also serve Denver. For information on getting from the airport see "How to Get Around," below.

Numerous airlines offer discounted fares with certain restrictions. For example, *Continental Airlines* sells at lower fares during off-peak hours and on certain prepaid plans. Other carriers have Super-Saver tickets. These must be booked in advance and may restrict the length of stay and departure/arrival dates. These special rates change almost weekly, so consult your travel agent for the best possible deal.

By bus. *Greyhound/Trailways* serves Colorado and has a terminal in downtown Denver. Discounts are available for children.

By train. *Amtrak* offers service from Chicago, San Francisco, Seattle, Portland, and Los Angeles. Amtrak also serves Winter Park, Granby, Grand Junction, and other Colorado towns.

By car. Main highways into Denver are I-25 from Wyoming in the north and New Mexico in the south; I-70 from Utah in the west and Kansas in the east; and I-80S from Nebraska in the northeast.

EMERGENCY TELEPHONE NUMBERS. In the Metro area dial either 911 or 0 for ambulance, fire, and police. The State Patrol number is 757–9475. The Poison Control Hotline can be reached at 629–1123. For road conditions phone 639–1111.

HOTELS AND MOTELS in Denver range from the old, established, world-famous Brown Palace, through its sister lodgings in the deluxe and expensive categories, then on to the many fine hotels scattered along the metropolitan area's highways and side streets. Many of the latter are connected to national chain operations. Cost figures here are generally for the minimum or moderate-priced rooms, unless a range is indicated. Listings are in order of price category.

The price categories in this section, for double occupancy, will average as follows: *Deluxe* $85–$210, *Expensive* $37–$84, *Moderate* $22–$36, and *Inexpensive* $18–$21. Note that all motels and hotels accept credit cards unless otherwise indicated.

DELUXE

Brown Palace. 321 17th St., 80202; 303–297–3111. Downtown. One of the world's well-known hotels, with good service, 500 guest rooms, and tasteful decoration. Elegant dining in the *Palace Arms* or *Ellyngton's,* relaxed meals in the *Ship Tavern,* where prime rib reigns. Beauty and barber shops, florist, drugstore.

The Burnsley. 1000 Grant St., 80203; 303–830–1000. Distinguished small hotel close to downtown and state capitol. Some suites and kitchenettes. Favored by upper-echelon business executives.

Cambridge Club Hotel. 1560 Sherman, 80203; 303–831–1252. Luxurious one- and two-bedroom suites, with Continental breakfast, 24-hour room service, many amenities. Helpful concièrge staff, health-club privileges. Appeals to business people.

Clarion Denver Airport. 3203 Quebec, 80207; toll-free 800–325–6064. At airport. A well-run, 588-room super motel with large indoor pool, sauna, and outstanding dining facilities. Complimentary airport limousine.

Denver Radisson Hotel. 1550 Court Pl., 80202; 303–893–3333. Downtown. A large establishment catering to conventions. Five dining areas and handsome cocktail lounge. Heated pools, saunas, radios, barber and beauty shops, drugstore, airport bus available.

Denver Marriott City Center. 1701 California, 80202; 303–297–1300. Centrally located 42-story, 612-room hotel, with 42 luxury suites in downtown financial center. Indoor pool. Ballrooms. Restaurants and bars. Ideal for conventions.

Hyatt Regency Denver. 1750 Welton, 80202; 303–295–1200. Downtown Denver's elegant $44 million, 550-room convention hotel. The hotel began an extensive renovation program scheduled for completion in 1989. All amenities. *Marquis* dining room. Superb Sunday brunches. Twenty-four-hour *McGuire's* restaurant and cocktail lounge. Rooftop pool, "sky court" tennis.

Loews Giorgio Hotel. 4150 E. Mississippi, 80202; 303–782–9300. Hotel with 200 rooms, 20 suites, Italian country villa decor. Complimentary breakfast, superb restaurant, nearby Cherry Creek Sporting Club.

The Oxford-Alexis Hotel. 1600 17th St., 80202; 303–628–5400. Downtown. Supremely elegant $8 million renovation of a small, grand hotel near Union Station. Restaurant, bar, entertainment, 82 rooms. Charming Sunday brunches.

Regency Inn. 3900 Elati St., 80216; 303–458–0808. I-25 at W. 38th Ave. A large hotel in north Denver, popular with conventions. Two pools, saunas, exercise rooms, barber and beauty shops, restaurant, and cocktail lounge.

Sheraton Denver Tech Center. 4900 DTC Parkway, 80237; 303–779–1100. At Tech Center, 12 miles southeast of downtown Denver. Built in 1980. Conference and banquet facilities, shops, health club, and 640 rooms.

Westin Hotel. Denver Tabor Center, 1672 Lawrence St., 80202; 303–572–9100 or 800–228–3000. Luxurious 430-room, 19-story superhotel with rooftop pool. Seventy shops, plus access to the mall meeting facilities.

Writer's Manor. 1730 S. Colorado Blvd., 80222; 303–756–8877 or 800–525–8072. Southeast Denver. A large, renovated, 350-room spacious motel with two heated pools, sauna. *Churchill* gourmet restaurant, coffee shops, and bars.

EXPENSIVE

Best Western Inn at the Mart. 401 E. 58th Ave., 80216; 303–297–1717. I-25, Exit 215. Popular with sales reps. Shops, cafés, post office on premises. Convention site.

Compri-Lakewood. 137 Union Blvd., 80228; 303–969–9000 or 800–426–6777. Cable TV, heated pool, health club. Free breakfast, late snacks, and beverages. Meeting facilities.

Golden Hours Motel. 11080 West Colfax, Lakewood, 80215; 303–237–7725. Ideal for families visiting Denver for more than a few days. Kitchenettes, playground, pool, and nearby shopping.

Holiday Inn Downtown. 1450 Glenarm Pl., 80202; 303–573–1450 or 800–423–5128. Four hundred-room hotel in excellent downtown location. Free indoor parking.

Holiday Inn Southeast. 9009 E. Arapahoe Rd., Englewood, 80112; 303–790–1421. At Denver Tech Center, I-25. Suites available. Indoor pool, sauna, exercise room, steam room. Live entertainment and dancing nightly (except Sunday and Monday). Dining room, cocktail lounge, and coffee shop. Good location, south of city.

Howard Johnson's Motor Lodge-West. 4765 Federal Blvd., 80211; 303–422–8442. Modern chain motel. Restaurant, cocktail lounge, hot tubs, coin laundry. Pets allowed.

Queen Ann Inn. 2147 Tremont Pl., 80205; 303–296–6666. Elegant bed-and-breakfast in three-story 1879 home near downtown. Ten rooms, afternoon tea or wine.

Raffles Hotel. 3200 S. Parker Rd., Aurora, 80014; 303–695–1700. I-225 and S. Parker Rd. Large, comfortable, well-designed hostelry with all amenities, including an indoor jogging track. Large convention area with ballroom. Good restaurants. Famous for Sunday brunch.

Ramada Inn Foothills. 11595 W. Sixth Ave., Lakewood 80215; 303–238–7751. Sixth Ave. and Simms, on the way to the ski areas. Pool and sauna. Attractive establishment. Elegant lobby. Plush rooms.

Rodeway Inn. 4590 Quebec, 80216; 800–228–2000. Five minutes from Stapleton International Airport, courtesy car. Special rooms offer private steambath, recliner chairs, office-size work desks. *Bijou Revue* restaurant and lounge. Entertainment.

Sheraton Denver, Airport. 3535 Quebec St., 80207; 303–333–7711. At Stapleton International Airport. This modern hotel offers heated indoor pool, sauna, health club, restaurant, and cocktail lounge. Free airport bus.

The Warwick Denver. 1776 Grant St., 80203; 303–861–2001 or 800–525–2888. Former Governor's Court Hotel. Attractive lobby and rooms, excellent meeting facilities. Near downtown attractions and city's business district.

MODERATE

Broadway Plaza. 1111 Broadway, 80203; 303–893–3501. Located 4 blocks south of State Capitol. In addition to 40 rooms, there is a rooftop sun deck and free coffee. Privately owned motel. Cafés nearby.

Colburn Hotel. 980 Grant St., 80203; 303–837–1261. Close to downtown area. All rooms with baths. Some kitchenettes and facilities for permanent guests. *Charlie Brown's* dining room, plus cocktail lounge.

Continental Inn Downtown. 2601 Zuni St., 80211; 303–433–6677 or 800–525–8110; from Colorado 800–332–8767. Located at Valley Hwy. at N. Speer Blvd. This large, easily accessible motel offers a large heated pool, free coffee, dining room, coffee shop, cocktail lounge, dancing. Recently refurbished.

Holiday Chalet. East Colfax at High St., 80218; 303–321–9975. Comfortable apartment hotel in eastern section of the city.

Kipling Inn. 715 Kipling St., Lakewood, 80215; 303–232–5000. Located 9½ miles southwest just off US 6. This motel west of Denver offers heated pool, playground, restaurant, and cocktail lounge. Some units have kitchens.

La Quinta. 3975 Peoria, 80239; 303–371–5640 or 800–531–5900. Chain motel with 112 rooms, not far from airport. *Denny's* café.

Relax Inns. 1680 Colorado Blvd., 80222; 303–691–2223. Comfortable rooms with free HBO, Continental breakfast. Indoor pool, covered parking. Special weekend rates, senior discount.

Sands Motel. 13388 E. Colfax, Aurora, 80011; 303–366–3581. Located across from Fitzsimons Hospital, near Lowry and Buckley. Waterbeds available. Some units have kitchens.

INEXPENSIVE

American Family Lodge North. 5888 Broadway, 80216; 303–296–3100. Located four miles north at I-25 Exit 215. Standard motel, near Merchandise Mart.

American Family Lodge-West. 4735 Kipling St., Wheat Ridge 80033; 303–423–0800. Located eight miles west on I-70 at Wheat Ridge (Exit 65). Heated pool. Twenty-four-hour café opposite.

Anchor. 2323 S. Broadway, 80210; 303–744–3281. Located four miles south on State 87. Small motel, free coffee, pets, sun deck. Twenty-four-hour café nearby. Good value.

Broadway Plaza Motel. 1111 Broadway, 80203; 303–893–3501. Near capitol, within walking distance of downtown attractions.

Cameron Motel. 4500 E. Evans, 80222; 303–756–9431. Not far from University of Denver. Thirty-five units, with phones and color TV's.

Motel Six. 480 Wadsworth Blvd., 80226; 303–232–4924. West Denver. Bargain rates for simple, nondescript, but clean rooms. Fills up early in the day. En route to mountains.

Regal 8. 12033 E. 38th, 80239; 303–371–0740. East Denver. Chain motel without luxuries.

Six Pence Inn. 9920 W. 49th, Wheat Ridge, 80033; 303–424–0658. At I-70 and Kipling. Across from *Furr's Cafeteria* and *Denny's.*

BED AND BREAKFASTS. Affectionately known as B and B's, these guest homes provide the personal touch in accommodations and are becoming more popular in the U.S. every year. A B and B offers the warmth of sharing someone's house, home-cooked breakfast, and the chance to get to know a local family. Rooms are infinitely varied—you may have to head down the hall to the bathroom but you will often enjoy antique furniture or find fresh flowers on your bedside table. For a directory of guest homes in Denver and reservation assistance, contact *Rocky Mountain Bed & Breakfast,* Box 804, Colorado Springs, CO 80901.

Y'S AND HOSTELS. Located in most major cities, these provide basic and economical alternatives for lodging. *YMCA,* 25 E. 16th Ave., Denver 80202; 303–861–8300. Downtown. Coffee shop in lobby; lobby open 24 hours. Check-in is 11 A.M.–10 P.M. on a first-come, first-serve basis. Rooms are small but clean and have telephones. Separate floor for women. Rates for a double with bath are $31.25. *American Youth Hostels,* 1452 Detroit St., Denver 80206; 303–333–7672. Dormitory-style, any age welcome, three-night limit, communal kitchen. Bring sleeping bag or rent linens, men and women on separate floors. Rates for AYH members, $6. Nonmembers pay $8. Reservations with half deposit. For **camping** information see *Practical Information for the Areas Beyond Denver.*

HOW TO GET AROUND. From the airport. Downtown is seven miles from Stapleton International. Taxi service is about $10; see "By taxi," below. Limousines to major hotels run $5 to city center; $7 to southeast area; phone 398–2284. Cabs, limousines, and city buses (see below) leave from lower level, door 5. Rental cars are also available at the airport; see "By car," below.

By bus. The *R.T.D. (Regional Transportation District)* operates the city's buses. Buses run not only within Denver proper, but also out into the suburbs and to Boulder. Route and schedule information is available by calling 778–6000. Basic city fare: 50 cents; 75 cents at peak hours; exact change. Seniors over 65 ride for 10 cents. A free shuttle runs along the 16th Street Mall downtown. A first-time rider's kit with system maps and information can be obtained by writing RTD, Department of Marketing, 1600 Blake St., Denver, CO 80202.

By taxi. Cabs in Denver may be hailed or requested by phone. Taxis are usually plentiful in the city. *Yellow Cab,* 292–1212, is one of the major operators, or call *Metro Taxi,* 333–3333. Cabs operate on a "live meter" system, which means in bad weather or heavy traffic rates change from by-the-mile to by-the-minute.

By car. Two interstate highways, I-70 and I-25, intersect near downtown Denver. Traffic usually flows smoothly, except during rush hour. From 6:30 to 8:30 in the morning and 4 to 6 in the afternoon, traffic can be stop and go, especially on I-25. (Most city AM radio stations provide traffic updates during the prime hours.) Parking downtown is hard to find and ranges from 50 cents a half hour to $5 a day. Parking in the suburbs is usually available. The designated Snow Route signs around the city indicate streets on which parking is not allowed during a snowstorm. On these roads during heavy storms parked cars will be towed. Handicapped parking is indicated by blue-and-white signs.

Rental cars. All major agencies have offices in Denver, including airport booths. *Avis* and *Hertz,* the two most expensive, have toll-free numbers: call Avis at 800–331–1212; Hertz at 800–654–3131. The city has hundreds of other rental companies, including everything from *Rent-A-Lemon* to offices that specialize in Porsches and other sports cars. There are also many companies renting limousines in the city. Try *Colorado Limousine* (832–7155) or *People's Choice,* with one-hour service available; 232–1699.

TOURIST INFORMATION. *Denver Metro Convention and Visitors Bureau,* 225 W. Colfax Ave., Denver 80202; 303–892–1112, provides an official *Visitors Guide* that lists area attractions, events, shopping areas, and provides a map. Hours are: winter: Mon.-Fri. 8–5, Sat. 9–1; summer: Mon.-Fri. 8–5, Sat. 9–5.

SEASONAL EVENTS. January: *National Western Stock Show and Rodeo* takes place for 12 days in mid-month. The world's largest single livestock exhibition, this trade show of the ranching industry draws visitors from Canada and Mexico as well as from the entire U.S. It is said that millions of dollars in business deals are settled here each year. Events include professional and amateur rodeo, several horse shows, and the judging of champion cattle. All stock show events are held at the Denver Coliseum, at I-70 and Washington Street. **February:** The Hyatt Regency Tech Center presents *Jazzfest '89. Garden and Home Show.* **March:** *Denver Symphony Run* (marathon benefit). *St. Patrick's Day Parade* downtown. **April:** *Easter Sunrise services* at Red Rocks. **May:** Lakeside Amusement Park and Elitch Gardens, *bands* begin summer performances, *Cinco de Mayo* is celebrated in Skyline Park. **June:** *Greyhound racing* at Mile High Kennel Club throughout the summer, with pari-mutuel betting. Annual *Cherry Blossoms Festival* in Sakura Square. *The People's Fair* is held in Civic Center Park. *Colorado Renaissance Festival* runs through July in Larkspur. **July:** Annual 4th of July *Zephyrs'* baseball game and fireworks are held at Mile High Stadium. The *Drums Along the Rockies* competition is held at Mile High Stadium. In Central City, the *Opera and Drama Festival.* **August:** *Rocky Mountain Bluegrass Festival.* **September:** *Denver Broncos* professional football season opens. *The Festival of Mountain and Plain* is held Labor Day. **October:** Early in the month is the *Larimer Square Oktoberfest.* The *Denver Symphony* opens a season filled with classical, pops, and children's concerts. **December:** The *Annual Parade of Lights* features brilliantly lighted holiday floats, bands, and Santa. Larimer Square has the yearly *Christmas Walk,* and arts, dance, and food highlight the *Colorado Indian Winter Market,* Currigan Hall.

TOURS. *Gray Line* offers a deluxe city and mountain tour that includes a drive to mountain parks, the main sights of Denver, and a lunch stop in Evergreen. Departs daily at 9 A.M., returning 3 P.M., at a cost of $15. Children receive a discount. They also offer special trips to Pikes Peak, Central City, and, in summer, Rocky Mountain National Park. Your hotel will contact Gray Line for your pickup, or call 289–2841. Mailing address is Box 38667, Denver 80238.

The preservation group, *Historical Denver, Inc.,* arranges tours of "old Denver." Walking tours cost $5; $4 for children and seniors. Van tours are $10; $8 for children and seniors. Each is two hours long. Contact Historic Denver at 1330 17th Street, 80202; 534–1858.

For information on tours into the areas outside Denver, see the following section, "Beyond Denver."

SPECIAL-INTEREST TOURS. *The Denver Mint,* 320 West Colfax, downtown. Tours depart at 30-minute intervals every weekday, except the last two weeks in June. 8:30 A.M.–3:00 P.M. Free. Call 844–3582.

Colorado State Capitol, Broadway and Colfax, downtown. Free guided tours. Open 9 A.M.–4 P.M. Mon.–Fri. Call 866–5000.

Colorado Governor's Mansion, at Eighth and Logan streets, downtown, is open for tours at announced times during the rest of the year. Call 866–3682.

The Denver Center for the Performing Arts, 14th and Curtis. Tours on Wed. and Fri. at 12:10 P.M., or by appointment. Phone 893–4200.

PARKS. Over 150 parks attract city dwellers in droves on the weekends; best time to go is on weekdays, particularly mornings. Most of the parks—especially *City Park,* (off 17th Ave., between York St. and Colorado Blvd.)—have show-quality flower gardens, pools, picnic areas, and plenty of trees.

A weekday may be the best day to stroll through Denver's *Washington Park,* at S. Downing and E. Virginia, not far from E. Alameda Avenue. These acres of greenery are almost unknown to tourists, in spite of the attractions: small creeks flow under the branches of willows and cottonwoods. Young lovers from nearby Denver University rendezvous along the trails; elderly gentlemen enjoy a game of *boccie;* a soccer match draws crowds of cheering onlookers; an energetic exercise class comes jogging past. Bring a lunch basket. People walk their dogs, of course, and children sway on swings.

On the drive from downtown to the mountains, consider the greenery surrounding *Sloan's Lake Park* at W. 26th and Sheridan (or reach it from W. Colfax Ave.). On a clear day, the view of the mountains is spectacular from here. Denverites take advantage of this lake for water skiing, sailing, motor boating (no swimming), fishing, bicycling, tennis (courts on both sides), or just walking around. The circle tour takes about one hour on foot.

THEME PARKS AND AMUSEMENTS. *Elitch Gardens,* 4620 W. 38th Ave.; 455–4771. This may be one of the most delightful amusement parks in the nation. Loosely patterned after Tivoli Gardens in Copenhagen, Denmark, Elitch Gardens charms both children and adults with its colors, its impeccable maintenance, and the imaginative rides. One of these, Mister Twister, is rated the second most exciting roller coaster in the world. Also a "Miniature Madness" section for tots, a well-known summer stock theater, and many refreshment stands. Open 10 A.M.–11 P.M. June–late August; special hours at the beginning and end of the season.

Hyland Hills Water World, one of America's largest water parks, in Federal Heights, has two wave-tech pools and 14 water slides. Open 10 A.M.–11 P.M., May–August.

Lakeside Amusement Park, at 4601 Sheridan Boulevard, is not far away from Elitch's. You can reach Lakeside via the Interstate 70. Lakeside has a different character altogether, somewhat noisier and faster and aimed more toward large crowds. The park is located next to a lake, and the lights reflecting in the water are mesmerizing. The season runs from June to September. Hours Mon.–Fri. are 1 P.M.–10 P.M. for the Children's Playland, 6 P.M.–11 P.M. for major rides; Sat., Sun. and holidays the park is open from noon to 11 P.M. Phone 477–1621.

Celebrity Sports Center, 888 S. Colorado Blvd.; 757–3321, features water slides, an Olympic indoor pool, steam rooms, bowling, and video games. Hours and costs differ for separate sections, and the whole family can enjoy a day's entertainment here. (Discounts for Seniors.)

ZOOS. *Denver's Zoological Gardens* are located in City Park (see "Parks," above). Several thousand animals are housed in native habitats. The Children's Zoo here sports a monkey island and cavorting seals. There are also several walk-through bird houses. Hours are 10 A.M.–5 P.M. Adults pay $4, children and seniors $2. Phone 331–4110.

GARDENS. *Denver Botanic Gardens,* 1005 York St.; 331–4010. Outdoor gardens and a conservatory offer beautiful arrangements of native and exotic plant life. Eight hundred species of tropical and subtropical plants thrive year round in the steel and glass conservatory. Enjoy trickling streams, waterfalls, and tall royal palms. Admission is $3 adults, $1.50 seniors over 65, $1 children 7 to 16. Daily 9 A.M.–4:45 P.M.

Elitch Gardens (see "Theme Parks and Amusements," above) has a 96-year-old tradition of some of the best displays in Denver.

Many of the areas parks, particularly *City Park* at 17th and York streets, and *Washington Park,* at S. Downing and E. Virginia, also have outstanding gardens.

PARTICIPANT SPORTS. With its 300 sunny days a year Denver is a marvelous place for active people.

Denver has an extensive network of paths for **bicycle** enthusiasts. A map is available from the *Bicycle Racing Association of Colorado,* 1290 Williams St., 80218; 303–333–2453.

Boating is popular at *Cherry Creek Reservoir,* just southeast of the intersection of Hampden and Havana. The reservoir is crowded on hot weekends. *Sloan's Lake,* at 17th and Sheridan, is for sailors and **waterskiers.**

Many city parks also offer **fishing.** A license is required and is available at most sporting goods stores around town.

The **golf** lasts for virtually 12 months in Denver. Among the array of courses, consider the scenic *Wellshire Municipal Golf Course,* 3333 S. Colorado Blvd. at Hampden Ave. Eighteen holes, lush grounds, rental equipment, a good restaurant and lounge. Phone 756–1352. Other Golf Links: *City Park,* E. 25th Ave. and York St., call 295–2585, and *Park Hill,* 3500 Colorado Blvd., call 333–5411, both in the northeast section of the city; *Willis Case,* W. 50th Ave. at Vrain, call 575–2112, in the northwest section; the *John Kennedy* course, 10500 E. Hampden Ave., call 751–0311, in the southeast section; and *Overland Park,* in the southwest section, West Jewell Ave. at S. Santa Fe Drive, call 777–7331.

If you belong to a golf or country club back home, you may be extended playing privileges at Denver's private courses. Some of the better ones are *Cherry Hills,* 4000 S. University Blvd., call 761–9900, and *Heather Ridge,* 13521 E. Illiff Ave., call 755–3550.

For **hikers:** The city maintains 45 mountain parks, many in Jefferson County. For a complete listing write Denver Mountain Parks, 2900 E. 23rd Ave., Denver, 80205 or call 575–3170. See also the next section, "Beyond Denver," for some other nearby hiking sites.

For **joggers,** there are paths in almost every municipal park. *City Park,* with its beautiful flower gardens, is especially nice. Or jog around *Sloan's*

Lake at 17th and Sheridan. *Cheesman Park,* E. Eighth Ave. and Franklin St., also affords lovely scenery.

Denver is located less than 90 miles from many of the best **ski** resorts and areas in the world. (For details, see the "Ski and Summer Resorts" chapter of the guide.) Ski equipment may be rented by the day or week in Denver, often at a lower price than the resorts charge. Discounted lift tickets to some areas are available at local grocery chains; some offer special lessons packages as well. *Colorado Ground Transportation* offers shuttle services to the major areas. From within the state phone 800–332–0202. Denver phone is 388–5669. Reservations are suggested. Many major centers have Denver phone numbers: check the yellow pages under "Skiing Center."

If your hotel or motel doesn't have a **swimming** pool, an Olympic-sized one exists indoors at *Celebrity Sports Center,* 888 S. Colorado Blvd. Steam rooms are offered too. Call 757–3321. The *YMCA* operates an indoor pool at 25 E. 16th Avenue, downtown. Call 861–8300. This facility also includes weight rooms, gyms, racketball courts, and aerobics classes. Fee is $8 for a day's use of all equipment; $4 for a YMCA member from any U.S. city. Many city parks also have swimming pools. Call 575–2552 for information on pools within the city.

Tennis thrives on free city-maintained courts in most parks, including *City Park,* E. 25th Ave. and York St.; *Berkeley,* W. 46th Ave. at Tennyson; *Washington Park,* Louisiana at Downing; *Eisenhower,* S. Colorado Blvd. at Dartmouth; *Crestmoor,* E. First Ave. at Monaco. A little-known spot: *Houston Lake Park,* W. Kentucky Ave. at S. Vallejo St., with four courts beside a lake. Call 575–3233 for information, including details on tennis lessons.

SPECTATOR SPORTS. Denver area's **auto racetracks** offer everything from Indianapolis-type formula cars to motorcycle competition. Nearest is *Lakeside Speedway* at the amusement park, W. 44th Ave. and Sheridan. The Sunday night programs run from early May through Labor Day. Call 477–1621. *Bandimere Speedway,* 3051 S. Rooney Rd., near Red Rocks (697–6001), is famous with drag racing fans, and *Colorado National Speedway,* 4281 Weld County Rd. 10 (I–25N, Exit 232); 665–4173, has Saturday night stock car meets on a ½-mile banked clay track.

Next to the stadium, the *Denver Nuggets* **basketball** team is based in *McNichols Arena* from October to May. Tickets are $8–16; call 575–5833.

If you have never seen a **dog race,** try the *Mile High Kennel Club* at Colorado Boulevard and East 62nd Avenue. The greyhounds run six nights a week, June through August, with matinees on Saturdays. Betting is legal for persons 18 or over. Admission is 50 cents, programs cost $1, and parking is free. Phone 288–1591 for more information.

The 74,000 seats of Mile High Stadium, Federal Blvd. and 17th Ave., are never enough to hold all the fans of the *Denver Broncos* **football** team. The team has improved greatly in recent years and is now a citywide passion. Fans wait years for tickets and brave traffic jams around the stadium at game times. For ticket info call 433–7466. Parking is usually adequate.

Each January Denver hosts the *National Western Stock Show,* northeast of Denver at I–70 and Brighton Blvd., with a rodeo, cattle displays, and myriad contests. Phone 297–1166 for ticket information.

CHILDREN'S ACTIVITIES. A full day may easily be spent in *City Park,* with its zoo, children's zoo, and playgrounds. The *Denver Museum* *of Natural History and Planetarium* are in the park and should not be missed. City Park is located at 17th and York streets. Zoo admission is $4 adults, $2 children. Hours are 10 A.M.–5 P.M. The museum is open 9 A.M.–5 P.M. daily. Admission is $3.50 adults, $1.50 children. Phone 370–6363. The Planetarium has evening and matinee shows. Call 370–6351 for program information. Ticket prices vary depending on the show.

Elitch Gardens, Lakeside Amusement Park, and the *Celebrity Sports Center* have long been favorites with the young; see "Theme Parks and Amusements," above.

The *Denver Public Library* often features special children's programs. The main Library is at 1357 Broadway, phone 571–2000.

The Children's Museum, 2121 Crescent Dr., offers story hours, hands-on displays, health screening, and much more. Hours are Sun.–Fri., 12–5 P.M.; Sat. 10 A.M.–5 P.M.; closed Mon. Admission $2.25 adults and children; $1.50 seniors. Phone 433–7444.

The *Colorado Railroad Museum,* in a depot-style building, houses many early Colorado railroad items. It's located in Golden at 17155 West 44th Avenue, phone 279–4591. Open 9 A.M.–5 P.M. daily. Family rate of $5.50. Both girls and boys will enjoy the *Forney Transportation Museum,* 1416 Platte, 433–3643. It features antique cars, carriages, and trains. Prices are $3.00 adults, $1.50 for children ages 12–18, 50 cents under 12.

HISTORIC SITES & HOUSES. The *Molly Brown House,* home of the "unsinkable Molly Brown," re-creates Denver's rich Victorian past. Molly, a survivor of the *Titanic,* bought the house in 1894. It has been beautifully restored. The address is 1340 Pennsylvania Avenue, phone 832–4092. Hours are Tues.–Sat. 10 A.M.–3 P.M.; Sun. 12–3 P.M. Cost is $3.00 adults, $1.00 children 6–18, $1.50 for those over 60.

Straight south of Molly's place, at Eighth Avenue and Pennsylvania, is another famous residence, the *Colorado Governor's Mansion.* It's surrounded by terraced gardens and ancient elms. The house is open on Tuesdays in summer; during the rest of the year, special days are selected. Admission is free. Phone 866–3682.

Four Mile Historic Park surrounds the oldest house in Denver. Located at 715 S. Forest, hours are 11 A.M.–5 P.M. Tues.–Sun. Modest admission price.

Denver has many beautiful Victorian homes. *Ninth Street Historic Park,* near the Tivoli Brewery, is a picturesque block of early Denver houses. *Pearce-McAllister Cottage,* 1880 S. Gaylord, phone 322–3704, is a historical home built in 1899. Guided tours on Tues.–Wed. 10 A.M.–2 P.M. Visit also *Larimer Square* downtown. A restored section including Denver's oldest streets, the square features courtyards, gas lamps, and Victorian buildings. Virtually every outlaw and desperado in the West once walked this street. Today it houses restaurants, galleries, and nightclubs.

MUSEUMS. Denver is a fast-growing city, and its museums and galleries reflect that growth. Here are some of the most notable.

Arvada Center for the Arts and Humanities, 6901 Wadsworth Blvd., Arvada 80003, phone 431–3080. Overlooking city, about 12 miles from downtown. Art and history exhibits. Hours are 9 A.M.–9 P.M. Mon.–Fri., 8 A.M.–5 P.M. Sat., 1–5 P.M. Sun. Free.

The Buckhorn Exchange, at 1000 Osage Street near downtown, is a nice lunchtime stop. Several generations have enriched this museum and dining emporium, which houses hundreds of historic photos, ancient western guns, trophies and antlers of every description, stuffed animals, Indian mementos, and paintings. Free. Phone 534–9505.

The Colorado History Museum, located at 1300 Broadway, phone 866–3682, houses artifacts and photos from Denver's early life, ancient Mesa Verde Indian pieces, and a fascinating diorama of Denver as it was in 1860. Contains the treasures collected by the Colorado Historical Society, including many permanent exhibits.

The Denver Art Museum, 100 S. 14th Avenue Parkway, houses a collection that includes African, Western U.S., Oriental, and pre-Columbian items, with some works by Rembrandt, Picasso, Matisse, Renoir, Rubens, and others. There are also textiles, costumes, pottery, jewelry, period rooms, and antique furniture. Museum hours are Sun. 12–5 P.M., Tues.–Sat. 9 A.M.–5 P.M., closed Mon. Cost is $2.50 adults; $1.50 seniors, students, and children. Phone 575–2793.

The Denver Museum of Natural History, Montview and Colorado blvds., in City Park, features four floors of dinosaurs, Indian artifacts, insects, birds, and animals from around the world. Don't miss the moose and elk displays and the whale exhibit. Headphones can be rented that plug into outlets at each display. The IMAX Theater, in the museum, is "the cinema of the future." Images explode on the huge screen with elaborate acoustics. Call 370–6300 for show times.

The Museum of Western Art, at 1727 Tremont Place, phone 296–1880, is outstanding and fits Denver's western image. Open Tues. through Sat., 10 A.M. to 4:30 P.M. Adults $3, children free.

MUSIC. Denver has a variety of music, from bluegrass to opera. Check the entertainment sections of the *Denver Post* and *The Rocky Mountain News* for up-to-date music listings. For information on the spectacular natural amphitheater at Red Rocks Park, see the section "Beyond Denver." Here are the major music venues in the city:

Arvada Center for the Arts and Humanities, 6901 Wadsworth Blvd., Arvada, 80003; 422–8050. The center books everything from jazz to chamber music.

Denver Symphony Orchestra, Boettcher Concert Hall, 950 13th; 592–7777. The DSO imports world-renowned conductors and musicians, and also performs a jazz series, a pops series, and special outdoor concerts. Tickets also through Datatix, 988–6712.

The *Paramount Theater,* 1621 Glenarm (825–4904), presents Gibson Jazz Concerts and various entertainers.

DANCE in Denver takes many forms. *Ballet Denver* is the city's oldest professional touring company. Located at 3955 Tennyson Street, it offers fine performances and daily dance and exercise classes.

Colorado Contemporary Dance, 1290 Williams, 80218, phone 321–6583, advertises performances by well-known companies several times each year.

Arvada Center, 6901 Wadsworth Blvd., Arvada, phone 422–8052, brings nationally known troupes for its fall-to-spring program.

New Dance Theater, 2006 Lawrence St., phone 295–1759, is home to the Cleo Parker Robinson Dance Troupe. Ultramodern dance performances take place at various times during the year.

THEATER. *The Denver Center for the Performing Arts,* 1050 13th St., phone 893–4000, offers playgoers their choice of entertainment. The *Denver Center Company* performs in repertory Mon.–Sat. fall through spring. *The Source,* a 158-seat theater, stages world premieres of locally written plays. *StageWest,* in the Galleria of the Denver Arts Center, offers professional off-Broadway–type productions in a 250-seat cabaret with bar. The center also presents nationally known touring companies. Weeknight performances are less expensive than weekends, and the first week of a production sees tickets at almost half the regular price.

The Arvada Center, 6901 Wadsworth, Arvada, phone 422–8050, features a variety of attractions in fall and winter.

The Changing Scene, 1527½ Champa, the *Victorian Theater,* 4201 Hooker, and *Germinal Stage,* 1820 Market, all rate highly among Denver's theaters.

The *Lowenstein Theater,* at 2526 E. Colfax, 893–4000, presents good actors from the community, September through June, with several children's shows. The *Bonfils' BoBan's Cabaret* presents mostly off-Broadway fare. Phone 399–5418.

ART GALLERIES. Denver has many fine galleries located throughout the city, though the Cherry Creek area perhaps boasts the largest concentration. Some examples are listed here.

Arctic Art, 2817 East Third Ave., phone 320–0469 (Cherry Creek area). Open Mon.–Sat., 10 A.M.–5:30 P.M. Exquisite ivory and soapstone sculptures, large collection of Eskimo masks.

Camera Obscura Gallery, 1309 Bannock St., 623–4059. Contemporary and vintage photographs.

Panache, 1071 Old S. Gaylord, phone 778–0519. Hours Mon.–Sat., 10:30 A.M.–5 P.M. An innovative collection of fiber, clay, and jewelry.

SHOPPING. Downtown, retail shops line the 16th Street Mall from Court Place to Arapahoe Street. Here you will find most major **department stores:** *May D&F Company, Fashion Bar,* and *Joslins.* Try also the *Tabor Center,* on the mall: 70 new shops and restaurants in an ultramodern setting. For good buys on **skis** and other **sporting goods,** there is *Dave Cook,* downtown at 16th and Market, 892–1929; and *Gart Brothers,* 1000 Broadway, 861–1122. For newly popular **western wear,** *Miller Stockman,* 1409 15th St., carries a full array of authentic cowboy garb. *Kohlberg's* at 1720 Champa is the best place in the city to find **Indian crafts.** The store was opened in 1888 and still has its own Indian silversmith. The Kohlbergs are authorities on Pueblo pottery, turquoise, and all Native American arts. You can lose yourself browsing among the rugs, bracelets, and other items. *Robert Waxman Camera,* 913 15th St., is a stop for discount **cameras, photo supplies,** and advice. For **antiques** there are two major areas: *Olde Towne Arvada,* northwest of Denver, a neighborhood of historic buildings that house antique shops; and *South Broadway Street.* This section of town has shops lining both sides of the street offering everything from Victorian furniture to art deco dishes and vintage clothing.

DINING OUT. The restaurants of Denver and its large metropolitan area are often underestimated. There are approximately 1,800 restaurants, cafés, bistros, pizza places, franchises, taverns serving food, cafeterias, and other establishments where you can eat. You can find every type of fare in Denver—from haute cuisine to the simplest cowboy chow. Foreign restaurants proliferate. Western steak houses are abundant and, practically everywhere, you can get excellent mountain trout.

While many excellent restaurants go in for international cuisine, those serving steak and lobster are prevalent and popular. Most good restaurants prefer that reservations be made for dinner. Dress is usually casual; ties are rarely required, for instance. Prices here are for the medium-priced meals on an establishment's menu unless a range is indicated. For other worthwhile restaurants, check hotel listings. Restaurants are listed in order of price category.

Restaurant categories are: *Super Deluxe* $38 and up, *Deluxe* $35 and up, *Expensive* $15–$34, *Moderate* $11–$14, and *Inexpensive* $6–$10. These prices are for one meal, including appetizer, salad or soup, plus entrée, exclusive of drinks and tips. All restaurants listed take major credit cards unless noted otherwise.

AMERICAN AND WESTERN

Deluxe

Palace Arms. Brown Palace Hotel, 321 17th St., downtown; 297–3111. This is the choice of Denver's Old Guard and favorite with business executives. Known for native steaks.

The Rattlesnake Club. 901 Larimer; 573–8900. Bright, classy California import; southwestern cuisine. Stylish decor, pure linen, fine glassware; stunning views of Denver skyline. A favorite with business people for lunch; fresh fish, duck, lamb, veal dinners, fabulous desserts. Long wine list. Sunday brunch.

Wellshire Inn. 3333 S. Colorado Blvd., southeast Denver; 759–3333. Elaborate menu served against a baronial manor backdrop. Overlooks golf course. Specialties include fresh fish, spinach salad, veal verona, chicken with almonds, Cantonese duck, elegant desserts, tasty "HealthMark" dishes. Under longtime management of Leo Goto. Lunch and dinner. Open seven days a week.

Expensive

Bobby Mc Gee's. 2852 W. Bowles Ave., Littleton; 730–0080. Traditional steaks, smokehouse specialties, fresh fish, served by entertaining waiters dressed as Cleopatra, Zorro, Cinderella, etc. Scrumptious soup and salad bar, dessert tray, kids' menu. Old-fashioned decor with eclectic mix of memorabilia. "Island motif" lounge has sunken dance floor, light show, and hot music. A unique experience.

Buckhorn Exchange. 1000 Osage St., near downtown; 534–9505. A Denver institution since 1893 (see also "Museums"). Friendly, informal, truly Western eatery. Famous bean soup and steaks of several sizes; also buffalo meat, quail, and trout. Nightly specials. Cordial bar. Hundreds of pictures, animal heads, and stuffed creatures decorate. Busy and informal.

Moderate

Apple Tree Shanty. 8710 E. Colfax, east Denver; 333–3223. Takes no reservations but usually enough room for families. Pit-prepared ribs a house specialty. Sizable dessert menu. Waitresses in Dutch-style garb.

Betty Rose. 1404 Larimer, at Larimer Square; 623–0123. Cute downstairs restaurant with a Cajun accent; spicy shrimp, Cajun pork, garlic chicken, good seafood. Talented chef. Liquor. Open weekdays until 10 P.M., until 4 A.M. weekends. Lively jazz club upstairs.

Hoffbrau Steaks. 13th and Santa Fe; 629–1778. Mostly steaks and meats. Big portions. Jukebox music. Liquor.

North Woods Inn, 6115 S. Santa Fe Dr., 12 miles southwest on US 85 in Littleton; 794–2112. This locally popular restaurant serves steak, beef stew, and logging-camp food with home-baked sourdough bread. The decor is north woods. Good value for big eaters.

Tabor Grill. Westin Hotel, 1672 Lawrence St., Tabor Center; 572–9100. Lively eatery with good values in chops, chicken, fresh fish. Cocktails. Open seven days a week.

White Fence Farm. 6263 W. Jewell Ave., between S. Sheridan and Wadsworth blvds.; 935–5945. In a meadow en route to mountains. Great American food with a southern accent—ham, turkey, chicken, ribs—prepared colonial style and served by waitresses in historic dress. Freshly baked goods. Liquor. Excellent quality food. Mostly local clientele. Dinner only. Closed Mon. Senior discount.

Inexpensive

Furr's. 3215 S. Wadsworth, Lakewood; 989–9188. Indoor parking. Clean and modern cafeteria. No credit cards.

King's Table Buffet. 6206 W. Alameda; 935–6101. All-you-can-eat buffet at one price is an outstanding deal for hungry people. No liquor.

Wyatt's Cafeteria. W. Alameda and Wadsworth; 934–5663. Prettily presented, quality foods at reasonable prices. No liquor.

FRENCH AND CONTINENTAL

Deluxe

The Augusta Room. Westin Hotel, 1672 Lawrence, downtown; 572–9100. One of Denver's most elegant gourmet outposts, with view of city. Splendid service; dishes prepared with an eye for color. Smoked sturgeon, pheasant mousse, poached salmon, Long Island duckling. French chef.

Churchill's. At Writers Manor, 1730 S. Colorado Blvd.; 756–8877. Candlelit, upscale, and cosmopolitan. Elegant appetizers include coquilles St. Jacques, goose liver pâté, escargots. Fresh salmon, halibut, sole; quail Forestière, duck. Tender prime rib. Fine veal, Cornish game hen, lamb chops served in Continental-cuisine style. European chef makes this one of Denver's best. Sunday brunch. Closed Sun. nights.

Deluxe to Expensive

Le Central. 112 E. Eighth Ave., near downtown; 863–8094. Genuine French restaurant at fair prices. Lunch and dinner. Extremely busy. Many entrées, all excellent. French wines. No credit cards.

Normandy Restaurant Francais. 1515 Madison, east Denver; 321–3311. A restaurant with a reputation among local gourmets. Interesting appetizers such as smoked trout, mousseline Neptune, excellent veal entrées, coq au Beaujolais. Fresh fish daily; goose at Christmas. Wine cellar with many vintages, including rare imports. Several private rooms. Under longtime ownership-supervision of M. and Mme. Gerstlé.

Quorum. 233 E. Colfax Ave., across from State Capitol; 861–8686. An elegant favorite with politicos. Features smoked trout, steak Diane, duckling, scallops, Dover sole, chateaubriand, veal Jean Pierre. For smaller appetites, "light menu" includes low-priced coq au vin, braised lamb, fresh fish, duckling strips. Multilingual owner/personality Pierre Wolf always on hand. Excellent choice for visitors from Europe. Open for lunch.

GERMAN AND SWISS

Moderate

Gasthaus Ridgeview. 4465 Garrison, in Wheatridge; 424–2161. Genuine German offerings for a hungry clientele. Sauerbraten, schnitzel, *Kassler, Rindsrouladen,* milk-fed veal dishes, elk, venison, rabbit in wine sauce, goose (in December), strudel. Peter Hellerman, proprietor and chef, is from Germany; hostess Elizabeth Hellerman is from Switzerland. Imported beers. Outdoor area for lunch. Low-priced specials.

Inexpensive

Das Essen Haus. Belmar Center, 1050 S. Wadsworth Blvd., Lakewood; 936–7864. Family dining. American version of German restaurant. Modest, bright, clean. No liquor.

Swiss Bells Restaurant. 7340 W. 38th Ave., Wheatridge; 421–6622. Ernie Eugster's longtime Swiss-American café. Diet dishes, too. Excellent value. No liquor. No credit cards, but checks accepted.

INTERNATIONAL

Deluxe

Bay Wolf. 231 Milwaukee; 388–9221. One of Denver's "in" restaurants. Ingenious dishes, beautifully displayed. Intimate booths. Smooth service. Bar. Live jazz, nonsmoking section.

Chateau Pyrenees. I–25, Exit 197 at Arapahoe, Englewood, 770–6660. Grandeur in furnishings, chandeliers, splendid French chateau ambiance, tuxedoed waiters. Colorado's most elaborate menu, in French. Outstanding French chef. Hors d'oeuvres include escargots, lobster, delicacies in champagne sauce; entrées feature tournados, chateaubriand, roast rack of lamb, fish, elegant fowl such as baby pheasant and roast duck, all beautifully presented. Half portions for dieters. Classical piano music, international wine list. Austrian proprietor Conrad Trinkaus a perfectionist and always on premises. Reservations essential.

ITALIAN AND MEXICAN

Expensive

Bella Napoli. 2245 Sheridan Blvd., Edgewater; 237–8991. Veal parmigiana, chicken cacciatore. Eggplant or zucchini dishes. Wine list. While small and a bit cramped, this ristorante is worth the drive. No credit cards, cash only.

Cactus. 601 S. Broadway; 733–5050. Spacious modern adobe restaurant with Mexican and Southwestern dishes. Good fish. Zesty sauces. Cocktails.

Josephina's. 1433 Larimer on Larimer Square, downtown; 623–0166. Roaring Twenties decor in a historic building with foods such as spaghetti, pizza, chicken. Excellent lasagna. Bar.

Transalpin. 416 E. 7th Ave; 830–8282. Imaginative, colorful cuisine with exotic touches. Eclectic menu: Spanish tapas hors d'oeuvres, oriental duck salad, vegetarian pasta, grilled ahi tuna. Excellent fresh fish; luscious desserts. Nonsmoking section. French wines. Accepts credit cards.

Tuscany. At Loews Giorgio Hotel, 4150 E. Mississippi; 782–9300. Elegant Italian fare prepared by an *Italiano* from Bari. Poached seafood, grilled fish, marinated pork, superb lamb. Fresh raspberries; pastries baked in house. European background music.

Moderate

Casa Bonita. 6715 W. Colfax Ave. at JCRS center; 232–5115. A busy "Mexican" restaurant for Americans. Great for tourists. Tasty food in multitiered surroundings decorated with murals. Entertaining mariachi music. Good for kids.

The Chili Pepper. 2150 Bryant (I-25 and Mile High Stadium exit), overlooking downtown Denver; 433–8406. Great Mexican food in a nice setting.

La Fontanella. 1700 E. Evans, near Denver University; 778–8598. Popular Italian ristorante for lunch and dinner. Young clientele. Large menu.

Garcia's. 1697 S. Havana, near Buckingham Square; 755–2670. All the south-of-the-border favorites. Mexican background music.

Inexpensive

Marble's Bistro. 504 E. Colfax; 832–4840. Small place with big portions of lasagna, fettuccine, tortellini, chicken cacciatore.

Old Spaghetti Factory. 1215 18th St. and Lawrence, downtown; 295–1864. Pasta served in the old Denver Cable Car Company. Lively and crowded. Great value.

MOROCCAN

Deluxe

Mataam Fez. 4609 E. Colfax, east Denver; 399–9282. Denver's only Moroccan restaurant. Genuine couscous, lamb dishes, *pastella*. Dim lights, heavy pillows. Good Moroccan wines. Reserve several hours for your complete supper.

ORIENTAL

Expensive

Gasho. 5071 S. Syracuse (Denver Tech Center), I-25 and E. Belleview; 773–3277. Dramatic tableside hibachi cooking. Good beef, chicken, sole. Popular with tourists. Sake or plum wine available.

Moderate to Inexpensive

Canton Landing. 6265 E. Evans; 759–1228. Three Chinese cuisines under one roof. Luncheon buffet; dinners daily until 10:30 P.M. Chinese beer.

Lotus Room. W. Ninth Ave. and Speer Blvd., near downtown; 534–7918. Busy family restaurant, frequented by many Denverites. Excellent chop suey, Chinese duck, and countless other dishes. Good value. Informal.

New Saigon. 630 S. Federal Blvd., southwest Denver; 936–4954. Small but outstanding Vietnamese café, with dishes from *Mi Tom Cua* to *Bo Vien* and *Goi Cuon*. Excellent value, friendly atmosphere. Closed Mon.

Red Coral. 1565 S. Colorado Blvd.; 758–7610. Efficient Chinese lunches and dinner. Locally popular.

Tommy Wong's Islands Restaurant. 4851 East Virginia, Glendale; 321–3207. Outstanding oriental luncheon and dinner buffet. Sunday brunches. Order from menu, too, if you wish.

SEAFOOD

Expensive

Fresh Fish Company. 7800 E. Hampden; 740–9556. Over 20 varieties of boneless, fresh fish fillets, broiled over mesquite. Live lobster, New Zealand cockles, sashimi and ceviche. Sourdough bread and tasty, low-fat, low-sodium dishes. Homey oak and brick decor and good food attracts crowds. Trendy wine list. Sunday brunch.

Marc's. 6920 W. 38th, Wheat Ridge; 422–6600. Well-run seafood restaurant and oyster bar. Mellow atmosphere. Scampi in garlic, blackened snapper, mountain trout specialties. Good salad bar. Some meat dishes, too.

NIGHTLIFE AND BARS. Denver's teeming nightlife can offer a visitor—even a resident—many choices.

Comedy: *The Comedy Works,* 1226 15th St.; 595–3637. Features well-known headliners and local talent. *George McKelvey's Comedy Club,* 7225 E. Hampden, 758–5275, showcases improv groups and famous comedians.

Jazz and Pop: *El Chapultepec,* lower downtown at 19th and Market, 295–9126, is the favorite of Denver's jazz lovers. Visit the *Denver Art Museum* on Wednesday evenings and enjoy live jazz bands and a cash bar. *The Burnsley Hotel,* 1000 Grant, 830–1000, features local jazz personalities, Thurs.–Sat., in its plush lounge. *Betty Rose,* 1404 Larimer, 623–8619, offers lively music upstairs from its restaurant.

Rock and disco: The scene centers in Glendale, a nearby suburb that has now been completely surrounded by Denver expansion. Leetsdale Drive east from Colorado Boulevard is the main area for action. Places to try include *Neo,* 320–0118; *Lauderdale's,* 756–4555; or *Packards,* 695–1752. *Ironworks,* 25 Larimer, 825–4901, in a restored factory near Mile High Stadium, has good music and great hot Buffalo wings. You can also try *Proof of the Pudding,* 694–4884. Big-name rockers appear regularly in the summer at *Red Rocks,* Morrison; 575–2637, and *McNichols Sports Arena,* 1635 Clay; 575–3217.

Dancing: *Park Hill Golf Club,* 35th Ave. and Colorado Blvd., 333–5411, has Sunday dances to big band, swing, and contemporary music. The *Regency Hotel,* 3900 Elati, Exit 213 off I–25, 458–0808, has free country and western dances nightly. *Conville's Pub,* 10133 W. Chatfield, Littleton, 973–2905, has a live contemporary dance band Wed.–Sat. nights.

EXPLORING BEYOND DENVER

The preceding section does touch on some of Denver's most immediate suburbs, but this section moves farther afield, within an approximate 50-mile radius of the Mile-High City.

Golden

Golden, Denver's farthest western suburb, spread along the banks of Clear Creek as a pioneer camp in 1859. It became the capital of Colorado Territory in 1862, and still boasts many buildings from pioneer days. According to a banner over the main street, Golden is "Where the West Remains." The internationally respected Colorado School of Mines is located on the west edge of the town.

The Railroad Museum, at 17155 West 44th Avenue, has an 1880s-style depot, historical exhibits, old narrow-gauge locomotives, railroad and trolley cars.

The Foothills Art Center, 15th and Washington, was built in 1892 originally as a Presbyterian church and later became a Unitarian church. The art center, which shows regional arts and crafts daily all year, was opened in 1968.

Colorado School of Mines' Geology Museum is nearby at 16th and Maple. The 1940 structure displays mineral ore, fossils, mining equipment, meteorites, and even a replica of an old gold mine.

Around Golden

Lookout Mountain, which is above Golden, just west on I-70, has the grave of Buffalo Bill Cody at the summit. Here also is a museum displaying relics of his cavalry and Wild West show days; it has a well-stocked gift shop. No charge.

Hikers and nature worshippers should drive up to the Jefferson County Conference and Nature Center at 900 Colorow Road. It offers a small botanical museum, plus trails.

On the way to Lookout Mountain you may wish to leave I-70 and visit the Mother Cabrini Shrine. There is no charge to enter the church, devoted to Saint Francis Xavier Cabrini. The setting includes a large number of meadows, summer flowers, surrounding forests, and quite a few steps that will make young walkers happy but can cause older ones to puff a little. It's all free.

Also consider a trip to Heritage Square, southeast of town and one mile west on the intersection of US 6 and 40. The rustic artisan and entertainment village has shops with metal smiths, jewelers, candy makers, and more. There is an alpine slide, a stable for horseback rides, a narrow-gauge train, and a large melodrama theater.

Red Rocks

Red Rocks Park can be found above the small town of Morrison on Denver's far western edge. The red sandstone formations, thrust skyward by the ancient upheaval of a prehistoric ocean bed, make an impact on the first-time viewer. There's lots of space for hiking and exploring although casual climbs on the rocks are not advisable.

Everything is giant at the Red Rocks Park, including the natural amphitheater. For years, the theater was used for ballet and classical music performances. The cost was formidable, however, and mountain gusts would carry away the sound. Now, with modern improvements, Red Rocks is the site of well-attended summer pop music, as well as rock concerts. Although expensive, tickets often sell out weeks in advance. It takes about

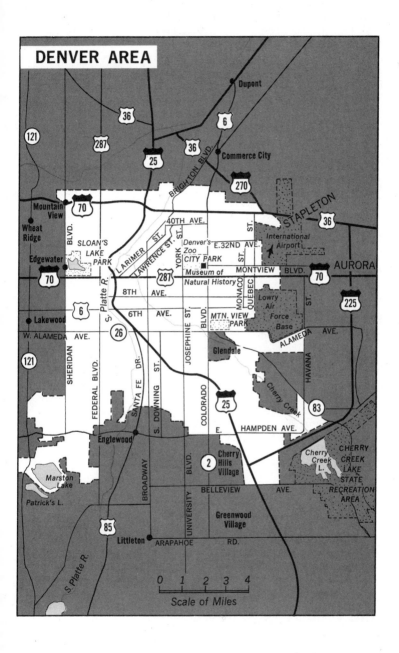

30 minutes to reach Red Rocks from Denver. Best route: the Sixth Avenue Freeway west to Interstate 70; turn south on I-70 and get off at the next exit so you'll be driving south on Hog Back Road toward Morrison.

Evergreen

Evergreen, "the Blue Spruce Capital of the World," was settled in 1859 as a lumber and supply center for the local mining camps. Today, it has become a mountain community for city workers (about 30 miles west of Denver on I-70 or via Colorado 74). Lots of specialty shops here in a busy, but small-town atmosphere. Evergreen is surrounded by several mountain parks, and nearby Evergreen Lake is a favorite spot for visitors, with boating in summer and ice skating in winter. There are modest fees for the activities.

Idaho Springs

Idaho Springs, above Evergreen on I-70, has been called "the buckle of Colorado's mineral belt." Families find a wealth of history here, and the community's hot springs—where the Ute Indians brought their old, sick, and wounded—are open year-round.

Nearby is the Indian Springs Resort. Built in 1869, it is now a complete tourist facility, with tennis courts, restaurants, and, of course, hot mineral baths.

The springs flow through two separate tunnels, one for men and one for women, carved into the mountains. You may wish to reserve a private bath for your family for an hour. Swimming pool, sauna, whirlpool are available, too. The dramatic Bridal Veil Falls is a short hike away. Idaho Springs is also the gateway to the nation's highest auto road, which climbs to 14,260 feet at the top of Mount Evans.

Central City

Central City, once known as "the richest square mile on earth," is now a National Historic Landmark, located on Highway 119 via US 67 west from Golden. It was here, on a spot now marked by a modest plaque, that John Gregory first struck gold in 1859 and began the rush to the Rockies. In summer, Central City and its companion village of Blackhawk come alive, looking like reborn boomtowns of a century ago. Winding Eureka Street sports saloons with swinging doors, gift shops, candy stores in a somewhat gaudy Old-West manner. A great number of the brick buildings were erected in the old boom days. Likewise, some of the old mines still exist and can be inspected.

Central City is most renowned for its summer operas held in the old 1878 Central City Opera House, with solid stone walls four feet thick. Fine murals and crystal chandeliers decorate the Victorian interior. Artists from the New York Metropolitan Opera and other leading companies fly out on occasion to sing here. The operas are often followed by hit Broadway musicals and plays, frequently with the original casts.

Georgetown

Georgetown, just over 50 miles west of Denver along I-70, was named for George Griffith, the first prospector to strike gold there in 1859 at the confluence of the two streams at what now is Tenth and Rose streets.

The discovery of silver after the gold played out gave Georgetown a continuing stability that other boomtowns lacked. Many miners built opulent Victorian mansions that have been preserved and added to the National Historic Register.

Unlike other old Colorado mining communities, Georgetown was never leveled by a major fire, thanks to the efficiency of its volunteer fire companies. Three of the antique fire houses still stand: the Alpine Hose Company on Fifth Street, the Star Hook and Ladder (now the Georgetown municipal offices) on Sixth Street, and Old Missouri on Taos Street, across from Georgetown City Park.

You can also take a giant step backward in time and board the old Colorado and Southern narrow-gauge train that runs the four miles between Georgetown and Silver Plume. The line was a main supply route 100 years ago. Now, visitors can make the 45-minute "loop"—so called because the track runs over and under itself repeatedly—on great bridges rising 600 feet above the valley floor.

Boulder

Boulder is a half-hour's highway drive north of Denver on US 36 from I-25. As you approach, you'll see the much-photographed reddish sandstone formations known as the "Flatirons," the abrupt border between the plains and the Rocky Mountains. The Flatirons are also a gateway to webs of popular hiking trails in the hills that rise behind the college town. And rock climbers favor these same rocks.

Boulder's tree-lined campus is worth visiting, especially in summer when the University of Colorado stages its yearly Colorado Shakespeare Festival. Several Shakespeare plays are performed here in repertory from mid-July through mid-August. Actors are chosen from national auditions.

Wander along the Boulder Mall, a brick-paved area of downtown closed to traffic; it boasts some unusual shops and restaurants.

Boulder is headquarters for the National Center for Atmospheric Research. Perched on a mesa southwest of town, the futuristic complex sits in a nature preserve open to hikers and picnickers. The respected National Bureau of Standards is also located in this university town.

PRACTICAL INFORMATION FOR
THE AREAS BEYOND DENVER

HOW TO GET THERE. By bus. *RTD* buses travel between Denver, Boulder, and Golden, and also serve Evergreen. For information call 778–6000. *Greyhound/Trailways* (292–2291) travels to Idaho Springs.

By car. Boulder can be reached most quickly on US 36 from I-25. This route affords a good view of the city nestled in its valley, the Flatirons towering above. From Golden, take Highway 93 north. Golden can be reached from Denver by taking I-25 North to I-70 West; take the Golden exit. Evergreen, Idaho Springs, and Georgetown may be reached by traveling west on I-70 from Denver. To reach Central City head west on Highway 6 from Golden, then pick up Highway 119. No buses currently travel this route.

For more information, write or call: Boulder Chamber of Commerce, 2440 Pearl St., 80203; 303–442–1044.

HOTELS AND MOTELS. Rates for double occupancy average as follows: *Deluxe* $80–$210, *Expensive* $40–$79, *Moderate,* $25–$39, *Inexpensive* $20–$24.

BOULDER

Hotel Boulderado. *Deluxe.* 2115 13th St., 80303; 303–442–4344. Elegant 1908 downtown hotel, restored to Victorian splendor. Genuine antiques in rooms, many suites, beautiful lobby. Health-club privileges, banquet facilities, entertainment. Three restaurants.

Best Western Boulder Inn. *Expensive.* 770 28th St. 80303; 303–449–3800 or 800–528–1234. Across from University of Colorado. Restaurant, bar, pools, 100 attractively furnished rooms, private baths, Chinese restaurant.

The Broker Inn. *Expensive.* 555 30th St. 80303; 303–444–3330. Near University of Colorado. Pool. Elegant Old West Restaurant on premises.

Clarion Harvest House Hotel. *Expensive.* 1345 28th St. 80302; 303–443–3850. A modern high-rise motel with landscaped grounds, dining facilities, cocktail lounge, swimming pool, 15 tennis courts. Shopping center nearby.

Holiday Inn of Boulder. *Expensive.* 800 28th St. 80303; 303–443–3322 or 800–HOLIDAY. Pool, sauna, exercise room, restaurant. Across from the University of Colorado.

University Inn. *Expensive.* 1632 Broadway 80302; 303–442–3830. TV. Pool. Free Continental breakfast; cafe nearby.

Highlander Inn Motel. *Moderate.* 970 28th St. 80303; 303–443–7800. Pool. Near University of Colorado campus.

CENTRAL CITY

(Zip Code 80427)

Gilpin Hotel. *Moderate.* 111 Main, Black Hawk; 303–582–5012. Tiny, historic miners' hotel built in 1900 and well restored.

Golden Rose Hotel. *Moderate.* 102 Main; 303–582–5060 or in Denver, 303–825–1413. Small, Victorian-style hotel built 1874, restored with elegant furniture. Hot tub, sauna.

EVERGREEN

(Zip Code 80439)

Bauer's Spruce Island Chalets. *Expensive.* 5987 S. Brook Forest Rd., Box 1678; 674–4757. From one- to four-bedroom houses, restful mountain atmosphere, lawn, ponds.

Davidson Lodge. *Expensive.* 27400 State Hwy. 74; 303–674–3442. Comfortable cabins along scenic Bear Creek. Open year-round. Fishing, skiing, sightseeing.

GEORGETOWN

(Zip Code 80444)

Georgetown Motor Inn. *Moderate.* On east edge of town, I-70 exit 228; 303–569–3201. Alpine-style inn in a scenic, historic location. Restaurant, cocktail lounge.

GOLDEN

(Zip Code 80401)

The Dove Inn. *Expensive.* 711 14th St.; 303–278–2209. Pleasant 1889 Victorian home, some private baths. Delicious breakfast provided.

Holland House. *Moderate.* 1310 Washington Ave.; 303–279–2536. On Golden's main street. Good location for mountain excursions. Has motel section, small café, bar. Clientele includes local mining engineers.

IDAHO SPRINGS

(Zip Code 80452)

Argo Motor Inn. *Expensive to Moderate.* One mile east on I-70 business route; 303–567–4473. Modernistic motel near mine. Tennis courts not far away. On river.

H & H Motor Lodge. *Moderate.* 2445 Colorado Blvd.; 303–567–2838. Nicely appointed rooms, some kitchens, hot tub, cable TV, laundry.

Indian Springs Resort. *Moderate to Inexpensive.* 302 Soda Creek Rd.; 303–623–2050. Old resort hotel with mineral pool, baths, exercise room, small café. Off of the beaten trail and good value.

BED-AND-BREAKFASTS. In the area around Denver, a number of residents are opening their homes to travelers.

BOULDER

One of the most charming of Colorado's guest homes is located in Boulder. *The Briar Rose,* 2151 Arapahoe; 303–442–3007, is a sunny country-style brick house where fresh flowers and fruit on your nightstand are just a hint of the hospitality to come. Rooms cost from $50–$75 per night, single; $65–$95, double.

CENTRAL CITY

Two Ten Casey. Box 154, 80427; 303–333–3340. Inexpensive and modest accommodations overlooking this historic Victorian mining town. Prices run $35–$45 a night. Separate entrance, private bath, and Continental breakfast.

GEORGETOWN

The Hardy House. 605 Brownell, 80444; 303–569–3388. A Victorian home ½ block from Main Street. A pleasant setting with cable TV, full breakfast, goose-down comforters, and a potbelly stove in the parlor. Rates run $34–$65 per night, single.

CAMPING. The Denver area offers a number of excellent camping sites. Here are a few of the better campgrounds in the area: *Chatfield State Recreation Area,* 11500 Roxborough Rd., Littleton, 80215; 303–797–3986. Summers only. On lake, with swimming, fishing, hiking trails. 150 sites. $10 per night. Reservations available through Mistix, 303–671–4500. Call park for group campsites. A popular area; it fills up quickly at holidays. *Chief Hosa Campground,* Rte. 3, Box 282, Golden, CO 80401; 303–526–0364. A pleasant campground in the mountains 20 miles from Denver on I-70 West. Laundry, groceries, pool. Open mid-May through October 1. Reservations accepted. *Denver North Campground,* Rt. 1, Box 149, Broomfield, CO 80020; 303–452–4120. 15 miles north on I-25. 157 sites, year-round. All amenities. Reservations accepted. *Shady Meadows RV Park,* 2075 Potomac St., Aurora, CO 80011; 303–364–9483. Store, pool, playground. 300 year-round sites. Reservations accepted.

HOT SPRINGS. *Indian Springs Resort,* 302 Soda Creek Rd., Idaho Springs, 80452; 303–567–2191; Denver telephone 623–2050. A popular spa located 22 miles west of Denver on I-70. Swimming pool, hot mineral baths, accommodations.

TOURS AND SPECIAL-INTEREST SIGHTSEEING. *Best Mountain Tours,* 11100 E. Dartmouth, 219, Denver, 80014; 303–750–0777, conduct a variety of four-wheel drive tours (summer and winter) which include Georgetown, Idaho Springs, and Central City. The Georgetown tour focuses on Guanela Pass and does not stop in town. Another tour includes a guided drive through both Idaho Springs and Central City, with a brief stop in the latter town for exploration of its many shops and historic buildings.

BOULDER

The *Walking Tour of Boulder* is a self-guided tour with an accompanying pamphlet outlining places of note. Contact the Bureau of Conference Services and Cultural Affairs, 2440 Pearl, 80302; 442–1044.

Boulder Beer Brewery, 2880 Wilderness Place, 80301; 444–8448, gives guided 45-minute tours of the facilities, culminating in a visit to the newly opened tasting room, where visitors receive a free sample. Thurs., 11 A.M.; groups of five or more may make special arrangements.

National Center for Atmospheric Research, 1850 Table Mesa Drive; 497–1174. Self-guided tours of the southwest Boulder facility are offered Mon.–Sat. Brochures, exhibits, and trail maps for the Center's nature preserve are available.

CENTRAL CITY

Brochures for a *walking tour* of this famous mining town are available at most hotels and from City Hall, 117 Eureka St., 80427.

GOLDEN

Coors Brewery, at 13th and Ford, offers free 30-minute tours of the "world's largest single brewery." Samples are served (must be 18 or older) and special handicapped- or foreign-language tours can be arranged. Call 303–277–BEER.

GEORGETOWN

Ride the historic *Georgetown Loop Railroad's* narrow-gauge train along its 100-year-old route. Board either at Georgetown or Silver Plume for the roundtrip, which leaves every 75 minutes and includes a stop at the Lebanon Mine and an adjoining museum. 1207 Argentine St., 80444; phone 569–2403; in Denver, call 279–9670. Operates Memorial Day through September 30.

A brochure for a *self-guided walking tour* can be picked up at businesses around town, or from the Georgetown Society, Box 667, Georgetown, 80444; phone 569–2840; in Denver 674–2625.

It's difficult to top the nation's highest auto road—paved all the way—to the summit of Mount Evans. (Follow the signs from town.) From 14,260 feet above sea level you can look down on passing clouds or see a sunrise. The road is closed in winter.

For an adventurous side trip from Idaho Springs, drive up Fall River Road (Exit 48 from I-70) for an intimate look at various mountain terrains. The road ends at St. Mary's Lake, and a 30- or 40-minute climb up a well-marked footpath will bring you to St. Mary's Glacier, which has snow all year long. The glacier is popular with summer skiers.

PARKS. The following make pleasant spots for a picnic or just a break from sightseeing.

BOULDER

Chautauqua Park, Ninth and Baseline; at the base of the Flatirons. Dining room, auditorium, music programs, tennis.

City Park. Next to Boulder Creek at Canyon and Broadway. Bandshell has summer music performances.

Flagstaff Mountain. At the western end of Baseline road, in the mountains. Beautiful views.

GOLDEN

Lookout Mountain Park, 5 miles west off US 6, has a spectacular view of Denver and the Rockies from atop Lookout Mountain. *Buffalo Bill Memorial Museum and Grave* are located in the 66-acre park.

Golden Gate Canyon State Park on Highway 93 outside town offers beautiful rock formations and spectacular panoramas of the Continental Divide.

IDAHO SPRINGS

Riley Cooper Park. Colorado and 23rd avenues; on Clear Creek. Tables.

SPORTS. The magnificent outdoors here means a wide range of sporting choices.

Boulder is an extremely health-conscious town, and *joggers* and *bicyclists* may be seen pumping away even in the worst of weather. Many trails are available throughout town. Rental bicycles are available from *University Bicycles,* 923 Pearl St., 444–4196. Free bike trail maps are provided by the Bank of Boulder, 3033 Iris Ave., 443–9090; they may also be picked up in person at the Chamber of Commerce, 1001 Canyon Blvd., 442–1044. Other maps are available from the *Bicycle Racing Association,* 1200 Williams St., Denver 80218, 333–2453.

For *hiking,* there is the Boulder Mountain Park system with 6,000 acres of open space; the "Mesa Trail" is especially enjoyable. For trail maps contact the Chamber of Commerce, 1001 Canyon Blvd.; 442–1044. Other hiking spots include Boulder Canyon (at the end of Canyon Blvd.), Eldorado Canyon (off Hwy. 93, seven miles south of town) and Flagstaff Mountain, at the west end of Baseline Road. The parks (see above) also provide good spots for *cross-country skiing.* For *swimming, raquetball, weight lifting* and other sports, try one of Boulder's fitness centers, listed below. Hours and fees differ for each activity: North Boulder Recreation Center, 3170 N. Broadway; 441–3444. Pool, gym, racquetball, tennis. South Boulder Recreation Center, 1360 Gillaspie; 441–3448. Usual activities plus lake with boating. YMCA, 2850 Mapleton, near Crossroads Mall; 442–2778. Pool, gym, weights, classes.

For *hiking* around **Golden** try *Golden Gate Canyon State Park* on Highway 93, with its beautiful rock formations and 100-mile panoramas of the Continental Divide.

Evergreen has a fine 18-hole public golf course which is adjacent to Evergreen Lake, a 55-acre reservoir popular with fishermen and boaters in summer and ice skaters in winter.

Echo Lake, on Mt. Evans, outside **Idaho Springs,** attracts *anglers* and overnight campers. Skiers use the *cross-country* trails in winter. Also outside Idaho Springs is St. Mary's Lake; a climb from it leads to St. Mary's Glacier.

MUSEUMS AND HISTORIC SITES. The area surrounding Denver is rich in the history of the country's western expansion.

BOULDER

Boulder Historical Society, 1206 Euclid; 449–3464. Harbeck House, built at the turn of the century by a banker and his wife as a summer residence houses the society's collection, which focuses on local history. Hours are Tues.–Fri. 10 A.M.–4 P.M.; Sat. noon–4 P.M.

University of Colorado Museum of Natural History, located in the Henderson Building, at Broadway between 15th and 16th streets. Phone 492–6165 weekdays; 492–6892 weekends. Biology, anthropology, and earth sciences halls, along with a changing exhibit.

CENTRAL CITY

This Victorian "gingerbread" tour boasts a wealth of historic sites.

The Teller House, 110 Eureka St., was built in 1872 at the staggering cost of $107,000. It became the most opulent hostelry of the gold fields, hosting Ulysses S. Grant, Oscar Wilde, Baron de Rothschild, and other notables. The famous "Face on the Barroom Floor" in the saloon is one of the highlights of the 45-minute tour, which also includes the renowned *Central City Opera House* next door. Tours are available daily from 11 A.M.–5 P.M.; 303–582–3200. Denver phone number: 279–8306.

Central City Gold Mine and Museum, 126 Spring Street, offers a 20-minute tour of the Bugher mine and a display of local historic memorabilia from railroad and mining days. Open daily, 11 A.M.–4 P.M., May–Oct. Fee charged.

St. James Methodist Church on Eureka Street is the oldest church in the state, dating back to 1859. The interior has been restored; if the door is open, look in at the intricate stenciling that decorates the sanctuary.

EVERGREEN

Downtown, take some time to visit the *Hiwan Homestead Museum,* 4208 S. Timbervale Dr.; 674–6262, a pioneer display in a 17-room log house. Included: a reconstructed 1880s assay office. Free tours in the afternoon, Tues. through Sun.

GEORGETOWN

Hamill House, 305 Argentine St. Mining czar William Hamill built this edifice in the late 1870s; it is now almost completely restored and open for public tours. Two stone buildings on the back of the property served as Hamill's office and counting house. (The vault and curved walnut counter are still there.) Today, the buildings house the Georgetown Historical Society, a good stop for visitor information, brochures, and guides to area shops, restaurants, and attractions. Open daily 9:30 A.M.–5 P.M. in summer, noon–4 P.M. in winter. Small fee.

Four blocks away on Sixth Street, in the commercial district, the *Hotel de Paris,* dating back to 1875, became famous throughout the West for its gourmet cuisine. Proprietor Louis DuPuy, a Frenchman, took 15 years to complete the inn. When DuPuy died in 1900, it turned out that he was actually a French army deserter named Adolphe Gerard and had lived in Georgetown for 30 years under a false identity. Located at 409 Sixth Street, the museum is open Tues.–Sun. 9:30 A.M.–5 P.M. in summer; noon–4 P.M. in winter. Phone 569–2311.

GOLDEN

Colorado School of Mines' Geologic Museum at 16th and Maple. The 1940 structure displays mineral ore, fossils, mining equipment, meteorites, and even a replica of an old gold mine. The museum's hours are 9 A.M.–4 P.M. Mon.–Sat., Sun. 1–4 P.M. Phone 273–3823. Free. Also in Golden, *The Railroad Museum,* at 17155 West 44th Avenue, has an 1880s-style depot, historical exhibits, old narrow-gauge locomotives, railroad and trolley cars. Hours are 9 A.M.–5 P.M. daily; a family rate of $5.50 is offered. Phone 279–4591.

The Buffalo Bill Museum, on Lookout Mountain off Highway 40 near Golden features the famed Westerner's grave and personal possessions. Closed Mon. Adults $1, children 25 cents. Phone 526–0747.

IDAHO SPRINGS

Don't miss the *Clear Creek Museum* and the *Argo Gold Mill,* 2350 Riverside Dr., downtown. Equipment and mining displays are shown inside an actual gold mine. There are tours of the shaft and adjoining ore mill, May–Labor Day. Small entrance fee. For information write Argo Town U.S.A., Box 1498, Idaho Springs 80452; 303–567–2421.

Underhill Museum, in the 1400 block of Miner Street, is open Tues., Thurs., and Sat. This is a historic old home with original furnishings, old mining relics, and maps.

MUSIC AND THEATER. *Red Rocks Park,* near Morrison, is a 30-minute drive from Denver but well worth it. For hard rock enthusiasts concerts are performed in a natural amphitheater formed by jutting red sandstone formations. Call 575–2638 for concert information. Open June to Labor Day.

Boulder. *Boulder Public Library,* 1000 Canyon; 441–3114. Free concerts throughout the year featuring both local and national performers in a broad range of styles. Mid-June through July sees the *Colorado Music Festival,* in Chautauqua Park, 900 Baseline Rd. Visiting performers and composers lend their talent and energy to the festival. You will need reservations. Write to the festival at 1245 Pearl, 80302, for details or call 303–443–1397.

Macky Auditorium, on the university campus, hosts performances by the *Boulder Philharmonic,* the *College of Music,* visiting musicians participating in the "artists series," and concerts by nationally known groups. For information write Campus Box 285, University of Colorado, Boulder, 80309, or call 492–8424.

Boulder is home to the *Colorado Shakespeare Festival* each summer. Write University of Colorado Department of Theater and Dance, Campus Box 261, Boulder, CO 80309; 492–7355 or 492–8181. The University Drama and Dance departments offer performances year-round. Write to them at Campus Box 261, Boulder, 80309, for more information or call 492–7355. *Nomads,* 1410 Quince St.; 449–0045, is a modern and experimental theater.

Central City. Summer performances at the *Central City Opera House* are world-famous and definitely worth a visit. Write Central City Opera Association, 1615 California, Suite 510, Denver 80202; 623–7167.

Evergreen. *Colorado Philharmonic Orchestra,* Box 975, 80439; phone 674–5161. Young musicians in summer repertory.

Heritage Square Opera House, Box D109, **Golden,** 279–7881, offers a change of pace with live "Western" melodrama. Open year-round.

ART GALLERIES. Boulder. *Boulder Arts & Crafts Cooperative,* 1421 Pearl St.; 443–3683. Ceramics, weaving, wooden toys, photography, and more by 72 local artists. Open 10 A.M.–6 P.M. daily.

Boulder Public Library, 1000 Canyon; 441–3100. The Bridge Gallery features several changing exhibits. Hours are 9 A.M.–9 P.M. Mon.–Thur. 9 A.M.–6 P.M. Fri. and Sat., noon–6 P.M. Sun.

Boulder Center for the Visual Arts, 1750 13th St.; 443–2122. Various media from local and visiting artists.

University of Colorado Galleries, Sibell-Wolle Fine Arts Building, University of Colorado at Boulder, 80309; phone 492–8300. Four gallery spaces featuring works from the Colorado Collection, student shows, and visiting artists. Mon.–Fri. 10 A.M.–4 P.M.; Sat. and Sun. 1–5 P.M.; closed on some university holidays.

The White Horse Institute, 1218 Pearl St.; 443–6116. Indian and primitive art and antiquities. Open 10 A.M.–9 P.M. Mon.–Sat., 11 A.M.–5 P.M. Sun.

Georgetown. *Saxon Mountain Gallery,* 408 Sixth St.; 674–0353. 10 A.M.–6 P.M. daily. Traditional art, with a large collection of Colorado landscapes and ski scenes, pottery, and bronzes.

Golden. *Foothills Art Center,* 809 15th St.; 279–3922. Hours Mon.–Sat., 9 A.M.–4 P.M.; Sun. 1–4 P.M. Features regional artists.

DINING OUT. For a full meal, exclusive of drinks, tax, and tip, the price categories are as follows: *Deluxe,* $35 and up; *Expensive,* $15–$34; *Moderate,* $11–$14; *Inexpensive,* $5–$10. All restaurants listed here take major credit cards, unless otherwise noted.

BOULDER

Flagstaff House. *Deluxe.* Flagstaff Rd.; 442–4640. On Flagstaff Mountain, offering fine views, award-winning Continental/American menu including oven-smoked salmon, venison, filet À la Wellington, duck, Alaska king crab. Prime rib a specialty. Cocktail patio, free appetizers. Overlooks city, mountains. A treat in summer.

Boulder Dinner Theater. *Expensive.* 55th and Arapahoe; 449–6000. Cheerful young actors, singers, dancers regale you after a well-cooked supper.

Franco's Ristorante y Pastatia. *Expensive.* 2115 13th (in Hotel Boulderado); 449–4819. Elegant Italian restaurant boasting pasta specialties. Choose from any or all six daily fresh-made sauces to top the spaghetti, linguini, fettuccine at the pasta bar. Liquor.

Harvest Restaurant and Bakery. *Moderate.* 1738 Pearl St.; 449–6223. Specializes in natural foods. Own baking. Beer and wine served. Background music and outdoor seating.

Jose Muldoon's. *Moderate.* 1600 38th St.; 449–4543. Mexican restaurant specializing in sizzling *fajitas* and a do-it-yourself tostada bar. Live entertainment. Takeout. A good place to bring kids.

Furr's Cafeteria. *Inexpensive.* 28th and Iris; 443–9211. In large shopping center. Excellent value. No bar.

CENTRAL CITY

Black Forest Inn. *Expensive.* 260 Gregory, three-quarters of a mile east on State 279 in Black Hawk; 279–2333. A well-managed Bavarian restaurant. Authentic German dishes expertly prepared. Goose liver pâté. Elk, venison, Canadian snow goose, pheasant, and other native game featured. Wiener schnitzel, calves' liver à la Berlin, good trout, herring, berries in season. Open noon to 9:30 P.M. Beer garden in summer. Accordion player; owner always on premises.

Chicago Spaghetti & Pizza Co. *Moderate.* 321 Main St.; 582–5242. Italian/American cuisine. Open seven days a week.

Poco's Mexican & American Restaurant. *Moderate.* 118 Lawrence St.; 582–3220. Top-notch Mexican food and margaritas. Open year-round.

EMPIRE

Peck House. *Expensive.* 83 Sunny Ave.; 569–9870. Distinguished dinners in authentic Old West setting. Steak and trout specialties. En route to Berthoud Pass.

EVERGREEN

El Rancho Colorado. *Expensive to Moderate.* Off I-70, Exit 252; 526–0661. In addition to steak and prime rib, it serves always fresh, boned rainbow trout. The rustic atmosphere includes a cocktail lounge with a fireplace. A popular restaurant in the heart of the mountains.

Evergreen Inn. *Inexpensive.* 27845 State Highway 74; 674–5495. Friendly local pub with reasonably priced food.

GEORGETOWN

The Place. *Expensive to Moderate.* 7th and Brownell; 569 2552. Large selection of steak specialties, with special sauce. Some seafood.

Happy Cooker. *Inexpensive.* 507 Taos Square; 569–3166. Quiches, stews, waffles, sandwiches for tourists and skiers. Cozy.

GOLDEN

Briarwood Inn. *Deluxe.* 1630 8th St.; 279–3121. Elegant country inn. Fine tablecloths, china, cutlery. Classical background music. Lazy Susan with free appetizers; great variety of American and Continental dishes. Each plate has visual appeal here—always an excellent dining experience. Reservations recommended.

The Chart House. *Expensive to Moderate.* 25908 Genesee Trail Road, I-70 Exit 254; 526–9813. Famous Sunday brunch. Dinner menu offers many cuts of meat. Clear mountain views.

IDAHO SPRINGS

Indian Springs Resort. *Moderate.* 302 Soda Creek Rd.; 623–2050. Home cooking.

Beau Jo's. *Inexpensive.* 1517 Miner's St.; 567–4376. Features mountain pie and great pizza. Incredible menu selection; beer, wine; rustic atmosphere.

The Cantina. *Inexpensive.* 2700 Colorado Blvd.; 567–2051. *Fajitas* (marinated meat, grilled, and wrapped in a flour tortilla), *chimichangas* (deep-fried pork burritoes), *rellenos* (cheese-stuffed green chilies, dipped in a batter and fried), Mexican pizza (topped with hot peppers and spicy sausage), and large combination plates.

SKI AND SUMMER RESORTS

by
DIANA HUNT

Diana Hunt writes for national and Rocky Mountain publications and is a member of the U.S. Ski Writers Association, and Public Relations Society of America. She has been editor for Pan Am's in-flight Clipper *magazine.*

Colorado is a dramatic state. Its beauty is sometimes harsh, sometimes overwhelming. The highest state in the nation, with nearly 1,200 mountains rising two miles or more, 53 peaks towering above 14,000 feet, Colorado has six times the mountain area of the Swiss Alps.

Denver is the gateway for Colorado and the entire Rocky Mountain region. Because of its central location, the city started as a transportation hub and remains so today. The majority of tourists heading for the mountain resorts will either fly into or drive around Denver (see the chapter "Denver and Environs") or, in winter, into Grand Junction. Once out of Denver's urban sprawl of the Front Range (so-called because the population spreads along the front, or eastern edge, of the Rocky Mountain foothills), the climb begins up to and over the Continental Divide. This rocky, ragged edge of mountain peaks wiggles down through the state, cutting it in half mentally as well as physically. These mountains of central and western Colorado are what the tourist posters are made of. Even in August, there is often snow on the highest mountain peaks, lending a brilliant contrast to the red earth, the green pines, and the electric blue sky.

Skiing originally put Colorado on the map. Miners toiling in the remote mountains in the late 1800s used to slide down the snowy slopes on boards ten feet long. Not much for turning, but they hit speeds of 90 miles per hour. During World War II, the famed Tenth Mountain Division trained at Camp Hale near Leadville, between Aspen and Vail. Their specialty was mountain survival, and skiing was an integral part of that training. Many of the men fell in love with Colorado, returned after the war, and did what they did best—skied. Aspen, Vail, Loveland, and many other ski areas were started by these former Tenth Mountain Men. Many of them are still active in the ski industry today.

The *White Book of Ski Areas* lists 31 ski resorts in Colorado. The major destinations, world-class resorts, as well as some up-and-coming ones, are described individually, in order of their distance from Denver.

Coloradoans have always known that summer in the mountains was just as glorious as winter skiing. It has just been the last few years that the ski resorts have actively marketed that "second" season and visitors increasingly have been enjoying the outdoor activities of summer—hiking, backpacking, river rafting, bicycling, outdoor music festivals, horseback riding—the list goes on. It's all here in Colorado.

Seasons and Prices

Winter is still "high" season in the mountain resorts. Most resorts are open for skiing from mid-November to mid-April (there are a few that open earlier and stay open later, depending on snow conditions). Summer season generally extends from the end of June until mid-October. The shoulder periods in between have become popular for meetings and conventions. If you're planning to travel to a resort between seasons, be advised that many establishments do close down.

The lodging prices given in this chapter reflect standard prices during the ski season. Nightly rates are given to reflect the general price range of the resort as a whole. However, every resort promotes package rates that can be as elaborate or as simple as a visitor wants. Early and late ski season discounts are available (from the opening date of the ski season to before Christmas; during January; and from April 1 to closing), and the shoulder and summer rates are usually the least expensive. Christmas and New Year are the most expensive holiday periods.

Except in Keystone, men will feel overdressed in a tie, no matter how elegant the restaurant or lounge.

In this chapter we have supplied addresses and phone numbers—but these resorts are very self-contained, and you should have no trouble finding anything. Visa and MasterCard are widely accepted; American Express less so.

To further explore the area around your resort, refer to the other chapters in this book.

WINTER PARK

Middle Park and the Fraser Valley were lush summer hunting grounds for the Ute Indians. Irish baronet Lord Gore heard of the paradise for hunters in this part of the American west and headed for what is probably

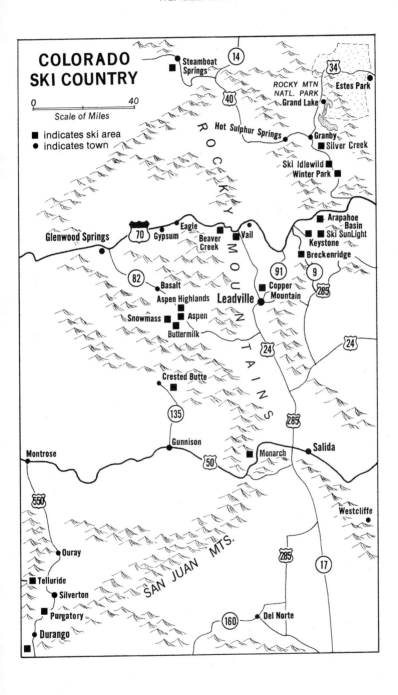

COLORADO
SKI COUNTRY

0   40
Scale of Miles

■ indicates ski area
● indicates town

Steamboat Springs

ROCKY MTN NATL. PARK
Estes Park
Grand Lake

Hot Sulphur Springs

Granby
Silver Creek

Ski Idlewild
Winter Park

Glenwood Springs

Eagle
Gypsum
Beaver Creek
Vail

Arapahoe Basin
Ski SunLight
Keystone
Breckenridge

Basalt
Aspen Highlands
Snowmass
Aspen
Buttermilk

Leadville

Copper Mountain

Crested Butte

Gunnison

Montrose

Monarch
Salida

Ouray

Westcliffe

Telluride
Silverton
Purgatory
Durango

SAN JUAN MTS.

Del Norte

the most bizarre hunting party ever to hit these shores. For two summers, 1854–56, Lord Gore, accompanied by the famous scout Jim Bridger, devastated the local wildlife while he lived like a king in a striped silk tent, with a brass bed and down-filled mattress, linen coverings, trunks of cloths, barrels of delicacies, leather-bound books, wines and liqueurs, pewter mugs, a bathtub, hand-carved and inlaid rifles, packs of hounds, a collapsible raft, and a fur-covered potty. The Baronet's personal possessions alone filled 28 vehicles. The mountain range and valley named for Lord Gore were never visited by him; instead, he spent his time east of the pass in Middle Park and its environs.

It wasn't the miners who overran the Indians' territory here; it was the railroad and ranching men. A railroad route linking the plains states to the west coast via Denver was built over the Continental Divide and through Middle Park. Later, the Moffat Tunnel was built for six miles under the Divide, eliminating the tortuous 11,600 foot Rollins Pass. It was the opening of this tunnel in 1928 that brought the first skiers to the area. (Robert Black's book, *Island in the Rockies,* gives a complete account of the fascinating railroad history of this remote country.)

Enthusiastic Denverites rode the train as far as West Portal Station (so named because it was the entrance on the west side of the Continental Divide). They would hike up the mountain and ski down, making perhaps two runs a day and staying overnight in the railroad construction shacks. Winter Park ski area was born. It became part of the Denver Mountain Parks system in 1940, making it the second-oldest ski area in the state. (The oldest area is atop Berthoud, a small area a few miles away on top of the Continental Divide.) Today Winter Park is still owned by the City of Denver, administered by a management company and run as a not-for-profit entity—unique in resort operations in this country. The little mountain town of Winter Park, two miles north of the ski area, grew after the ski area was in existence.

Winter Park prides itself on being a "people's resort": rates are consistently less than those at other Colorado resorts.

PRACTICAL INFORMATION FOR WINTER PARK

HOW TO GET THERE. Winter Park is 67 miles northwest of Denver in the Arapaho National Forest.

By air. Denver's Stapleton Airport is the closest gateway for all major airlines. See also *Practical Information for Denver.* From the airport, *Vanex* and *Home James* are on-call taxi services, leaving from Door #7; $30 per person round-trip. For complete schedule and reservations, call the Transportation Center, 726–8015, or Central Reservations, 726–5587.

By bus. *Greyhound/Trailways* serves Winter Park from the airport, (303–726–8015).

By train. *Amtrak's* transcontinental California Zephyr serves Winter Park daily; train depot is Fraser, two miles from the town of Winter Park, four miles from the ski slopes (800–USA–RAIL). Some lodges provide free shuttle service. The area shuttle bus, *The Lift,* meets all trains, no charge during ski season. *Home James* taxi service is also available (303–726–5060) as well as *Vanex* (303–726–5776). On weekends, January through March, the *Denver and Rio Grande Railway* runs a ski train between Denver's Union Station and the Winter Park base area. Arrival is 9:30 A.M.; the train waits on a siding for the return trip at 4:15 P.M. Since the early '50s, the ski train has climbed 4,000 feet in altitude, gone through 29 tunnels and carried hundreds of young skiers each weekend. The eight vintage coaches recently have been upgraded for more comfort and service. First-class tickets are $35 round-trip; standard class, $25 ($20 if purchased in advance). Call 623–TIXS or 298–1000 for information and reservations.

By car. Winter Park is 67 miles northwest of Denver via I–70 to Exit 232 onto US 40, over Berthoud Pass to the ski area; the town is two miles farther. All major rental car agencies are represented at the Denver airport (see *Practical Information for Denver*). In Winter Park there are *American International* (800–527–0202 or 303–726–4500), *Hertz* (303–726–8993 or 800–654–3131), and *National* (303–726–4879 or 800–328–4567).

ACCOMMODATIONS. Winter Park Central Reservations handles the majority of lodging in the Fraser Valley; write Box 36, Winter Park, CO 80482, call 303–726–5587 or 800–453–2525 outside Colorado.

Expensive

Crestview Place. Vasquez Rd. at US 40; 726–9421. Two- and three-bedroom units with fireplaces, some one-bedrooms without fireplaces; shopping galleria, underground parking. Range is $116 for one bedroom; $174, two-bedroom; and $232, three-bedroom.

Iron Horse Resort Retreat. 257 Grand County Rd. 70; 303–726–8851. Winter Park's only ski-to, ski-from property offers full hotel service, a health club, restaurant, and lounge. Studios to premium two-bedrooms range $90–$140 a night, double occupancy.

The Vintage. 100 Winter Park Drive; 303–726–8801. The hotel is something right out of a Swiss resort, oozing European charm. 121 elegant rooms ranging in price from $79 to $270; restaurant, exercise room; breakfast buffet, and free shuttle to ski area and town included in room rates. View of Mary Jane trails.

Winter Park Tennis Club, 628 Cranmer, Fraser; next to Meadow Ridge complex, 726–9703. Huge condominiums with wonderful views, but only one tennis court. $80 a night, double occupancy.

Moderate

MeadowRidge Resort. 102 E. Meadow Mile, Fraser; 303–726–8822 or 303–726–9401. Condominium resort community, four and one-half miles west of ski area. One- to three-bedroom units, each with fireplace and sun deck. Restaurant, bar, pool, sauna, and whirlpool, tennis courts, racquetball courts, ice rink. One- to three-bedroom condos go for $100–$150 a night.

Snowblaze Athletic Club. Box 404, 79104 U.S. Highway 40; 303–726–8501. Full athletic club facilities, sauna in every condo. Studios to three-bedroom units cost $90–$270 a night.

Timber Run Condominiums. Box 3095, Winter Park, 80482; 303–726–9435. Studios to three-bedrooms are $100–$235 a night, depending on the season.

A number of Mountain Inns serve breakfast and dinner family-style; most cost in the range of $42–$60 a night per person with two meals; contact: *Arapahoe Lodge,* 78594 U.S. Highway 40; 303–726–8222; *Beaver Village,* 79303 U.S. Highway 40; 303–726–5741; *Brenner's Lodge,* Box 15; 303–726–5416; *Gasthaus Eichler,* 78786 U.S. Hwy. 40; 726–5133; *Millers*

Inn, Box 53, 219 Vasquez Rd.; 303–726–5313; *Timber House,* 196 Grand County Rd. 716; 303–726–5477.

Inexpensive

Alpenglo Motor Lodge. 78641 U.S. Highway 40; 303–726–5294. Basic accommodations for $30–$40 a night per person.

Olympia Motor Lodge. 78572 U.S. Highway 40; 303–726–8843. $25–$30 a night per person.

Sundowner Motel. 78869 U.S. Highway 40; 303–726–5452. $25–$30 a night per person.

YMCA of the Rockies (Snow Mountain Ranch). Box 558, Granby 1344 Grand City Rd.; 303–887–2152. A real bargain, 20 minutes from Winter Park with miles of cross-country trails and Olympic-size pool. Rustic cabins are $10 a night per person.

CAMPING. All are U.S. Forest Service campgrounds, individual sites on a first-come, first-serve basis. Follow the Experimental Forest Road past Fraser to *St. Louis Creek Campground:* well water, small trailers, good hiking; $6 fee. *Byers Creek* lies at an elevation of about 9,700 feet, beyond St. Louis Creek on the Experimental Forest Road; from here the trail goes up to Byers Peak, an incredible view but steep climb; no fee. *Robber's Roost* is near the base of Berthoud Pass, five miles south of Winter Park, a wide spot in the road, no facilities, no fee. North of Winter Park, near the town of Grand Lake, are numerous campsites. For groups of 25 or more, *Cutthroat Bay,* just off the east side of Rte. 34, has two loops accommodating 100 people; no water, vault toilets, picnic tables, and fire grates; space for tents or campers. There is a $25 reservation fee and you must put in an application for a yearly, random drawing. Write U.S. Forest Service, Box 10, Granby, CO 80446, or call 303–887–3331. *Willow Creek* is west of Rte. 34 five miles on Willow Creek Reservoir; piped water, vault toilets, fire grate, picnic tables; $6 fee. *Arapahoe Bay Campground* is close to Monarch Lake, has fireplaces, pit toilets, small boat launching area; $6 fee. *El Navajo Trailer Park* on Shadow Mountain Lake has RV hookups, swimming pool; commercial campground with fee. *Green Ridge* on Shadow Mountain Reservoir has dump station, picnic tables, launching ramp; $7 fee. *Shadow Mountain* has modern rest rooms, running water, picnic tables; no fee. *Stillwater* on Lake Granby has modern rest rooms, running water, picnic tables, fireplaces, dump station, boat launching ramp; $7 fee. On Rte. 125 toward Walden there are two small campgrounds, *Sawmill Gulch* and *Denver Creek,* each with water, pit toilets, and a $6 fee. *El Navajo Trailer Park* is a commercial campground on Shadow Mountain Reservoir with RV hookups, swimming pool, fee.

HOW TO GET AROUND. During ski season the free lift connects all the lodges to the town and to the ski area of Winter Park; runs every 20 minutes; 726–8253.

TOURIST INFORMATION. For snow conditions, call 303–726–5514, or from Denver dial direct, 666–4502. KTLD is the county's local radio station for news, events. WPTV Channel 5 is local cable for activities, weather, shopping information. Pick up a copy of the weekly *Manifest* newspaper for features and news. Check the Chamber of Commerce in Cooper Creek Square for town activities: 726–4118; Box 3236, Winter Park, CO 80482.

SEASONAL EVENTS. There always seems to be something happening at Winter Park. Because of its status as a nonprofit entity, the area hosts more than its share of civic and amateur, as well as pro events. The *Chef's Cup Race* is held in early December. *Winter Wild West Week* is the town's Old West version of winter carnival the end of **January.** The *First Interstate Bank Cup* is the pro race held in early **March,** while a variety of pro and amateur races are held throughout the ski season. The *Golden Bunny Race* for kids highlights **Easter,** the *Chip's Invitational Mascot Ski Race,* in which the nation's college mascots compete in full regalia, is in early **April,** with *Spring Splash* (skiing into a pond of water) closing the season mid-April.

Summer activities include Friday night socials in the park, featuring performance from mimes to music; *Alpine Art Affair,* a juried arts festival, in **July;** also each July is the *Winter Park Jazz Festival; Cool Water Revival Windsurfing Regatta* on Lake Granby in **August.** Rodeos take place every other weekend throughout the summer and the *Famous Flamethrower High Altitude Great Chili Cook-off* is over **Labor Day;** *"Bert and Ernie" Fraser Valley Golf Classic* at Pole Creek Golf Course is mid-**September. December** festivities include a torchlight parade down the mountain, a visit by Santa Claus, and Christmas Eve services.

PARTICIPANT SPORTS. Winter Park grew up as a **ski** area and skiing is still primary. Nineteen chairlifts carry skiers into nearly 1,100 acres of skiing, from intermediate cruising on the Winter Park side to knee-wrenching mogul fields on the Mary Jane side. Also **Snow-Cat skiing** (conditions permitting) in Parsenn Bowl, above the Mary Jane area. Racing clinics, mountain guides, freestyle and jumping programs are available; for some little-skied, hard-to-find, challenging terrain, sign up with the "Jane Gang," the ski instructors on the Mary Jane mountain. Never-Ever skier packages, STAR test, NASTAR, and Ski Blast Weekend workshops are offered through the ski school. For all ski lessons, rentals, and information call 726–5514.

Cross country enthusiasts can head for nearby *Idlewild* (726–5564), a Nordic center in the town; *Snow Mountain Ranch/YMCA of the Rockies* with 26 miles of groomed trails (887–2152); *C Lazy U Ranch* near Granby for outstanding trail systems (887–3344); or to *Soda Springs Ranch* near Grand Lake, about 30 miles from Winter Park (627–3486). Cross-country trails are also available at *Silver Creek Resort,* a few miles north of Winter Park (887–3384), or in *Grand Lake,* at the edge of Rocky Mountain National Park (627–8226).

For those who like ungroomed **alpine skiing,** drive 15 minutes to *Timberline Ski Area,* set high atop Berthoud Pass. There are only two lifts, but they access nearly 1,000 acres of controlled but ungroomed terrain. Ski down to US 40 and a shuttle bus brings you back to the Timberline lifts.

Snowboarding lessons are available through the ski school (726–5514) for $24 for a half-day group lesson, private lessons for $35 for the first hour. Rentals at Winter Park Ski Shop at the base area and Golden Spike Ski Shop at Mary Jane for $12 a day.

Snow Tubing at *Fraser Valley Sports Center* is uncontrolled fun; $5 an hour for an innertube and rope tow (726–5954). **Snowmobiling** is available from *Beaver Village,* $40 for a 2½-hour guided trip up to the summit of the Continental Divide (726–9247); also available from Snow Mountain

Ranch/YMCA. **Ice skating** is available at *Beaver Village,* 726–5741 (skate rental for a small fee), and Meadow Ridge, 726–9401 ($2.50 for skate rental from *Ski Depot Sports* on premises, 726–8766); at *Snow Mountain Ranch,* 887–2152, small fee plus deposit for skates. **Sleigh rides** are scheduled from *Meadow Ridge,* 726–9401, *Beaver Village,* 726–5741, *Idlewild,* 726–5564, and from McLean Real Estate Office by *Winter Park Sleighrides,* 726–5557. Reserve *Dinner at the Barn* sleigh rides at 726–8605. Indoor sports of **racquetball, swimming,** and **weights** can be enjoyed by guests of *Snowblaze,* Meadow Ridge, and *Iron Horse;* year-round. **Roller skating** and **basketball** are available year-round at *Snow Mountain Ranch,* 887–2152; indoor **miniature golf** is at the *Fraser Shopping Center.*

In summer, people head off for day **hikes, backpack trips, bicycling** (Winter Park/Fraser boasts the state's most extensive mountain bike trail system). Fat-tired stump jumpers are for rent at *Ski Depot* on US 40, 726–8055, $12 all day; at *SportStalker,* Cooper Creek Square, 726–8873, and *Winter Park Sports Shop,* King's Crossing, 726–5554. For a scenic **chairlift ride,** take the *Iron Horse Lift* up Mary Jane, $3.50; self-guided nature hikes head off from the summit; walk or ride down. The *Alpine Slides* swing under the Arrow Lift on the Winter Park side Memorial Day through late September, weather permitting; $3.75 a ride, $9.50 three rides. **Jeep** tours leave from the Winter Park base area; rates $15–$27, depending on the tour; call for information, 726–5514. **Volleyball** and **horse shoes** are popular at the Mary Jane base area. **Rafting** on the Colorado River, half- and full-day trips; *Mad River Rafting,* Inc., 726–5290, *Timber Rafting,* 726–9550.

For **golf,** *Pole Creek Golf Course* has spectacular vistas, long fairways, challenging greens; open early June–early Oct., weather permitting; call 726–8847 for tee times. Greens fees are $32 for 18 holes, $20 for 9 holes, cart rentals $18 for 18 holes, $12 for 9 holes; five miles from Winter Park. *Grand Lake Metropolitan Recreation District Golf Course* is about 30 miles from Winter Park; call 627–8008 for information.

Boat marinas line Lake Granby, Grand Lake, and Shadow Mountain Reservoir; Grand Lake claims the highest yacht club in the country at 9,000 plus feet above sea level.

Stream fishing is superb in the Fraser Valley. President Eisenhower's favorite fishing haunts were right here; contact *Nelson's Fly and Tackle Shop* in nearby Tabernash for licenses, information, 726–8558.

HISTORIC SITES AND OTHER LANDMARKS. Hiking along the Continental Divide is one of the most spectacular walks you can take. Bring a warm sweater. Shorter walks are on marked trails from the Iron Horse Lift, Mary Jane. Look for trailheads on the Experimental Forest Road for St. Louis Creek and Byers Peak, see "Camping," above.

Drive up to Rollins Pass for a look at the old Corona Station from the days the railroad struggled up and over the pass, before Moffat Tunnel was built. Hiking trails go from here along the Divide.

For recommended hiking and driving trips, contact the Winter Park Resort Chamber in Cooper Creek Square on US 40, 303–726–4118. Numerous trails take you over the Continental Divide. One of the prettiest places is Meadow Creek Reservoir; take Rte. 129 off US 40 and drive the rough road up to the lake; great for fishing, canoeing, hiking trails, horsepack trips. Indian Peaks Wilderness Area is nearby. For maps and information, check with the U.S. Forest Service at the corner of US 40 and US 34 in Granby (303–887–3331).

Drive the highest continuous highway in the U.S. through Rocky Mountain National Park; the west entrance is 35 miles from Winter Park near Grand Lake; for information and road conditions, contact the Chamber of Commerce in Grand Lake (303–627–3402). See the chapter "Northwest Colorado."

The Overlook, just off US 40 at the ski area, affords a view of historic Moffat Tunnel, the larger bore for the train and the smaller bore for water. The big, green pipe snaking down the mountainside at the ski area carries western slope water under the Continental Divide in the tunnel to thirsty Denver residents.

CHILDREN'S ACTIVITIES. The 32,000-square-foot *Children's Center* houses all children's programs, rentals, a toddler nursery, cot room, kitchen, and even an isolation room for sick youngsters. The center is next to Mt. Maury, the children's ski garden. The Nursery is for 1–8-year-olds, $30 lunch included. *Penguin Peak* is for children 3–4 years old with all-day supervision, lunch, ski lessons, $38 a day, $98 for three days, $140 for five days. *Ski Scouts* are for 5–7-year-olds with four hours instruction, all-day supervision, lunch, lift ticket, progress card, and pin; cost is $38 a day, $98 for three days, $140 for five days. *Ski Rangers* are children aged 8–13; class lessons, lift tickets, lunch, and pins for $38 a day, $98 for 3 days; $140 for five days. Call for reservations, 726–5514, ext. 214.

SHOPPING. Copper Creek Square is the main shopping center in Winter Park, and other stores are located at the ski area and along US 40 in town. Sports clothes and gear are carried in *Ski Depot,* 78727 U.S. Highway 40; *Sports Etc.,* 78885 U.S. Highway 40; *Vasquez Sports,* Park Place Center; *Winter Park Sports,* 78336 U.S. Highway 40; *Nelson's Fly & Tackle* (for fishing gear, summer only), 72149 U.S. Highway 40; *Alpine Sun Ski Shop,* 78876 U.S. Highway 40; *Gear Up,* in Fraser. Children's clothing is in the *Little Caboose,* at the ski area. Sweets and other goodies are in *The Satisfied Sweetooth* at the Winter Park base area. Gift items are found in *The Shop,* 78897 U.S. Highway 40, *The Frame Shoppe,* 78336 U.S. Highway 40, *Stoney Lonesome* (a kitchen boutique), and *Safeway Shopping Center,* which has gift boutiques and a hair salon. Get your boots orthopedically fitted—custom ski tuning at *Le Ski Lab,* 78941 U.S. Highway 40.

DINING OUT. There is a broad selection of eateries for a small town. At the ski area, the *Mary Jane Center* has a cafeteria and a sit-down restaurant, the *Club Car.* In the lower level of Mary Jane Center is *Pepperoni's Pizza and Sports Bar.* On the Winter Park side, midmountain *Snoasis* is a cafeteria, and downstairs is *Mama Mia's* pizzeria; at the base, *West Portal Station* is a cafeteria and the *Derailer Bar* is an après-ski lounge. *Coffee and Tea Market* serves croissant sandwiches, homemade soups, salads, divine pastries for sitdown or takeout; a small bar carries the beverage of your choice. For a change of pace, try *Dinner at the Barn* (726–4311), a sleigh-ride "gourmet" dinner. $25 includes entertainment.

Entrées at the *Expensive* restaurants listed below run $17–$30; *Moderate* $7–$17; *Inexpensive,* under $6. All restaurants listed take Visa and MasterCard unless otherwise noted.

Expectations at the Slope. *Expensive.* 1161 Winter Park Dr., Old Winter Park; 726–5727. Fine continental food served in a small dining area. Dinner only. Reservations suggested.

Gasthaus Eichler. *Expensive.* U.S. Hwy. 40; 726–5133. Classic German food in a European atmosphere. Good fattening desserts. Breakfast and dinner.

The Hideaway. *Expensive.* 78260 U.S. Highway 40; 726–9921. Darkly dramatic with madrigal music in the background. Excellent service. Entrées include Tasmanian lobster, Alaskan king crab, Nova Scotia scallops, veal, lamb, shrimp, prime rib (with advance notice). Dinner only; reservations needed.

The Peck House. *Expensive.* Empire; 569–9870. Thirty miles southeast of the ski area on U.S. 40 (but worth the trip), this original stage coach house is the oldest hotel still operating in Colorado (established in 1862). Fine dinners served in the Victorian dining room. Reservations recommended. Rooms are available—some are said to be haunted.

Carousel. *Moderate.* Cooper Creek Square Shopping Center, 3d level; 726–4900. Elegant atmosphere in which to enjoy Italian specialties, seafood, reservations.

Crooked Creek Saloon. *Moderate.* 401 Zerex Ave., Fraser; 726–9250. Steaks, burgers (try the 10-oz. Awesome Fatboy Burger), sandwiches, seafood. Breakfast, lunch, dinner; no credit cards.

Deno's Coachman Tavern and Restaurant. *Moderate.* 78911 U.S. Hwy. 40; 726–5332. A favorite local hangout featuring American dishes, late-night snacks, burgers.

Fontenot's Cajun Restaurant and Deli. *Moderate.* 78711 U.S. Hwy. 40 in Park Plaza Shopping Center; 726–4021. Specialize in Po'Boys, spicy stews, and other Louisiana dishes.

Lani's Place. *Moderate.* Cooper Creek Square; 726–9674. Light, cheery oaken surroundings. Mexican specialties, also takeouts. Lunch and dinner.

Marcello's Italian Restaurant. *Moderate.* In Park Place, next to Cinema on U.S. Hwy. 40; 726–4034. Authentic Italian chef who creates delicious soups, veal, and pasta dishes. Casual atmosphere.

New Hong Kong. *Moderate.* 331 Cooper Square; 726–9418. 99 selections from mild to hot and spicy. Eat in or takeout. Lunch and dinner.

The Shed. *Moderate.* 78672 U.S. Hwy. 40; 726–9912. Good steaks; also chicken and burgers. Breakfast and dinner. No reservations; no credit cards.

Carver Brothers Bakery. *Inexpensive.* 93 Grand County Rd.; 726–8202. Egg breakfasts, fresh pastries; lunch and dinner selections include soups, stews, sandwiches; no credit cards.

Fred & Sophie's. *Inexpensive.* 78884 U.S. Hwy. 40; 726–5331. Soups, sandwiches, barbecued ribs. Lunch and dinner.

The Kitchen. *Inexpensive.* 78542 U.S. Hwy. 40; 726–9940. Hearty breakfasts, some Mexican specialties served at this local favorite. Casual spot for breakfasts only. No credit cards.

NIGHTLIFE. Night time activities are as casual as the life-style in Winter Park. After skiing, late evening usually finds music and dancing at *The Slope,* 1161 Winter Park Dr., in Old Town Winter Park. The *Stampede,* Cooper Creek Square, has recorded disco music, dancing, oyster bar, and is a good meeting place. If you want to run into your ski instructor or other locals, head for *Deno's* on Highway 40, no entertainment but lots of lively conversations and TV sports programs. *Gasthaus Eichler,* on US 40, celebrates "Stammtisch Hour" from 5–6 P.M. by the fireplace with special German après-ski treats. *The Balcony Theatre,* 3rd Level of Cooper Creek Square on U.S. Hwy. 40, features musical revues and comedies starting in December through the ski season. Curtain time is 8 P.M. Wednesday through Sunday, but doors open at 7 P.M. for cocktails and the music of a jazz pianist. Call 726–4037 for schedules. In the summer, the company moves to nearby Grand Lake. Call 726–4037 for schedules and times.

HINTS FOR THE HANDICAPPED. Winter Park operates the largest handicapped program in the world, with both winter and summer activities. Ski lessons, equipment, lift tickets for $5 a day; all physical and mental disabilities; racing programs, camps, hiking, rafting, crafts. For information and scheduling call Hal O'Leary, Director Handicap Program, Winter Park Recreational Association, Box 36, Winter Park, CO 80482; 303–726–5514.

COPPER MOUNTAIN

Like so many other modern resorts in Colorado, Copper Mountain originally was a small mining town. John Wheeler moved his family to the Snake River Valley in 1879, where he seemed to town or run all the necessities in the little settlement. The mining camp, set amidst the 13,000-foot peaks of the Ten Mile Range, soon became known as Wheeler. Mines yielded only low grade copper ore, but one mine at the summit of the sloping mountain dominated the valley, hence the name Copper Mountain.

There were even a few skiers in the area, hardy men like Father Dyer (an itinerant preacher) and contract mail carriers. The ore ran out and only a few weathered cabins remained of Wheeler. In 1969 the valley was rediscovered by ski-area developers and Copper Mountain opened its first lift in 1972.

Copper is a planned community at the foot of Copper Mountain, and each year more condos and amenities are built. The mountain terrain naturally divides into areas for expert skiers, intermediates, and beginners. In fact, the U.S. Forest Service has called Copper Mountain a "mountain created for skiing." Copper is one of four resorts in the "Ski the Summit" promotion—the other three are Arapahoe Basin (a day-ski area owned by Keystone), Breckenridge, and Keystone—with interchangeable lift tickets and free shuttle service connecting all four resorts.

Copper is considered to be at the high end of affordable resorts, popular with families and groups. Because it's visible from I–70, it gets a lot of drop-ins for day skiing.

PRACTICAL INFORMATION FOR COPPER MOUNTAIN

HOW TO GET THERE. Copper Mountain is in the Arapaho National Forest, 75 miles west of Denver.

By air. Denver's Stapleton Airport is the gateway with connections by bus (see below) or rental car. All major rental car agencies are represented at the airport (*see* Practical Information for Denver). Ground transportation to Copper Mountain on *Resort Express,* 303–968–2882, ext. 6820.

By bus. *Greyhound-Trailways, American Limousine,* and *Resort Express* all shuttle between Stapleton Airport and the ski area. Call Apex Travel at 303–968–2310 or 800–231 3425 for information.

By car. I–70 west from Denver 75 miles through Eisenhower Tunnel to exit 195. The resort claims that there are no mountain passes to cross from Denver, but this is misleading: Eisenhower Tunnel cuts through the Continental Divide at 11,600 feet and climbing the hill from 5,280 feet at Denver is sometimes no small task. Loveland Pass is an alternate if one does not drive through the tunnel. From Colorado Springs it is 90 miles via U.S. 24 and Colorado Route 9; from Grand Junction 180 miles east on I–70 to Exit 195.

ACCOMMODATIONS. There are approximately 3,572 pillows in 24 hotel and condominium units plus a 225-room Club Med in the village. There are four management companies. The largest with deluxe properties is *Copper Mountain Lodging Services,* Box 3001, Copper Mountain, CO 80443; 800–458–8386 (outside Colorado), 800–332–3828 (in Colorado). However, the best bet is to call *Copper Mountain Resort Association* (the Chamber of Commerce), 800–525–3891 nationwide, Denver direct 303–825–7106 or 303–968–6477; write Box 3003, Copper Mountain, CO 80443. They will book for all properties.

Nearly all the lodges have a similar choice of *expensive* to *moderate* hotel rooms and condos; all are within walking distance to the ski slopes and guests of two management companies have complimentary access to the Copper Mountain Racquet & Athletic Club. The average price runs $65 for a hotel room to $235 for a two-bedroom condo per night, double occupancy.

Club Med. 50 Beeler Place, Copper Mountain, CO 80443; 968–2161. For reservations/information write 7975 N. Hayden Rd., Scottsdale, AZ 85258; 800–CLUB MED. The club is open during the ski season, November–April. Weekly, Sunday-to-Sunday stays $880 per person, double occupancy, include lift ticket, Club Med ski school, and three meals. In summer *Kids of the World* summer camp operates from July 2 to end of August (it is the only one in the U.S.). For children 8–13, two- to eight-week stays, prices range from $1,200 for two weeks to $3,400 for eight weeks; included are airport transportation, meals, lodging, excursions, circus school, riding, volleyball, biking, hiking, sailing, canoeing, and skateboarding, to name a few activities. Five percent discount for siblings.

Inexpensive

Alpen Hutte. 471 Rainbow Dr. (mail to Box 919), Silverthorne, CO 80498; 468–6336. Newly built to look Old World Bavarian, this is the best bargain with class. $15 a night; breakfast or packed lunch $2.50, dinner $4.50. Popular with Front Range skiers.

CAMPING. For nearby camping facilities, see Breckenridge.

HOW TO GET AROUND. Once in Summit County, the *Summit Taxi Service* (668–3565) and the free Summit Stage operate throughout the county. Within Copper Mountain Resort there is a free shuttle service. Much is within walking distance from the base of the mountain.

TOURIST INFORMATION. Snow report numbers are: *Colorado Ski Country USA* 303–831–SNOW or 303–837–9907; from Denver 303–893–1400; in Summit County and at Copper call 968–2100. Pick up a copy of *Copper Cable* published bimonthly or tune in to Channel 11 for up-to-date activity information. *This Week at Copper Mountain Resort* gives current event listings. Contact the resort at P.O. Box 3001, Copper Mountain, CO 80443, (303) 968–2882.

SEASONAL EVENTS. Early season ski clinics for recreational skiers of all abilities are held in **December.** *Let's Go Skiing America* free ski days are in **January.** *Women's Ski Seminars* are in January and early **February.** The *Rocky Mountain Trade Fair* in February is at the bottom of the base lifts; in **March** the *Snowboard* Race Series and *Telemark* clinics are scheduled. The *Carpenter/Finney Cycling* camp in early **June** starts off the summer season. Fourth of **July** celebrations include tennis tournaments, concerts, a Volksmarch, barbecues, five- and ten-kilometer runs, fishing derbies. The *Copper Mountain Fair* is in July and the *Copper Mountain Creteriums* and the *Copper Mountain Stage of the Coors Classic* are mid-**August. Labor Day** is another long weekend full of celebrations, including *West-Fest.*

PARTICIPANT SPORTS. Ski season is from early November through late April. Twenty lifts carry skiers to 76 trails, 40 percent of which are intermediate. Copper is part of "Ski the Summit" pass, and interchangeable lift tickets with Arapahoe Basin, Breckenridge, and Keystone are available. Group lessons, workshops, and racing camps are available through the ski school. Racing programs include NASTAR, Copper Mountain self-timer, club racing, and a recreational race camp. Call the ski area at 303–968–2882 for details.

Cross-country skiing is available on 25 kilometers of maintained double tracks at *Copper Mountain/Trak Cross Country Center.* Track fees are $5 for adults; a ticket for K lifts and tracks is $10. Lessons, clinics, and a women's cross-country skiers are part of the Nordic program. Rentals available. Call 968–2882, ext. 6342.

Ice skating on West Lake is held noon to 10 P.M., no charge; skate rentals at *Turning Point Sports/Gorsuch Ltd.* in Village Square; 968–2048. **Sleigh rides** follow the base of the mountain daily except Sunday; call 968–2232 for reservations.

The Racquet and Athletic Club offers **racquetball, weight room, aerobics, pool** with four 25-yard lap lanes, **sauna, hot tubs,** a **massage therapist,** two **indoor tennis courts,** nursery, restaurant, and bar; call 968–2882. Resort seminars offer programs on a variety of professional and personal subjects December to mid-April.

Summer Sports

For information on summer sports call 968–2882, ext. 6322, unless otherwise noted.

The *Copper Creek Golf Course,* designed by Pete and Perry Dye, is the highest **golf** course in the U.S. (9,650 ft.). Bordered by snow-capped mountains, divided by West Ten Mile Creek and with eight acres of water, the scenery is spectacular on every hole.

Other summer activities include free **chairlift rides, jeep tours, horseback riding, rafting, volleyball, hiking, bicycling** on 47 miles of maintained

asphalt bike paths (rentals from *Christy Sports,* 968–6250), Six **outdoor
tennis courts** complement the indoor tennis and other activities at the Racquet and Athletic Club. **Fly fishing** is excellent at nearby Ten Mile Creek
and West Ten Mile Creek; equipment rentals and lessons available.

HISTORIC SITES, AMUSEMENTS, AND ACTIVITIES. Visible history of the area's mining past is found in Breckenridge (see that section).
A scenic chairlift ride is great fun. Art shows and workshops are generally
scheduled during the summer months as well. Call 968–2882, ext. 6322.

CHILDREN'S ACTIVITIES. Call for day-care information 968–2882
ext. 6345. *Belly Button Babies* is for tots two months to two years. Cost
is $30 a day, $20 for a half-day; operates year round. *Belly Button Bakery*
operates daily for kids two years and up to teach them cooking, baking,
arts and crafts, and outdoor snow play. Cost is $30 a day, $20 for a half-
day. (Kids 3 and up may have limited skiing play on snow.)

Junior Ranch is a learn-to-ski program for four-, five-, and six-year-olds.
A full day of supervised indoor and outdoor activity cost $25; a half-day
(12:45–3:30 P.M.) is $19. Ski equipment and lunch money are needed—
reservations recommended (968–2882). *Senior Ranch* is a ski-school program for 7–12-year-olds, beginners to hot-shots. All-day instruction—
lunch money needed; cost is $25 a day and $19 a half-day (12:45–3:30 P.M.).
Newcomer packages for children who have never skied before are also
available. At press time only one price was available: a one-day program
with life ticket, lessons, lunch, and ski rental is $40. Programs, including
lunch, lift ticket, and lesson, for children who have skied before were slated
at press time to cost $42 for one day and $114 for three days. Most likely
there will be other programs available during the season, so check before
you go. During December and January, children under 12 stay free in their
parents' lodging and they ski free.

SHOPPING. Ski and sports shops include *Breeze,* 104 Wheeler Pl.;
Christy Sports, Copper Junction Bldg.; *Turning Point Sports/Gorsuch Ltd.,*
Village Square; *Rec Sports,* 760 Copper Rd. Gift items are found in *Foggs
Shirt Emporium,* Village Square; *A Country Garden,* Village Square; *Hello
Colorado,* Village Square; books in *Mountain Books and Gifts,* Mountain
Plaza. There are several stores for groceries and necessities. Many more
stores are found in nearby Dillon, Silverthorne, Frisco, or Breckenridge.

DINING OUT. *Solitude Station* at **midmountain** offers the skier hearty
fare cafeteria style, as does the *Center Cafeteria* at the **base area;** upstairs
is *Jacques' Loft,* a full-service restaurant and après-ski lounge. *B-Lift Pub*
is open for three meals a day, mostly burgers. *Union Creek* also has a cafeteria.

Ten other restaurants in town offer a variety of cuisines at reasonable
prices. Entrées at *Expensive* establishments run $9–$17; *Moderate,* $6–$10;
Inexpensive, under $5. All restaurants listed take Visa and MasterCard
unless noted otherwise.

Expensive

Barkleys. 620 Main, Frisco; 668–3694. Good steaks, prime rib, chicken,
fish. Reservations recommended.
Blue Spruce. 120 W. Main, Frisco; 668–5243. A fine Continental restaurant. No reservations.

Farley's. 104 Wheeler Pl., Copper Mountain; 968–2577. Specializes in prime rib, steaks, nightly specials. Reservations recommended.

The Plaza. Mountain Plaza, center of the base area; 968–2882, ext. 6505. An elegant restaurant featuring Continental cuisine, classical guitar music during dinner. Reservations needed.

B-Lift Clubhouse. At B-Lift; 968–2282, ext. 6514. Breakfast and lunch; hot and cold sandwiches, outdoor barbecue. No reservations.

Moderate

Rackets. In the Copper Mountain Racquet and Athletic Club; 968–2882. Features prime rib and salad bar. Reservations recommended.

Tuso's. 104 Wheeler Pl.; 968–6090. A wide menu, including Mexican and Italian food.

Inexpensive

The Copper Still. Snowbridge Square; 968–2020. Deli foods, snacks, and soups. No reservations.

Copper Deli & Ice Cream Shoppe. Mountain Plaza Building; 968–6168. Croissant sandwiches, old-fashioned soda fountain; no credit cards.

That Soup Place. Village Square; 968–2629. Known for the stuffed potatoes, chili, and soups. Breakfast, lunch, and dinner.

Vlasta's Café. Snowbridge Square; 968–2323. Sicilian-style pizza, burgers, takeout. Breakfast, lunch, and dinner.

NIGHTLIFE. The nightlife won't overwhelm you at Copper Mountain, but some good sounds come from the guitar music at *Plaza Restaurant.* Sports on wide-screen TV, rock, and Top 40 are featured at *Jacques' Loft,* third floor of the Center, Tues.–Sat. 9 P.M.–1 A.M. *O'Shea's,* in Copper Junction Bldg. at base area, has live country/western music, winter only. Movies are put on twice-weekly by the Resort Association; call for schedules and location, 968–6477. VCR rentals and two game rooms (Snowbridge Building and Copper Junction) round out après-ski life.

KEYSTONE

Keystone is the ultimate planned village. This "full-service," four-season resort consists of The Keystone Lodge and 900 condominium units mostly clustered around a central lake and immaculate village. Every building has been built with materials and colors to blend with the environment, maintaining a feeling of the natural landscape. It is almost too perfect—and those coming from high-stress situations could decompress too quickly.

Like most mountain communities, Keystone first saw the light of day with the quest for gold. The settlement was established by 1880 in a wide valley bisected by the Snake River, the craggy Continental Divide towering above. With the wane of the gold and silver booms, Keystone had little more than a few weathered boards to show for its former life. In the 1950s a strange breed started coming to Arapahoe Basin, hard against the Divide a few miles from Keystone, to slip and slide down the snow. Skiers. It wasn't until the late sixties, though, that skiers started having an impact on the economy. Even then, Summit County was the high place to drive through on the way to Aspen.

The Keystone mountain resort was created in 1970; the mountain itself is perhaps a mile from the planned village, while Arapahoe Basin is five miles away, at the base of Loveland Pass. The entire operation is under the management of Ralston Purina Company, and the corporate hand can be felt, particularly in the efficient, formal service and employee attitudes. Today, the Summit County ski areas, marketed as "Ski the Summit," form the biggest resort cluster in the country and host more skiers than the Aspen complex of mountains.

Keystone is considered to be at the upper end of affordable, with enough elegant dining and shopping for those who want to spend a few more dollars. The resort attracts well-to-do and upper-middle income families, mostly from the midwest, southeast, Texas, and Oklahoma.

PRACTICAL INFORMATION FOR KEYSTONE

HOW TO GET THERE. Keystone is in the Arapaho National Forest, 75 miles west of Denver. **By air.** Denver's Stapleton Airport is the closest gateway with scores of airlines from all major American cities and rental cars available. (*See* Practical Information for Denver.) Scheduled chauffeured van service via *Resort Express* (800–334–7433) is available between Denver's Stapleton Airport and Keystone for $25 per person one way.

By car. Drive 68 miles west of Denver via I–70, through Eisenhower Tunnel, to exit 205, then six miles east on U.S. 6. In good weather, take scenically spectacular Loveland Pass by exiting I–70 just before the tunnel onto U.S. 6, past Loveland Ski Area and Arapahoe Basin to Keystone. From Colorado Springs it is 145 miles via I–25 and I–70; from Grand Junction it is 180 miles east on I–70 over Vail Pass to Exit 205, then six miles east on U.S. 6.

By bus. *Greyhound-Trailways* has daily bus service from Denver's airport to Frisco with some schedules direct to Keystone. It's a short taxi ride from Frisco to Keystone.

ACCOMMODATIONS. For reservations, call 800–222–0188 outside Colorado, 468–4242 in state . . . or write *Keystone Central Reservations,* Box 38 Keystone, CO 80435. In Denver, call direct: 534–7712. Average cost of a double room during ski season is $110.

Expensive

Ask for "Premium" when making reservations.

Keystone Lodge. Box 38; 800–222–0188 nationwide; 534–7712 from Denver, toll-free. Keystone's full-service hotel, the Lodge holds awards for the superiority of its guest facilities. Each of the 152 rooms has a mountain view; the heated indoor-outdoor pool has complete cocktail service; there is a sauna and whirlpool. No pets. $125–$135 double occupancy in regular winter season.

Most of the following establishments have accommodations ranging from studio units to four-bedroom condos. Private homes are also for rent. Rates range from $110–$310 a night. *Argentine, Plaza, Mall, Edgewater,* and *Lakeside* are all on Keystone Lake at the center of the village; a two-minute shuttle ride to the mountain.

Willows, Decatur, Montezuma, and *Lenawee* are on the east side of Keystone Lake, two-minute walk to village center, two-minute shuttle ride to mountain.

Chateaux d'Mont and *Lancaster Lodge* are at the base of Keystone Mt.

Moderate

Ask central reservations for "Deluxe." Studios to four-bedroom condos are available, $105–$270, a night. Five minute walk from village center. No pets. These include: *Pines, Soda Springs, Homestead/Lodgepole, Quicksilver, Tennis Townhouses, St. John.*

Inexpensive

These are standard accommodations, but hardly cheap. Studios and four-bedrooms that are farther from the Village and don't have the wonderful views, at $95–$230. Among these are: *Flying Dutchman, Wild Irishman, Keystone Gulch.*

CAMPING. Green Mountain reservoir, north on CO 9, about 18 miles from Dillon is a popular fishing and camping spot, with a store and cabins. First-come, first-serve. See Breckenridge section, below, for campsites around nearby Lake Dillon.

HOW TO GET AROUND. A free shuttle operates continually from the Keystone Lodge and all condos to the Village, Mountain House, River Run Plaza, Arapahoe Basin, and the Keystone Ranch for dinner. For information, call *Transportation* at 468–4130. Within Summit County the free bus service, *Summit Stage,* runs from Keystone to the neighboring "Ski The Summit" areas of Breckenridge and Copper Mountain from mid-November until late April.

TOURIST INFORMATION. For snow conditions call 303–468–4111 or Colorado Ski Country, 303–831–SNOW. The *Summit County Sentinel* carries local news and sports. The Keystone Central Switchboard is open 24 hours a day every day; 800–222–0188 nationwide. Write the Resort at Box 38, Keystone, CO 80435. Watch the local cable station, KSMT Channel 13, for mountain conditions and local activities.

SEASONAL EVENTS. *Colorado Special Olympics* for mentally handicapped athletes holds regional championships in March.

Special at **Christmas** is an Elizabethan-style dinner with madrigal entertainment, reminiscent of Tudor England. Presented in the Conference Center of the Keystone Lodge, this is an unusual and memorable way to spend Christmas—$38 per person; call 468–4130.

Keystone Music Festival features the National Repertory Orchestra in late **December.** Dance to a 40-piece orchestra on **New Year's Eve.** For information, call 468–4294. Children's *Easter Egg Hunt* is put on by the Activities Center each Easter day.

The *Keystone Summer Music Festival* begins early **June** and runs until early **September,** with performances on Wednesdays, Fridays, Saturdays, and Sundays. The 90-piece National Repertory Orchestra, Summit Brass, and nationally known guest artists and conductors are featured. Tickets range from $10 to $24. Call the box office at 303–468–4294 or the orchestra office at 303–674–5161 for ticket information. For lodging packages, including performances, call 800–222–0188 or from Denver, 534–7712. *Summitfest* at the end of **July** is a nonstop celebration on land and water to raise money for AMC Cancer Research Center. Early **August** is *Western Wildlife Camp* for children 9–13.

PARTICIPANT SPORTS. The activities center at Keystone Lodge is the place to call for sports info, even if you're not staying at a Keystone property: 468–4130. Visitors have three **ski** mountains from which to choose. The expert and adventurous skiers head a few miles east on U.S. Six to *Arapahoe Basin.* Top elevation is 12,450 feet, making it the highest lift-served ski area in North America. It is known for its excellent late spring, above-timberline skiing, often lasting into late June. Skiing really started here in the 1940s and hard-core Denverites still seek it out for day skiing. Five lifts serve mostly intermediate and expert terrain.

Skiing *Keystone Mountain,* until a few years ago, had been for the beginners and timid of the ski world. Wide, immaculately groomed slopes took their easy, winding courses down the mountain. Now, with the addition of North Peak on the back side of Keystone, a whole new world of expert terrain has opened up. A six-passenger gondola goes from River Run Plaza to the summit, directly accessing North Peak as well as Keystone Mountain. Three triple chairlifts, eight doubles, one beginner lift, and a poma carry skiers into 680 acres of maintained trails. Lift tickets are interchangeable with Arapahoe, Keystone, and North Peak. "Ski the Summit" lift tickets are valid at these areas, plus Copper and Breckenridge.

The *Mahre Training Center* provides week-long sessions taught by the World Cup and Olympic winners, Phil and Steve Mahre and their personally trained instructors. The purpose is to teach the Mahre technique, allowing students to build a technical base and allowing them to ski with greater confidence and comfort; included are technical and tactical exercises, free skiing and slalom course skiing, dry land training, seminars on physical and mental preparation for racing, video taping, and social events. The package includes lodging, the price depending on accommodations and the number of people in the party. Call the Mahre Training Center, 303–468–4172, for information; for reservations call Central Reservations at 800–222–0188 nationwide or 534–7712 in Denver, toll-free. Rentals available at area ski shops, or call *Keystone Rentals,* 800–255–3715 or 468–4180 in Colorado.

Cross-country skiing is on 26 miles of prepared trails. Lessons and tours by day or evening offered; telemark lessons with lunch and lift tickets are $40/day. Contact Jana Hlavaty, Keystone Resort, Box 38, Keystone, CO 80435; 468–4188.

Helicopter skiing is available through *Rocky Mountain Heli-ski* out of Dillon; call 468–8253.

Ice skating is popular on Keystone Lake; the *Keystone Center* is the largest maintained outdoor facility in the country. Rink admission is $2.50; skate rental $2.50. 468–2316, ext. 3980.

Summer Sports

Mahre Training Center offers summer race camps, including a special junior race camp in June. Call the Ski School, 468–4172.

The Keystone Tennis Center features 14 championship courts, two of which are indoors, plus a complete pro shop and lounge area. Courts are open to all guests and private instruction, group clinics, and tournaments can be arranged. Weekend clinics are held year-round, including eight hours of instruction. Five-day clinics begin every Sunday with 20 hours of instruction, use of ball machines and all the court time you want. For reservations for clinics and lodging call 303–468–4220.

Summer is full of activities besides tennis. The *Robert Trent Jones Jr. Championship* **Golf** *Course* rambles for 7,090 yards, incorporating a nine-acre lake, and features a "linksland," patterned after early Scottish courses. Two pros host clinics, offer lessons, and supervise play from early June to mid-October. Call the Pro Shop, Keystone Ranch, 303–468–4250.

Colorado is known for its exciting **whitewater rafting** expeditions. Keystone takes full-day excursions on the Colorado River for first-timers and novice rafters, on the Arkansas for more experienced rafters. Elaborate, shoreside lunches are served. Call Keystone Resort for details, 303–468–3130.

Keystone Stables (468–4156) are a half-mile from the village, and offer one- and two-hour **horseback rides** through the Snake River Valley and along high ridges for spectacular views of the Gore and Ten Mile ranges; breakfast rides also available. **Jeep tours** (468–4130) will take you into the backcountry if you don't hanker after a horse. **Hayrides** head behind Keystone for snacks and refreshments at an old ranching homestead. Also call 468–4156.

Lazy **paddleboating** on Keystone Lake in the Village has been likened to punting on the Thames. All you need is at the *Boat House,* 468–4245. For more ambitious water sports, Lake Dillon is only five miles west of Keystone. With 25 miles of shoreline, it is popular with sailors; Keystone's 25-foot *Cal* sailboat offers three skippered cruises daily. There's good **fishing** in Dillon Reservoir, but guides from Keystone will take anglers to their favorite lakes and streams for brook, rainbow, and brown trout; sign up for a guide and equipment or for space on Keystone's sailboat at the Activities Center at the Lodge, 468–4130; fishing licenses are for sale at local sports shops.

Bicycling along the fairly flat paved bike paths is a good way to see the area; rentals are available from the Sports Desk at The Lodge. **Hiking** and **backpacking** into the High Country of the Arapaho National Forest takes one into dramatic mountain terrain; just follow well-marked trails in the immediate village area.

HISTORIC SITES. Driving to the summit of Loveland Pass offers a dramatic view of the Continental Divide; there is an overlook and a picnic area—it's always windy so bring a jacket or windbreaker. At the base of Loveland Pass just off U.S. 6 is an old mining town, *Montezuma,* which is being brought back from the dead by mountain lovers. Young people are staying, fixing up the run-down buildings, and making a small community. Hikers and cross-country skiers come through on day trips. A country store has a few necessities and is worth the stop, just for the atmosphere and throw back to a previous century.

Keystone's six-passenger gondola takes visitors to a mountain summit at 11,640 feet for spectacular views of the mountain ranges and Lake Dillon. Take your own lunch or enjoy lunch and Friday dinners at the seven-level Summit House. Take the lift down or walk down the easy terrain to the base area of Keystone Mountain.

CHILDREN'S ACTIVITIES. Children 12 years old and under stay free in the same lodge room or condo unit with their parents, with minimum occupancy. Children's lift tickets are $10 a day for multiple days. The *Children's Center* in the Mountain House at the base of Keystone Mountain will take care of children from two months, open 8 A.M.–5 P.M. daily;

advance reservations required, call 800–255–3715 or, in Colorado, 468–4182. Care for infants 2–11 months is $32 a day or $5 an hour; you supply baby food. All-day child care—12 months and up—is $28, lunch included, or $4.50 an hour. Evening babysitting may be reserved through the Children's Center.

At Arapahoe Basin, the Center accepts children 18 months and older from 8:30 A.M.–4:30 P.M. daily; call 800–255–3715, or; in Colorado, 468–4182 for reservations. Prices are the same as Keystone Center.

Snow Play Program (800–255–3715 or, in Colorado, 468–4182) is for children three years and older. It offers sledding and skating. Children should be toilet-trained and dressed for outdoors, Keystone Mountain only. $32 a day, including lunch; half-day for $25 (8 A.M.–1 P.M. or noon–5 P.M.).

Junior Ski School is for ages 3–12, $40 a day includes lift ticket, rental equipment, lunch and four hours of lessons; reservations required at Ski School, 800–255–3715 or, in Colorado, 468–4170.

In summer, children 18 and under stay free in the same room or condo with parents. Preschoolers are treated to picnics, crafts, pony rides; older children can swim, ride, fish. An outdoor *Youth Activities* program is offered; check the Resort Activities Center, 468–4130.

Western Teen Adventure, a program of the Keystone Science School and the National Wildlife Federation, is a 12-day backpacking program for 14–17-year-olds; students learn wildlife, botany, wilderness issues, minimum impact camping, outdoor leadership skills. *Western Wildlife Camp* is a 10-day program for children 9–13 teaching geology, energy, folk history, astronomy, hiking. Call the Federation at 703–790–4363 for prices and dates.

SHOPPING. The Village at Keystone Resort has shops for the luxuries of life on a three-level pedestrian mall. *La Cima* carries ladies' and men's clothes; *Children's Shop* carries just what it says; *Cures & Curiosities* is fine for unusual gift items, as is *Rainbow Potpourri; Gorsuch* and *Sports Stalker* carry sports and ski attire; *Scoble Galleries* carries a variety of gifts, Indian crafts, original art, greeting cards, pottery. *Country Christmas Cottage* is a year-round Christmas shop. For the necessities of life, head for Dillon or Frisco.

DINING OUT. There are 10 restaurants in the village, including those in the Keystone Lodge, in the Keystone Ranch, and in the historic Ski Tip Lodge.

At the base of the mountain is *Gassy's,* open in winter for lunch and dinner. In summer, it becomes the *Pavilion Café* serving gourmet buffets before Keystone Music Festival performances. Good crêpes can be had from the *Greatest Crêpe Wagon* parked at the base area. *Last Lift Bar* is good for snacks and drinks. The *Summit House* at the top of Keystone Mountain is a multilevel cafeteria and soup bar, with outdoor barbecues in spring weather. *Mountain House* and *River Run Plaza* offer cafeteria food.

Entrées in *Expensive* restaurants will run $17–$20; $10–$15 in *Moderate;* under $10 in *Inexpensive.* All restaurants listed take Visa, MasterCard and American Express unless otherwise noted.

Garden Room. *Expensive.* In the Keystone Lodge; 468–2316. For Continental meals prepared tableside. Reservations recommended.

Keystone Ranch. *Expensive.* At the Keystone Ranch golf course in the resort, a few miles from Keystone Village; 468–4161. Outstanding six-course dinners; fixed price of $30. All in an elegant ranch setting. Reservations recommended.

Ski Tip Lodge. *Expensive.* Montezuma Rd., 2 miles east of Keystone Village; 468–4202. This is a cozy guest ranch—formerly a stagecoach stop in the 1860s. Reservations.

Bentley's. *Moderate.* Overlooking Keystone Lake; 468–6610. Burgers as well as Italian-American dishes. Reservations accepted.

Bighorn Steakhouse. *Moderate.* In the Keystone Lodge; 468–2316. Serves steaks and offers a 28-item salad bar.

The Navigator. *Moderate.* At Keystone Lake; 468–5600. For seafood. Reserve in advance.

Alpentop. *Inexpensive.* Keystone Plaza; 468–2774. A gourmet deli.

Edgewater Cafe. *Inexpensive.* In Keystone Lodge; 468–4127. For family dining; open in winter for three meals; in summer for breakfast and lunch only, with umbrella tables at lakeside. Reservations accepted.

Last Chance Pizza. *Inexpensive.* Argentine Plaza, Keystone Village; 468–4186. Good pizzas and a young crowd.

OUTSIDE KEYSTONE RESORT

Blue Spruce Inn. *Expensive.* 12 West Main, Frisco; 668–5243. Known for its Continental menu; steaks and ribs.

La France. *Expensive.* 25 Chief Colorow, Dillon; 468–6111. Elegantly French. No credit cards.

Old Dillon Inn. *Moderate.* 305 Dillon Lane, Silverthorn; 468–2791. Mexican food, loud music, and weekend entertainment make this *the* most popular hangout for locals.

Claim Jumper. *Inexpensive.* 805 North Summit Blvd., Frisco; 668–3617. For pizza and chicken; also serves breakfast.

Whiskey Creek. *Inexpensive.* 912 North Summit Blvd., Frisco; 668–5595. For Mexican food and fine margaritas.

NIGHTLIFE. You won't disco the night away in Keystone, but there are several lounges for après-ski and aprè-dinner drinks. The *Tenderfoot Lounge,* in The Lodge, is elegant with a spectacular view of the Gore Range. *Bentley's* ocassionally has live entertainment and *Last Chance Saloon* usually has nightly entertainment. See "Dining Out," above for addresses.

HINTS FOR THE HANDICAPPED. Ski instruction is given by appointment only for the blind and those with some physical disabilities. Contact Gordon Briner, Ski School Director, Keystone Resort; 303–468–4170.

BRECKENRIDGE

Breckenridge was the center of a thriving group of villages and mining camps that sprang up in the grip of gold fever during the 1860s. The largest single gold nugget ever found in the United States was unearthed here (weighing 13 pounds, 7 ounces) in 1887.

After World War II, the mining dwindled and the town was almost forgotten. As late as the midfifties, Breckenridge was included in listings of Colorado ghost towns. In fact, through a surveyor's oversight, Breckenridge was not even a part of the Union until 1936. Special ceremonies included what was called, for publicity's sake, the "Kingdom of Breckenridge" into the United States.

Early visitors were charmed by the Victorian buildings and miners' cabins (some date back to the 1840s), and in 1961 the Breckenridge Ski Area opened.

Over the years Breckenridge grew slowly, but in the past few years it has gained in popularity with the addition of ski terrain, state-of-the-art lift equipment and high-rise condos and hotels. Today it is a lively vacation spot, both summer and winter. Century-old businesses line the main street, and there are hundreds of shops and restaurants of all descriptions and price ranges. With 354 buildings, Breckenridge has one of Colorado's largest historic districts. The ski mountain is just at the edge of town, and each of the three peaks is no more than a three-minute bus ride from the center of town.

PRACTICAL INFORMATION FOR BRECKENRIDGE

HOW TO GET THERE. The resort is located in the Arapaho National Forest, 85 miles west of Denver.

By air. Stapleton Airport in Denver is the gateway (*see* Practical Information For Denver). Limousines, taxis, and charter coaches are available from Stapleton upon request.

By bus. *Greyhound-Trailways* operates daily service to Frisco and Breckenridge from Denver's Stapleton Airport and Denver downtown; about $11 one way. *Resort Express* (800–334–7433) and *Summit Taxi* (800–321–5246) operate chauffeured vans. Cost is approximately $25 one way.

By car. A nearly two-hour drive west via I–70 from Denver, through the Eisenhower Tunnel to exit 203, Colo. Rte. 9, about nine miles from Frisco. From Colorado Springs it is 105 miles via Hwy. 285, and Rte. 9. *Hertz* (800–645–3131) has drop-off services in Breckenridge.

ACCOMMODATIONS. The Breckenridge Resort Chamber represents 95 percent of the available lodging and is the central reservations facility. Call in Colorado 800–822–5381 or 303–453–2918; write Box 1909, Breckenridge, CO 80424.

There are more than 100 condominium complexes, motels, and family-style lodges in the town and base area of Breckenridge, which can house 23,000 people. The following list should give you some idea of what's available. Summer lodging rates are approximately 30–40 percent lower than winter rates.

Expensive

Beaver Run. Box B; 303–453–6000. Top-of-the-line ski-in, ski-out property at the base of Peak Nine. It includes a complete commercial center, pool, hot tubs, saunas, steam and exercise rooms, miniature golf course, day care. During ski season a two-bedroom condo goes for $225–$275 a night; a hotel room is $110 a night.

Park Place. 325 Four O'Clock Rd.; 303–453–6922. Spacious two-bedroom units, hot tubs, for $170–$230 a night. Easy access to shuttle, town and slopes; access to amenities area for pool, whirlpool, hot tub, sauna.

Village at Breckenridge. Main St. and South Park Rd.; 303–453–2000. Condominium resort complex between the banks of the Blue River and the base of the ski lifts. Fishing, hiking, horseback riding, cross-country skiing, ice skating. $100 hotel room, $110–$140 studios, a one-bedroom $130–$150, 2- and 3-bedrooms also available.

Moderate

Four O'Clock Lodge. 550 Four O'Clock Road in Upper Four Seasons Village; 303–453–6228. Within walking distance to the slopes and to town, one-bedroom loft is $135, two-bedroom loft $175. Access to an amenities area with pool, whirlpool, sauna, hot tub.

Hilton Lodge. 550 Village Road; 800–321–8444 nationwide, Denver direct 825–3800 or 453–4500. Has indoor pool, Jacuzzis, saunas, exercise room, masseuse, restaurant and lounge, day care center, and ski rental shop. Rooms, some with decks, have refrigerator and wet bar. $65 a night for a queen bed to $135 a night for three beds.

Wedgewood Lodge. 535 Four O'Clock Rd. Victorian townhomes; two-bedrooms for $190.

Inexpensive.

Brass Bed Inn. 229 S. Main St.; 303–453–0843. Victorian bed-and-breakfast inn built in the late 1800s, now restored. One-bedroom suite, including a Swedish breakfast, $55–$65 per night.

Fireside Inn. 114 French; 303–453–6456. Restored Victorian home in town with dorms, private rooms, and family-style group dining. A dorm room is $16.50 a night; a one-bedroom (sleeps four) is $55–$80; higher during holidays.

Ridge Street Inn. 212 N. Ridge St.; 303–453–4680. Dorm rooms are $15, private rooms (up to three bedrooms) are $60–$70 per person.

CAMPING. *Tiger Run RV Resort* is three miles north of Breckenridge on County Road 315; call 303–453–2231. A year-round, commercial campground, it provides hookups, jeep and snowmobile tours, horseback riding, raft trips, and a convenience store. The other campgrounds, run by the *U.S. Forest Service,* charge a nightly fee with a limit on the number of nights one can stay; no shower facilities; operated on a first-come, first-serve basis. Call 303–668–3314 or 945–3295 for opening dates and fee information. Around or near the Dillon Reservoir, about nine miles from Breckenridge are the *Blue River Campground,* 945–3295, *Frisco Bay, Heaton Bay, Peak One,* and *Prospector.*

HOW TO GET AROUND. Everything in the town of Breckenridge is within walking distance. There is free shuttle service to the three base areas, to town, and between lodges. *The Summit Stage* is a free service to the other ski areas in Summit County—Keystone and Copper Mountain. Call the *Summit Stage,* 453–2368, for schedule information; operates between the end of November and the end of April.

TOURIST INFORMATION. The local radio station for news and weather is KSMT, at 102.3 FM. Snow conditions telephone is 453–6118. For road conditions call 453–1090. There are three health clinics, a vet, laundromat, and any other essential services in Breckenridge. The *Summit*

County Journal is the local newspaper. The *Information Booth* at Bell Tower Mall is open year round, 303–453–6018. Contact *Breckenridge Ski Area* at Box 1058, Breckenridge, CO 80424; 303–453–2368 and *Breckenridge Resort Chamber of Commerce,* Box 1909, Breckenridge, CO 80424; 303–453–2918.

SEASONAL EVENTS. First highlight of the **winter** season is the Christmas lighting with Santa arriving by horse-drawn sleigh followed by carolers. Every ski season is punctuated by the *Freestyle World Cup Competition* in **January.** The *ULLR Festival,* a Norwegian winter carnival honoring the Norse God of Snow, is also celebrated in January. *Telemark Returns* and the *Summit Telemark Series* features cross-country competitions in early **March.** The annual *Mogul Challenge* is at the end of March; the **April** *Fool's Party* has long been a tradition. In early April the *Figure 8 Contest* is held in Horseshoe Bowl on Peak 8, as two skiers make their way down the fall line, intersecting each other's tracks in newly fallen snow, to form figure 8's over and over again.

Summer sees the usual complement of mountain activities, such as the *Bicycle Classic* in **July,** *Colorado Mountain College* programs, *Genuine Jazz,* a two-day free jazz fest in the Village at Breckenridge, in July. *Arts and Crafts Festival* is held July Fourth weekend. *Run the Rockies,* the highest certified marathon and 10 kilometer races in North America are held at the end of **August.** *No-Man's Land Celebration* in August is when the town again becomes a "kingdom." The **Labor Day Weekend** festivities, *Gathering at the Great Divide,* include burro races, parades, arts and crafts, music. The *Festival of Film* and *Summit Jazz Festival* in **fall** bring the summer to a close.

PARTICIPANT SPORTS. Both **cross-country skiing** and **downhill** are well organized here. The *Breckenridge Nordic Center* (453–6855) offers 22 km of groomed, double-track trails for cross-country skiing.

Fifteen lifts take skiers to 1,460 acres of ski terrain on three interconnected peaks, most of it intermediate and cruising runs with expert bowl skiing, and advanced terrain on Peak 10. Equipment and instruction available for juniors and adults, powder, racing, cross country. Guided mountain tours are offered free five days a week and are a good way to learn the three mountains and three base areas in a hurry. Call 453–2368.

Breckenridge is part of the "Ski the Summit" promotion and lift-ticket coupon booklets can be purchased for four or six days. Coupons are interchangeable at Breckenridge, Copper Mountain, Keystone, and Arapahoe Basin. The free Summit Stage runs eight times a day among the resorts for skiers.

For groups of 25 or more, the Obstacle Course Race is great fun. There is also **helicopter skiing** (668–5600) on nearby peaks, **ice skating** (453–2000; rentals at Rec Sports, 453–2194), **ice fishing** (453–2194 for information), **sleigh riding** with *Alpine Adventures* (453–1520), *Tiger Run Tours* (453–2231), and *Breckenridge Nordic Center* (453–6855), **Snowcat riding** and **snowmobiling** from *Tiger Run RV* (453–9690).

Summer Sports

Summer sports include **golf**— The *Breckenridge Municipal Golf Course* is the only Jack Nicklaus-designed municipal course in the world. For details on tee times and costs, call the town of Breckenridge, 453–9104. The

Alpine Slide at the ski area is a fast exit off the mountain. **Bike paths** go for miles, some of the most extensive in the state. Bike rentals are available at *Knorr House,* 303 S. Main, 453–2631. **Hiking, fishing, horseback riding, jeep tours, and rafting** can be enjoyed with *Joni Ellis River Tours* (468–1028), *Colorado Adventures* (879–2039), *Rec Sports* (453–9408), and *Alpine Adventures* (453–0111). **Tennis** is available on four public courts in Carter Park on the southeast corner of town (no reservations) and private courts at the Breckenridge Inn, 600 S. Ridge St., 453–2333, and at the Four Seasons Tennis Club, 201 W. Washington St., 453–2425.

HISTORIC SITES, OTHER LANDMARKS, AND AMUSEMENTS.
Breckenridge reeks with history. Horse-drawn buggy tours of century-old buildings leave every afternoon on the hour, and the Resort Chamber has an illustrated walking tour of the town. The *Breckenridge Country Explorer's Kit* gives details on accessible but often offbeat places. Pick up a copy from the Information Center, 453–6018.

Drive up Boreas Pass Road from the south end of Main Street to the top of the continental divide. *Boreas Station,* at 11,497 feet, was once the highest railroad station in the country. Some preserved sections remain.

Hoosier Pass between Breckenridge and Fairplay originally was a trail used by the Indians in their hunting expeditions. It is a spectacular summer drive. Turn right onto a four-wheel drive road at Goose Pasture Tarn; at the end of the road hike up to Moon and Mohawk lakes.

Gold and river dredging is what Breckenridge was all about. Well-preserved remains of the fleet of dredges are found at the north end of town near French Gulch Rd. Tiger Townsite north of Breckenridge once was the most active of all the mining towns; now the assay office and parts of the Royal Tiger Mine remain. Call the Breckenridge Historic Commission, 453–9022. Tiger Run schedules tours to old ghost towns and remains of mining operations: 453–2231.

CHILDREN'S ACTIVITIES. Special children's rates (12 and under) for lift tickets are $13 a day (also the rate for seniors over 60) and a half day (starting at 12:30 P.M.) is $9. Nursery and child care is available for children two months of age and older; call 453–2368 for rates.

In winter the *Kinderhut* provides ski classes and in the summer, outdoor programs; call 453–0379.

SHOPPING. *Bell Tower Mall* at the base of Peak Nine, *Village at Breckenridge* (Main St. and South Park Rd.), and *Georgian Square* are shopping complexes. In addition, hundreds of stores line the street in town. The more unusual stores are *Quandary Antiques,* 304 S. Ridge, and *Tapp Antiques,* 407 South Ridge, *Twisted Pine Fur & Leather Co.,* 900 North Summit Blvd., Frisco, *The Walking Yei,* 311 South Main, for Indian artwork and jewelry, the *Knorr House,* 303 South Main, and *Ski Stop,* 114 South Main, for skiing, biking, and hiking clothes and gear. *Tigerrrrrags,* 221 S. Main, has high fashion women's clothing and accessories, the *Yankee Peddler,* 400 South Main, for handmade ladies clothing and, upstairs, for kids' stuff, *Ciao,* 100 South Main, for ladies' apparel; the *Near Gnu,* 301 North Main, a second-hand store. Gifts, soaps, sundries, imports are found in *Crabtree & Evelyn,* 124 South Main, *Bay St. Company,* 323 South Main, and *Breckenridge Rose,* 100 South Main. For art, posters, and photography check out *Cunningham's,* 107 Main, *Gallery II,* 121 S. Main,

Indian Spirit, 100 South Main. *Foxy Lady,* 222 S. Main, and *Silver Cloud,* 311 S. Main, for jewelry. Ski and sports clothes and gear are found in *Racer's Edge,* 655 S. Park, *Bahnhof,* 100 S. Main, and *Norway Haus,* 110 Lincoln, to name just a few. Children's clothes are carried in *Happy Valley Toy Co.,* 100 S. Main St.

DINING OUT. There are five on-mountain restaurants and 17 picnic tables, plus a brown-bag room and a bar; three at the base area, and over 70 restaurants in town. Entrées at *Expensive* restaurants listed below run $12–$19; *Moderate,* $6–$12; *Inexpensive,* under $6. All restaurants listed take MasterCard and Visa unless otherwise noted.

Briar Rose. *Expensive.* 109 E. Lincoln St.; 453–9948. Wild game, prime rib, seafood, and steaks. Reservations.

Brown Restaurant. *Expensive.* 208 N. Ridge St.; 453–0094. Old traditional steak house in a restored Victorian hotel.

Polo Club. *Expensive.* At Village at Breckenridge, Main St. and South Park Rd.; 453–2000. Continental elegance serving beef, veal, poultry. With a good wine selection and view of Maggie Pond. Reservations recommended.

St. Bernard. *Expensive.* 103 S. Main St.; 453–2572. Italian food.

Webers. *Expensive.* 200 N. Main St.; 453–9464. Hearty German and American dinners, complete with homemade breads and desserts.

Whitneys. *Expensive.* Corner Ridge and Washington sts.; 453–6921. Steak and seafood.

Buffalo Flats. *Moderate.* 435 S. Columbine Rd.; 453–1760. Caters to the American food crowd; good for lunch and late-night dining.

Fatty's. *Moderate.* 106 N. Ridge; 453–9802. The oldest pizzeria in town. Also features other Italian dishes. Takeouts available.

Mi Casa. *Moderate.* 600 Park Ave.; 453–2071. Spicy Mexican lunches and dinners, also burgers named after the ski area's various departments.

9600 Ft. Club. *Moderate.* 450 S. Columbine; 453–6759. Overlooks Maggie Pond. Family priced roast beef, fondues, sandwiches, nachos.

Tillie's Restaurant. *Moderate.* 215 S. Ridge; 453–0669. Victorian atmosphere with stained glass and marble. Steaks, burgers, daily specialties. No credit cards.

Sweet Surrender. *Inexpensive.* 325 S. Main St.; 453–0969. Soups, salads, sandwiches, and ice cream treats.

Zachariah's. *Inexpensive.* 111 S. Main; 453–4806. Features a variety of burgers and 57 kinds of beer.

NIGHTLIFE. For those who can stay up and party after a day of skiing, Breckenridge does have bars, discos, and live entertainment. *Shamus O'Toole's Roadhouse Saloon,* 115 S. Ridge, features rock 'n' roll and live entertainment; *Flipside Nightclub* at the Village, 453–2004, is a bit more elegant, with a good sound system. *Village Pub* in the Bell Tower Mall, 453–2000, has live entertainment, good après-ski and late night; *The Mogul Georgian Square,* 109 S. Main St., 453–0999, features live rock 'n' roll, with a large dance floor. *Village Pub,* Bell Tower Mall, 453–0369, has live entertainment, good après-ski conviviality until late night.

There's live theater at *Backstage,* 355 Village Rd., 453–0199, and, summers only, at the *Music Institute,* base of Peak 8, 453–9142.

HINTS FOR THE HANDICAPPED. The *Colorado Outdoor Educational Center for the Handicapped* offers instruction; call 303–453–6422.

Cost Range. Moderate. It's an affordable area geared to families with a lot of alternative activities.

VAIL

What is now known as Gore Creek Valley was once a high mountain pasture, cradled by the Gore and Sawatch mountain ranges, that provided a rich summer hunting ground for the Ute Indians. Sir St. George Gore, a baronet from Ireland known as Lord Gore, spent the summers of 1854–56 with famous mountain man Jim Bridger on the east side of the Gore Range. Gore killed every animal he could raise his rifle to before he was "requested" to return home (see Winter Park section). It was five years later, when Bridger returned to the area, that he named the mountain range and valley after Lord Gore; Gore never set foot as far west as the range and valley that now bear his name.

The intrusion of the white man searching for gold and silver in the 1870s and 1880s was the last straw for the Utes. Leaving the mountains, they set "spite fires" that burned thousands of acres of timber (see Snowmass section). Years later, the wide open terrain so devoid of trees became Vail's famous back bowls. Like the "Big Burn" at Snowmass, Vail's "back bowls" are a magnet to skiers of intermediate and advanced ability.

With the exception of a few sheep ranchers, the Gore Creek Valley slept until 1940 when US Highway 6 followed the passes from Denver and wound through the valley. Charlie Vail was in charge of construction for the state department of highways, hence the name Vail Pass. The Tenth Mountain Division trained 20 miles away near Leadville during World War II, drawing many of the men back to these mountain valleys after the war. It was one of these veterans who saw the possibilities of the incredible ski terrain in the Vail Pass area.

Land was bought up and in one summer Vail rose from the ground, opening in December 1962. Today, the simulated Swiss village is the largest single mountain skiing complex in Colorado. Vail became the Western White House during President Ford's term of office. Gerald Ford and his family continue to vacation in Vail and maintain a second home in Vail Associates' Beaver Creek, ten miles west. Vail Village has 5,000 permanent residents and this year Vail celebrates its 25th anniversary. While there is plenty of glitz and glamor here, it seems a bit more conservative than its cousin and archrival up the road, Aspen.

PRACTICAL INFORMATION FOR VAIL

HOW TO GET THERE. Vail is in the White River National Forest, 100 miles west of Denver. **By air.** All major airlines serve Denver's Stapleton International Airport. (See also *Practical Information for Denver.*) *Continental Express,* operated by Rocky Mountain Airlines, makes connections to the Avon Stolport, 10 miles west of Vail at Beaver Creek. There is a general aviation airport at Eagle, 30 miles west of Vail. The following companies provide ground transportation between Stapleton and Vail: *Airport Transportation Service* (800–247–7074), *Colorado Ground Transportation* (800–824–1104), *Colorado Mountain Express* (van, limo, and taxi, 800–525–6363), *Colorado Western Stages* (charter bus, 800–332–6363),

Louie's Casual Cabs (taxi, 303–476–TAXI), The *Transporter* (800–722–2177 or 303–398–2177), *Summit Taxi/Going Places* (taxi, bus, limo, 303–476–LIMO), *TCG Limousines* (303–790–4004), and *Vans to Vail* (800–222–2112).

By bus. *Greyhound* (800–445–5287) and *Trailways* (303–398–5303) serve the Vail Transportation Center from downtown Denver and Stapleton, *Trailways* also from Grand Junction.

By car. From Denver, Vail lies 100 miles west on I–70. From Grand Junction it is 150 miles east on I–70; Colorado Springs is 145 miles away via I–25 and I–70. *American International* (800–527–0202), *Hertz* (800–654–3131), and *Thrifty* (303–949–7787) rental cars are located in the Vail area; all major rental companies are at Stapleton Airport (*see* Practical Information for Denver).

ACCOMMODATIONS. 25,000 guests can be accommodated within a five-mile radius of Vail Village. Contact Vail Resort Association, 241 E. Meadow Dr., Vail, CO 81657; call outside Colorado 800–525–3875; in state 303–476–1000 or Denver direct, 628–6624.

Expensive

All properties are in the village, within walking distance of slopes, shopping, and dining.

Antlers Lodge at Vail. 680 West Lionshead Pl.; 303–476–2471. Spacious lodge with studios to three-bedroom units, equipped with fireplaces and balconies. Saunas, heated outdoor pool, and Jacuzzi overlooking Gore Creek. Units range in price from $125–$360 a night, per unit.

Landmark Condominiums. 610 W. Lionshead Circle; 303–476–1350. One- to three-bedroom units range $125–$400 a night, per unit.

The Lodge at Vail. 174 East Gore Creek Dr.; 303–476–5011. A European-Alpine design houses hotel and one- to three-bedroom units that range $130–$550. Restaurant and lounge, swimming pool, saunas.

Vail Athletic Club. 352 East Meadow Dr.; 303–476–0700. Rooms and suites with balconies; many with kitchens, fireplaces. Swimming pool, sauna, massage, and steam rooms, exercise room, racquetball, handball, and squash courts. Prices range $159–$675 a night.

Moderate

These range from $100 to $400 a night for double rooms, one-, two-, and three-bedroom condos.

Christiana. 356 E. Hanson Ranch Rd.; 303–476–5641. Located at foot of mountain within walking distance of shops, restaurants, and lifts. Rooms and apartment units. Heated pool, sauna.

Enzian Lodge. 705 Lionshead Circle W., Box 1776; 303–476–2050. Two blocks from gondola ski lift. Heated pool, Jacuzzi, bar, and lounge. Some rooms with fireplaces.

The Lodge at Lionshead. Drawer 1868, 380 E. Lionshead Circle; 303–476–2700. Studios and apartments facing Gore Creek. Most units with fireplaces and balconies. Two heated pools, saunas, laundry facilities.

Marriott's Mark Resort. 715 W. Lionshead Circle; 303–476–4444. Rooms and condominium units 200 yards from Lionshead gondola. Restaurants, lounges, athletic club, racquetball and tennis courts.

Vail Racquet Club Condominiums. 4690 Racquet Club Dr.; 303–476–4840. At base of Vail pass in east Vail. Units with fireplaces and balconies with barbecues. Restaurant, 13 tennis courts (with three for winter play), squash and racquetball courts, health spa, swimming pool for summer, exercise room.

The Westin Hotel. 1300 Westhaven Dr.; 303–476–7111. In Cascade Village, to west of Vail Mt. Rooms and suites with balconies; some with fireplaces. Formal restaurant for northern Italian and Continental cuisine; *The Café* for light meals; lounge and bar. Two outdoor heated pools, golf courses, indoor tennis courts, racquetball, handball, and squash courts. Limo service to lifts; ski trail to return to hotel. Within a few feet of the Cascade Lift.

The Willows. 74 East Willow Rd.; 303–476–2231. 300 yards from chairlift. Units with fireplaces, balconies. Sauna and whirlpool.

Inexpensive

Best Western Raintree Inn-Vail. 2211 N. Frontage Rd.; 303–476–3890. Two miles west of Lionshead ski area. Health club with pool and sauna. Free shuttle service. $90–$99 a night for a double room.

Roost Lodge. 1783 N. Frontage Rd. W.; 303–476–5451. A longtime favorite of those on a budget, with rooms $65–$74 a night. Bus or drive to the village.

Sitzmark Lodge. 183 Gore Creek Dr.; 303–476–5001. Comfortable rooms with balconies. Restaurant and lounge, outdoor pool, whirlpool, and sauna. Rooms for $85–$115 a night.

Vailglo Lodge. 701 W. Lionshead Circle, Drawer 189; 303–476–5506, 800–541–VAIL or in Colorado 800–492–6533. Located in the center of Vail, walking distance to the gondola, chair lifts, shops, and restaurants. Complimentary Continental breakfast, cozy atmosphere; rooms $85–$130 in winter, $50–$68 in summer.

CAMPING. All the campgrounds in the area are operated by the U.S. Forest Service with nightly fees and ten-day limits on length of stay. For information call 945–3297. Ten miles southeast of Vail is *Black Lakes,* just off I-70 at 10,500 feet; drinking water, trailers up to 16 feet. South of Vail are several campgrounds: three miles south of Redcliff on Highway 24 is *Blodgett,* trailers up to 16 feet; no drinking water, nearby stream. *Hornsilver Campground* is a mile and a half south of Redcliff with drinking water and a nearby stream, trailers under 15 feet. *Halfmoon Campground* is six miles from Minturn off Highway 24, near a stream, with drinking water, campers and trailers up to 16 feet. Nearby *Tigiwon* at 9,000 feet is along the same stream.

HOW TO GET AROUND. Within Vail Village is a free shuttle-bus service, the third-largest municipal bus system in the state. Between Vail and Beaver Creek the shuttle costs $1. For information call 476–7000. The village is planned as a pedestrian mall and shops, dining, lodges, and the base area are all within walking distance; however, if you're carrying skis and boots, it can sometimes be a long walk.

TOURIST INFORMATION. Vail is a full-service community with any business, retail outlet, service, or luxury one could ask for. Channel 13 on cable TV has continuous updates on weather, snow conditions, upcoming events. Radio stations KVMT 104.7 FM, KGMJ FM, and KRVV, KZYR, and TV–2, the Vail/Aspen TV station, carry local information and good music. *Vail Daily* and *Vail Trail* newspapers, and *The Vail Mag-*

azine are dedicated to bringing you the latest local news and activities. Snow condition reports are available by calling locally 476–4888; from Denver 534–1245. The resort can be reached by writing Vail Resort Association, Box 7, Vail, CO 81658; call 303–476–1000.

Information booths are located at Vail Village, near the Transportation Center, and in the Lionshead Parking Structure Bldg.

SEASONAL EVENTS. *WinterFaire* is the annual winter carnival in mid-**January;** the end of January is the *Professional Mogul Classic.* **January** 29 to **February** 12 Vail/Beaver Creek hosts the *World Alpine Ski Championships,* held in this country for the first time in 40 years. Early **March** is the *American Ski Classic* with World Cup races, the *Gerald Ford Cup,* and *Legends of Skiing.*

The **summer** kicks off with the *Governor's Annual Invitational Sports Tournament;* the *Coors International Bike Classic* comes through Vail in **July;** the *Paine Webber Tennis Classic* is at the end of July; **August** features the *Gerry Ford Invitational Golf Tournament* and the *Eagle County Rodeo;* **Labor Day** celebrations always include lawn parties, music festivals, and a mountaintop dinner at Lionshead and Eagle's Nest; **September** is the *Vail Symposium,* where national issues are discussed, and *VailFest* to issue in autumn. Former President Ford starts the Christmas season at the annual *Tree Lighting* ceremony **December** 22; New Year's Eve is the *Torchlight Ski-down and Fireworks.*

PARTICIPANT SPORTS. Skiing, of course, is where it all started. A gondola, 19 chairlifts, and a children's poma carry skiers into ten square miles of groomed trails plus 700 acres of ungroomed powder bowls; another 800 acres of bowl skiing are being opened up over the next few years in China Bowl. Cascade Village is the fourth base area (Golden Peak, Vail Village, and Lionshead are the others); a quad lift takes skiers from the West End of Vail to midmountain. Classes are designed for all levels of skiers, from advanced expert powder skiers to first-timers. Call Vail Associates, 476–5601, for lesson and rental information. Ski shops also have rentals. Sybervision is a technique used in the Vail Ski School to improve skiing through imaging; race classes, technique evaluation programs, and Meet-the-Mountain groups are available by contacting the *Vail Ski School* for details and locations (there are six ski school meeting places), 476–5601.

MAX will accept your credit card in return for a lift ticket. Four automated ticket machines in Vail and two in Beaver Creek are the first on-line machines at any U.S. ski area. Also designed to save the skier time are the lift status signs located at major decision points on the mountain, advising skiers approximate waiting time in each lift line. Lift tickets cost $30 a day, $22 for a half-day.

The **cross-country** skiing center (476–5601) teaches basic to advanced track skiing and use of touring skis; and Telemark clinics are held; full- or half-day tours available. Gourmet lunches (Thursdays only) and a Vail-to-Red Cliff tour for six or more people can be planned by advance registration; call (303) 476–3239, ext. 4380. *Eagle River Mountain Guides* offer half- and full-day and supper tours; call Western Sports at 476–3296 for reservations. Experienced cross-country skiers can head out from the top of China Bowl or from the top of Vail Pass for backcountry skiing.

If you can ski Vail's back bowls with confidence, then **helicopter skiing** might be for you. *Vail Heli-ski* takes skiers to out-of-bounds areas in the Vail Valley, Resolution Peak, and other spots: $250 a day; write Box 54, Vail, CO 81658 or call 949–5113 for information.

Piney River Ranch, eight miles from Vail, offers **snowmobile** excursions, **snowcat** tours, and backcountry ski tours: 884 Spruce Court, Vail, CO 81658; 476–3941. **Sleigh rides** start from the golf course every night, 476–1154. **Snowshoe walks** and backcountry **hikes** are offered through *Vail Nature Center,* 476–7000, ext. 227; *Vail Mountaineering,* 476–1414; *Eagle River Mountain Guides,* 476–3296. **Ice skating** is available at *Dobson Ice Arena,* $2.50 admission, $1 skate rental; 321 E. Lionshead Circle, 476–1560.

Workouts, swimming, racquetball are available at the *Vail Racquet Club* (476–4840) and *Vail Athletic Club* (476–0700).

Summer is **golf** time. Five courses are within a 20-mile radius with play generally possible late May through late October. *Eagle-Vail* is a par-72 links course located off Highway 6 at Eagle-Vail; call 949–5267 for greens fees and tee times. *Vail Golf Club* is home of the Jerry Ford Invitational; 18 holes, par 71. Greens fees $25, cart rentals $15, call for tee times 476–1330. *Singletree Golf Club* is just west of Beaver Creek, facilities include sun deck, swimming pool, tennis courts, pro shop; greens fees $30, cart rental $16; 926–3533 for tee times. *Beaver Creek Golf Course* is for use by Beaver Creek resort guests; limited tee-times for public. *Arrowhead at Vail* opened in 1985, private to Arrowhead owners and guests, restaurant and pro shop open to public; 476–1972 for information.

The Town of Vail has 24 **tennis** courts for public use at $6 an hour; call 476–5823 for details. *Eagle-Vail* has eight tennis courts, ball machines, rentals, lounge, grill; 949–5356 for reservations, $6 an hour.

Horseback riding is available at *Spraddle Creek Ranch,* 476–6941, and *Piney River Ranch,* 476–3941. **Bicycle paths** head in all directions from town: for the energetic, bike east up and over Vail Pass; rentals from most sports shops. There are a number of **rafting** companies that lead guided trips on the White, Colorado, Arkansas, Crystal, and Roaring Fork rivers; check at a Vail Information Booth or call 476–2266 for a current list of outfitters. **Float fishing** and **alpine lake fishing** trips are available, check Vail Information booth; if you head off on your own, be sure you are fishing on public lands, not private property; licenses at any sports store.

Take a gondola ride to midmountain for miles of **hiking** trails; guided hikes from Eagle's Nest daily at 1 P.M. Call 476–5601. *Vail Nature Center* has guided nature walks and recreational programs in summer, some require advance registration; for information call 303–476–7000, ext. 227 on weekdays, 476–7005 on weekends. For **backpacking** on your own, trails fan out from the top of Vail Pass; from Gore Creek Campground into Eagle's Nest Primitive Area; from Red Sandstone Creek; and from Tigiwon Campgrounds. Maps and information are available from most sports shops in Vail and from the U.S. Forest Service office, 401 Main St., Minturn, CO 81645, 303–827–5715 or in Eagle at Fifth and Wall streets, 303–328–6388.

MUSEUMS AND ACTIVITIES. The *Colorado Ski Museum and Hall of Fame* is between Vail Village and Lionshead, 15 Vail Rd.; 476–1876.; exhibits portray the history of Colorado skiing and the individuals who made it happen; no charge, call 476–1876 for hours.

Drive up to *Mount of the Holy Cross* by taking US 24 through Minturn to Half Moon Campground; then walk the trail to Notch Mountain for the best view of the white cross of snow at 14,000 feet. Longfellow was so inspired, he wrote a poem about it.

The *Vail Public Library,* across from Dobson Ice Arena, 75 South Frontage Rd. W., schedules film series, art shows, and other programs during the summer months; 476–7000. Take a look at the sculpture garden near the footbridge. You'll also see a piece of the famous Matterhorn Mountain. A 400-pound chunk was removed by helicopter and brought to Vail by the Swiss Resort Tourism directors in the fall of 1984 to commemorate 100 years of skiing in America and as a token of friendship from Switzerland.

Sunday mornings nondenominational worship services are held on Vail Mountain at Eagle's Nest.

The *Vail Institute for the Performing Arts* presents a summer series of programs from community theater to musical productions to major festivals; call 476–1000 for information.

The *John Curry Skating Company* schedules performances throughout the year at Dobson Ice Arena, 476–1560.

CHILDREN'S ACTIVITIES. Summer offers a range of special children's activities. The Town of Vail Recreation Department sponsors events at the Lionshead Bratskeller weekdays June through August, call 476–2040 or 476–2626 for details. The town also sponsors camps for children (and adults), with camp focuses including gymnastics, running, golf, soccer, football; the *Vail Youth Center* is open daily with foosball, pool, films, field trips; call 476–2040.

There are a number of babysitting services; lodges maintain lists of qualified sitters, and the Vail Youth Center in Lionshead Parking Structure Bldg. provides sitters, call Robin Olsen at 476–1365. *Small World Playschool* is for ages 2 months to 6 years; call 476–1088. *Vail Babysitting, Inc.* 827–5279. *Children's Skiing Center* is day-care for ages 3 to 6, toilet trained, 476–2626; *ABC Children's Acres* for ages 2 to 5, 476–1420.

Vail's Children's Skiing Center has ski programs for kids 3 to 6, toilet trained, and youngsters 6 to 13 at Golden Peak and Lionshead. $30 a day for lessons with supervision, without lunch; $115 for three days.

SHOPPING. There are more than 100 shops, art galleries, jewelry stores, and boutiques in the town of Vail; if you can't find it here, you can't find it anywhere. Fine jewelry is found in *Vail Village Jewelers,* 254 Wall; *Fools Gold Boutique,* 2780 Lupine; *Alpine Gold,* 17 E. Meadow Dr.; *Hughes Precious Metal,* 304 Bridge; and the *Squash Blossom* (for American Indian arts, jewelry, sculpture), 198 Gore Creek Dr. Children's clothing is carried in the *Children's Corner,* 278 Hanson Ranch Rd.; *Kidsports,* 122 E. Meadow Dr.; and *Younger Generation,* 500 E. Lionshead. Ladies' and men's apparel is found in *Caroselli's Vail Factory,* 291 Bridge and 531 Lionshead Mall; *Designer Furs,* 285 Bridge; *Helga of Vail,* 234 E. Gore Creek Dr.; *Marcet's,* in the Vail Run Building; and *Nord Hus,* 500 E. Lionshead Circle, among others. Gift and specialty shops include *Krismar,* 465 W. Lionshead Mall and 193 E. Gore Creek Dr.; *Gourmet Cheese Shop,* 225 Wall; *Covered Bridge Store,* 227 Bridge; *Chocolate Mountain,* 675 Lionshead Pl.; *Baggage Claim,* 616 Lionshead Circle; *Alpine Collector,* 500 E. Lionshead Circle; *Gaslight,* 225 Wall; *Meadowlark Gifts,* 675 Lionshead

Pl.; *Mountain Mercantile,* 2111 N. Frontage Rd. W.; the *Rucksack,* 288 Bridge.

Sports clothes and equipment are carried in *Banner Sports,* 568 Lionshead Mall and 714 W. Lionshead Circle; *Aspen Alley,* 225 Wall; *Flexible Fisherman,* 278 Hanson Ranch Rd.; *Gorsuch Ltd.* (all over town); *Pepi Sports,* 231 Bridge; *Snug at Vail,* 227 Bridge; *Timber House,* 201 Gore Creek Dr.; *Western Sports,* 143 E. Meadow Dr., to name a few.

DINING OUT. Dining in Vail presents another array of choices—72 to be exact. **On-mountain** food service includes cafeterias at *Mid-Vail* (outdoor barbecues in good weather), *Eagle's Nest, Golden Peak,* and *Lionshead Gondola Building.* Snack facilities are at *Far East Shelter* at Lift 14 (also outdoor barbecues, weather permitting) and *Wildwood Shelter* at Lift 3. Full-service, sit-down restaurants are *The Cook Shack* at Mid-Vail (nouvelle cuisine), *The Stube* at Eagle's Nest (international dishes), and *Trail's End* is at the bottom of the gondola, at Lionshead (homemade soups, breakfasts, sandwiches).

The *Expensive* restaurants listed here have entrées ranging from $17.50–$45; *Moderate,* $12–$18; *Inexpensive,* under $12. All restaurants listed take Visa and MasterCard unless otherwise noted.

Alfredo's. *Expensive.* In the Westin Hotel, 1300 Westhaven Dr.; 476–7111. Northern Italian cuisine in an elegant setting. Serving dinner and Sunday brunch. Reservations suggested.

Ambrosia. *Expensive.* 17 E. Meadow Dr.; 476–1964. Extensive Continental menu and good dessert selection served in a French provincial setting. Dinner only. Reservations recommended.

Cyrano's. *Expensive.* 298 Hanson Ranch Rd.; 476–5551. Full Continental menu and good California wine list. Serves breakfast, lunch, dinner, and brunch. No reservations.

The Left Bank. *Expensive.* 183 Gore Creek Dr.; 476–3696. Très French and très expensive, with only two seatings each night. Reservations needed several weeks in advance. Dinner in winter only.

Maison Creole. *Expensive.* In the Vail Athletic Club, 352 East Meadow Dr.; 476–0700. New Orleans-style cooking served in mountain art deco surroundings. Open for three meals, plus Sunday brunch. Reservations recommended.

Tea Room Alpenrose. *Expensive.* 100 E. Meadow Dr.; 476–3194. German specialties and mouth-watering pastries. Lunch and dinner.

The Wildflower. *Expensive.* In the newly renovated Lodge at Vail, 174 E. Gore Creek Dr.; 476–5011. Sunny spot with silk flowers all around, serving nouvelle cuisine. Price-fixed dinner for $45. Reservations recommended.

Windows at the Top of the Mark. *Expensive.* 715 W. Lionshead Circle; 476–5011. Gourmet dining in a refined and formal atmosphere. Dress for dinner here. Reservations suggested.

The Chart House. *Moderate.* 610 W. Lionshead Circle; 476–1525. Known for its steaks and salad bar, this is one of the largest restaurants in Vail. No reservations.

Sweet Basil. *Moderate.* 193 E. Gore Creek Dr.; 476–0125. A local favorite. Sunny restaurant with local art on display. Homemade desserts.

Tyrolean Restaurant and Lounge. *Moderate.* 400 E. Meadow Dr.; 476–2204. Specializes in game dishes served in Austrian rustic elegance. Reservations recommended.

Los Amigos. *Inexpensive.* 318 E. Hanson Ranch Rd.; 476–5847. Vail's oldest Mexican restaurant serves huge portions and good margaritas. No reservations.

Blu's Beanery. *Inexpensive.* 193 E. Gore Creek Dr.; 476–3113. Offers a choice of omelettes, pasta, salads, steaks for brunch and dinner. No reservations.

Bully III Chop House. *Inexpensive.* 20 Vail Rd.; 476–4152. A breakfast buffet and a prime rib dinner buffet; also nightly specials. Make reservations.

Szechwan Lion. *Inexpensive.* 304 Bridge; 476–4303. Extensive Chinese menu. Serves lunch and dinner. Reservations accepted.

Torino's. *Inexpensive.* 2111 N. Frontage Rd. W.; 476–0122. Features Italian dishes, pizza, sandwiches. Takeout for lunch or dinner, too.

NIGHTLIFE. *Sheika's Night Club,* 220 E. Gore Creek Plaza, is a wild and glitzy disco, also has live entertainment. The *Clock Tower Café,* 232 Bridge, has a romantic piano bar Tues.–Sat. evenings. *Shadows at the Mark,* 715 W. Lionshead Circle, is a disco; and *Mickey's,* at the Lodge at Vail, 174 E. Gore Creek Dr., is lively. Call *Vail Institute for the Performing Arts* for information on local theatrical and musical productions: 476–1000.

HINTS FOR THE HANDICAPPED. Ski instruction by appointment for blind and other physical disabilities; contact Vail Ski School, Box 7, Vail, CO 81658, call 303–476–5601, ext. 4324.

BEAVER CREEK

Beaver Creek is the home of multimillionaire families. With second homes costing $600,000 for starters, these people have some cash to spend. The masses can enjoy the resort both winter and summer, but it's not the cheapest vacation. The 1987/88 winter will be its eighth season and the lift lines are still short; summer is elegantly quiet. There is an unhurried, European up-scale atmosphere to the narrow valley.

Beaver Creek had been selected as the site of the 1976 Winter Olympics but the Colorado voters vetoed any such antics in their backyard. As a result, Vail Associates (developers of the new ski area) took time to plan and develop a balance between the pristine environment, lodging and recreation needs, and private homes to create what they considered the perfect resort experience to complement their own sprawling Vail Valley. Since its opening in 1980, every house, condominium complex, hotel, and support building has been carefully blended into the pine and aspen trees. Cars are directed immediately to underground parking garages and that's the last anyone will see of a car until they leave. If you *must* ride, horse-drawn sleighs will pick you up.

The resort is due for completion in the mid-1990s at a price tag of more than one billion dollars. Among those who were the first to build at Beaver Creek are former president Gerald Ford, his secret-service bodyguards, and former ambassador to Belgium Leonard Firestone.

PRACTICAL INFORMATION FOR BEAVER CREEK

HOW TO GET THERE. By air. *Continental Express* flies two to nine flights daily from Denver into its private airport at Avon Stolport, just one mile from the entrance to Beaver Creek. Some lodge shuttles meet flights at no charge; make advance arrangements when booking accommodations; for schedules call 303–534–2291. Taxi service provided by *Louie's Casual Cabs,* 303–476-TAXI, and *Going Places,* 303–476–6816 or 800–321–5246. *Carey American Limousine* provides service to Avon; charters available, 303–393–0653.

By bus. *Trailways* provides service from Denver and Grand Junction to Vail, where a shuttle bus connects to Beaver Creek during the winter season for $1. *Colorado Mountain Express* (303–949–4227 or, outside Colorado, 800–525–6363), limo to your door service, makes regular trips from Stapleton Airport in Denver; also *Summit Taxi/Going Places* (303–467–LIMO or, outside Colorado, 800–321–5246).

By car. Beaver Creek is 10 miles west of Vail just off I-70 in the White River National Forest. By car it is 110 miles, or a little over a two hour drive from Denver west on I-70. From Grand Junction it is east 130 miles on I-70. Rental cars from agencies at Denver's airport (see *Practical Information For Denver*); in nearby Avon there is *Budget* (800–527–0700), *Avis* (800–332–0169), *Hertz* (800–654–3131) and *National* (800–328–4567).

ACCOMMODATIONS. Currently, Beaver Creek has accommodations for 1,600 guests, with projected room for 10,500 at completion, in condos, hotels, and private houses. There are eight condominiums or hotels plus luxury private houses with five to seven bedrooms for large groups. Reservations can be made by contacting Central Reservations, Box 915, Beaver Creek, CO 81620; call 303–949–5750 or 800–525–2257.

All rooms are pricey. One-bedroom condos range from $120–$265 a night; a hotel or lodge room ranges from $80–$180 a night, double occupancy. Superdeluxe five-bedroom homes rent for $425 a night; six-bedrooms for $550 a night; seven-bedrooms for $650 a night. The following list will give you an idea of what's available. All have whirlpools and saunas; none accept pets.

The Centennial. 180 Offerson Rd., Avon; 303–845–7600. Condos and lodge rooms; swimming pool; ski-back access.

The Charter at Beaver Creek. At base of Beaver Creek Mt., 120 Offerson Rd., Box 5310, Avon; 303–949–6660. The first to open with one- and two-bedroom condos and lodge rooms, indoor and outdoor swimming pools, golf course, and two restaurants; ski-back access.

Creekside at Beaver Creek. 1156 Village Rd., Avon; 949–7071. Two-bedroom condos, pool indoors and out; ski-back access.

Kiva. 135 Offerson Rd., Avon; 303–949–5474. Condos and lodge rooms; restaurant; tennis courts; ski-in, ski-out.

Park Plaza. Box 36, Avon; 845–7500. Newest lodge with 36 two- and three-bedroom luxury condos. Pool, restaurant; ski-in, ski-out.

Poste Montane. 76 Avondale La., Avon; 303–845–7500. Hotel rooms and suites; restaurant. European-style.

Ridgepoint Townhomes. Two miles from the area, Willis Pl., Avon; 303–949–7150; free shuttle to lifts.

HOW TO GET AROUND. Beaver Creek is a pedestrian village. It is compact and it is easy to walk between condos and the village and the mountain. For those who visit for a day but don't stay overnight, cars are parked at the Beaver Creek entrance, and a free shuttle bus winds the two miles up the valley to the village; service runs to and from the town of Avon. Daily *shuttle bus service* plies between Beaver Creek and Vail in the winter season for $1.00 a ride. During the summer, the free shuttle takes people from the village core to the Robert Trent Jones II 18-hole golf course (you can also walk) just a mile away. *Horse-drawn carriages* take folks around the village year-round; pick them up in front of the Village Hall. *Dial-a-Ride,* 949–1938, is available at no charge for guests staying in private houses within the resort.

TOURIST INFORMATION. Contact the resort at Box 7, Vail, CO 81658; 303–949–5750. *SnowWatch* provides daily, updated snow information: in Denver 303–534–1245. In nearby Avon there is a post office and all the convenience stores and businesses you might need. Local city magazines and newspapers carry the latest news and activities.

SEASONAL EVENTS. *WinterFaire* helps beat away the **January** blahs. The *Mountain Man Triathlon* (entrants include women) tests the skills of the most superb winter athletes each **February.** The *World Alpine Ski Championships* are scheduled here January 29–February 12 (see Vail). Early **March** is the *American Ski Classic,* featuring amateurs and pros alike competing in the Gerry Ford Cup and Legends of Skiing (featuring skiing greats). The last several **Junes** have seen an unofficial gathering of world leaders from government and business meet in *The World Forum* at the invitation of former President Ford. He believes the relaxed casual atmosphere of the mountain setting in summer lends itself to a free-flowing exchange of ideas. As in all resorts, there are **Christmas** and **Easter** events. *Women's Ski and Spa Weeks* are wellness programs with a variety of activities held in **December,** January, and February; for skiers of all abilities. Contact Central Reservations for information, out of Colorado 800–525–2257 or in state 800–525–9132.

PARTICIPANT SPORTS. **Skiing,** of course. Ten chairlifts open up 796 acres of skiing, 40 percent intermediate terrain. Lift tickets are interchangeable with Vail. MAX is the first automated lift ticket machine in the U.S. Beaver Creek has two (the others are at Vail). Just feed it your credit card and off you ski. *Bird of Prey* workshop takes skiers down the three most challenging runs, anywhere in the country, over a mile of nothing but moguls. Rentals are available at local ski slopes.

Nordic skiing goes along the golf course on gentle trails; instruction available; phone cross-country center, 949–5758. Accessible from Chair 12 is 12 miles of cross-country track along the edge of the ski area boundary; instruction and rentals from the cross-country center. $10 to ride the chair and use the track system.

Ice skate on the rink next to the Poste Montane and Park Plaza lodges; open 10 A.M. – 9 P.M. daily, no charge. Lighting and music. Skate rentals for $5 at the *Sports Stalker;* lessons for $6 for a half-hour; call 949–5750 ext. 5206, or 926–2013. **Sleigh rides, snowmobiling, snowshoeing,** gourmet **ski tours,** and overnight ski tours from the area or from Vail Valley; call 949–5750 for information.

Summer revolves around the par-70, 6,400-yard **golf** course, which winds along the private road connecting the village of Beaver Creek to Highway 6. The Club House provides cart rentals and a pro shop, the half-way house offers snacks and sells accessories. Call 949–5750. There are three other 18-hole courses within a ten-mile radius (see Vail section).

A chair lift ride to midmountain Spruce Saddle lets people take guided lunch **hikes** or a self-interpretive hike through the forest. Each Sunday, worship services are held at Spruce Saddle at 11:30 A.M. The chair is free in the summer or you can hike up to Turquois Lake.

Four **tennis** courts at The Kiva (949–5474) are available for public play. Fifty additional courts are within a ten-mile radius.

One-hour to all-day **horseback rides** head out daily; also **wagon rides, barbecues,** and **overnight pack trips;** call Beaver Creek Stable 845–7770.

HISTORIC SITES. The *historic farmhouse* at the entrance to Beaver Creek, now Mirabelle Restaurant, is a good example of 19th-century mountain architecture.

CHILDREN'S ACTIVITIES. A toddler's program, called *Small World Play School,* is for nonskiing infants and toddlers. The play school is located at the Golf Course Clubhouse and parents can register infants from two months of age; advance registration is recommended. Infants and toddlers cost $28 per day, $76 for three days, $115 for five days, includes lunch and snacks. Parents should supply any special food and diapers. Contact Small World Play School at 949–5750.

For toilet-trained children, the *Children's Skiing Center* meets at the Village Hall; lunch and ski lessons provided, ages 3–12; call 303–949–5750. Prices are $30 for one day, $115 for three days.

SHOPPING. Beaver Creek has a sampling of the usual alpine shops in the Village Hall. *Caroselli's* carries clothing and gifts; *Gorsuch* is a well-known sports shop with full-line shops in many mountain resorts; *The Sport Stalker* in Post Montane Hotel is another string of sport stores with clothing and equipment; *Images, Unlimited* carries posters and prints; *Sugar Babies* tempts your sweet tooth; the *General Store* sells groceries and sundry items. In nearby Avon and in the Vail Valley you'll find a full complement of stores and other retail businesses.

DINING OUT. Continental breakfast and lunch are served at the **mid-mountain** *Spruce Saddle* with a cafeteria setup and outdoor barbecues for warm spring-ski days; real plates and cutlery. In summer, there are evening barbecues. *The Rafters* has sit-down dining, Continental menu, and an extensive wine list in Spruce Saddle; reservations suggested; 949–6050. At the base area, *McCoy's Bar and Restaurant* serves breakfast and lunch cafeteria-style and après-ski cocktails, hors d'oeuvres, and entertainment; outdoor barbecues in good weather. Try *Beano's Cabin* at the bottom of Larkspur Bowl and the famous "Birds of Prey" runs; 949–5750, ext. 4636 (Beaver Creek Resort Activities desk). Take a moonlight sleigh ride for a dinner of prime rib or rotisseried chicken with all the trimmings, including beverages and carafes of wine. Seatings at 6 and 8 P.M. Reservations required.

At *Expensive* restaurants listed below, entrées cost $20–$35; *Moderate,* $12–$18; *Inexpensive,* under $12. All restaurants listed take Visa and MasterCard unless otherwise noted.

There are a number of less-distinguished and less-expensive restaurants in nearby Avon. See also Vail section.

Mirabelle. *Expensive.* At the entrance to Beaver Creek, 55 Village Rd., Avon; 949–7728. By far the most outstanding restaurant at the resort. French cuisine served in a restored wooden farmhouse, once the largest residence in the town of Avon and a place of some social importance at the turn of the century. Some claim it is the finest restaurant in the mountains—no small compliment. Cash only.

First Season. *Moderate.* In the Charter House at base of Beaver Creek Mt.; 949–6660. Continental cuisine seven nights a week; reservations required.

Kiva Club. *Moderate.* In the Kiva, 38340 U.S. Hwy 6 and 24, Avon; 845–7793. Lunch and dinner southwestern style. Reservations.

Legends Restaurant. *Moderate.* In the *Post Montane,* 76 Avondale La, Avon; 949–5540. Three meals, plus weekend brunch.

Drinkwater Park. *Inexpensive.* In the Village Hall. A favorite of locals, offering Mexican food seven days a week. No reservations.

NIGHTLIFE. Evenings in Beaver Creek tend to be on the quiet side, with people lounging in front of a fire or broiling in hot tubs. *Drinkwater Park* in the Village Hall has live entertainment, mostly folk, some rock, during the busiest months of the ski season and summer. To find the action, head to Vail where you can dance the night away.

HINTS FOR THE HANDICAPPED. Ski instruction is in Vail, by appointment only for the blind and physically disabled; contact Ski School, Box Seven, Vail, CO 81658; 303–949–7154.

STEAMBOAT SPRINGS

The Ute Indians considered the Yampa Valley their summer playground, with the numerous hot mineral springs, the abundant hunting and fishing. Trappers came upon the area in the mid-1800s, giving present-day Steamboat its name because of the chugging sound made by the mineral springs bubbling through the rock formations.

Mining had its turn in the valley, but it has been farming and ranching that have been the mainstay of the economy. Even today, the alfalfa hay from here is widely known for its high quality. Steamboat Springs is truly a thriving western town of over 6,000 inhabitants. There happens to be a big mountain nearby—and Steamboat throughout the years has produced more than its share of Olympic and National Ski Team champions. The feel is wide open and sunny, the mood is friendly, the dress casual; if you don't own a cowboy hat when you arrive, you probably will before you leave.

Steamboat is geared to families, as are its prices—at the low end of affordable.

PRACTICAL INFORMATION FOR STEAMBOAT SPRINGS

HOW TO GET THERE. Steamboat is in the Routt National Forest, 157 miles northwest of Denver.

By air. All the major airlines serve Denver's Stapleton Airport. *Continental Express* makes connections to the Bob Adams Field/Routt County Stolport two miles west of town and five miles from the ski area. Taxis from the airport to the lodges cost between $5 and $10, depending on the lodge location. There are also rental cars at the airport: *Budget* 800–527–0700 and *National* 800–328–4567. Regularly scheduled jet service from Dallas/Ft. Worth, Chicago, Los Angeles, and San Francisco on *American Airlines* (800–433–7300); from Minneapolis/St. Paul on *Northwest* (800–225–2525). Comes into the Yampa Valley Regional Airport, 22 miles from the resort. Shuttle service available between Steamboat Springs and the airport; call 303–879–0740 or 800–332–3204 in Colorado. Local taxi service includes *Alpine Taxi/Limo,* 303–879–2800, or *Ultimate Limousine,* 303–879–7417.

By bus. *Steamboat Express Bus* runs an express bus between Denver's Stapleton Airport and Steamboat Springs from mid-December to early April; fare one way is $29. Advance reservations during February and March recommended, call 303–879–0740 or in Colorado 800–332–3204; write Box 774408, Steamboat Springs, CO 80477.

By car. From Denver, Steamboat is 157 miles via I–70 through the Eisenhower Tunnel to Exit 205, follow CO 9 to US 40, over Rabbit Ears Pass and into the Yampa Valley. From Grand Junction drive east on I–70 to Highway 131 at Wolcott, then onto US 40 in the valley, a total of 200 miles. From Laramie, Wyoming, it is 122 miles via WY 230, CO 127, Route 14, and US 40.

ACCOMMODATIONS. The Resort Association serves as the Central Reservations office for lodging; call 303–879–0740 or 800–332–3204 in Colorado; or write Box 774408, Steamboat Springs, CO 80477. Twenty lodges are within walking distance of the slopes, and another 55 hotels, condominiums, and townhouses make up a total of 15,300 pillows in town and at the base area.

Expensive

Bear Claw Condominiums. 2420 Ski Trail Lane; 303–879–6100. Top-of-the-line accommodations, right against the lifts and part-way up the mountain. A one-bedroom condo goes for $220–$305 per unit, per night.

La Casa. 2700 Village Dr.; 303–879–6006. $220 per unit, per night for two people in a one-bedroom condo.

Chateau Chamonix. 2340 Après Ski Way; 879–7511. Fireplace, pool, whirlpool, pets allowed. $260–$275 per night for a one-bedroom.

Sheraton at Steamboat. 2200 Village Inn Ct.; 303–879–2220 or 800–325–3535. A luxury hotel at the base area next to the Silver Bullet Gondola; two restaurants, two lounges. Tennis and golf. Good après-ski activities, and close to restaurants and shopping. $89–$119 for a double room.

Moderate

Harbor Hotel. 703 Lincoln Ave.; 879–1522. Newly renovated Victorian-style rooms for $68–$90 a night, double occupancy.

The Inn at Steamboat. 3070 Columbine Dr.; 879–2600. ¼ mile from base area, free shuttle; swimming pool, washer/dryer. $72 a night, double occupancy.

Overlook Inn. 1000 Highpoint Dr.; 879–2900. One mile south of town; shuttle service. Most units with mountain views. Dining room and lounge with entertainment. Indoor pool, whirlpool, and sauna; tennis courts. $58–$86 for a double room.

The Ranch at Steamboat. 1 Ranch Rd.; 879–3000. About a mile to base area, free shuttle; fireplaces, pool, whirlpools, meeting rooms. $155–$190 per unit per night.

Scandinavian Lodge. 2883 Burgess Creek Rd.; 879–0517. Above the ski area—ski to the lifts and ski-tour out the back door. A large one-bedroom is $68–$132 a night per person, double occupancy with three meals.

Ski Time Square. 2155 Resort Dr.; 879–3700. At base area, fireplaces, whirlpools; close to shops, restaurants. $115–$160 per unit per night.

Vista Verde Guest Ranch. Seedhouse Road, Clark, CO 80428; 879–3858. Cozy log cabins with kitchens, fireplace; family-style meals in main lodge. Surrounded by wilderness area and national forest. Cross-country skiing, sleigh rides, horseback riding, fishing; overnight ski or horseback packages; special activities for children. $95 a day per cabin double occupancy; transportation from the two Steamboat airports; 18 miles to Steamboat ski area.

Inexpensive

Dream Island Motel. 1401 Lincoln Ave.; 879–0261. In the town of Steamboat Springs, your basic room for $36–$41 per night, double occupancy.

Whistler Village Townhomes. 2304 Après Ski Way; 879–1730. ¼ mile from the ski hill on the bus route; $115 for a two-bedroom condo.

CAMPING. The U.S. Forest Service maintains many campgrounds within a 30-mile radius of Steamboat. First-come, first-serve. Most popular are on Rabbit Ears Pass, off US 40, and in Steamboat Lake State Park, 25 miles north of town off County Rd. 129.

Dumont Lake Campground is near the top of Rabbit Ears, 24 miles southeast of Steamboat at 9,500 ft. Piped and lake water, no trailers over 22 feet. Good hiking; 14-day limit, fee. Just east of town off US 40 is *Fish Creek Campground;* bathhouse, nearby restaurant, close to town; commercial, with fee; 303–879–5476. *Meadows* is ten miles southwest of town at 9,300 feet up Rabbit Ears Pass; no trailers over 22 feet; piped drinking water; 14-day limit, fee. *Walton Creek* is in the same area, good stream fishing and hiking; 14-day limit and 22 feet trailer limit; fee. *Steamboat Lake State Park* contains numerous campsites with complete facilities; sailing, fishing, boating, water skiing, hiking in the Routt National Forest and Mount Zirkel Wilderness; crowded in summer, particularly holidays. Call 879–3922. All limit trailers to 22 feet, have 14-day stays and charge fees: *Hahn's Peak Lake Campground* lies at 8,500 feet. *Seed House* has extensive hiking trails and good fishing. *Summit Lake Campground* is ten miles northeast of Steamboat off Buffalo Pass Road at 10,300 feet. Lake water, good fishing in high country lakes, and hiking; 14-day limit, no trailers over 22 feet. No fee.

HOW TO GET AROUND. *Steamboat Springs Transit* (SST) connects points west of the city limits to town and to the ski area; check schedules at lodge, but extra buses are put on during ski season; 50 cents a ride, but for savings buy tokens in quantity at any lodge or merchant. For schedule information call 879–3717. Call *Steamboat Taxi Service* at 879–3111.

TOURIST INFORMATION. Radio KBCR 1230 AM, 96.5 FM, is good for local news; the world's only wind-powered radio station is in Oak

Creek, 17 miles south, KFMU 103.9 FM. Local cablevision reports weather and daily and weekly activities. The *Steamboat Pilot* is the weekly newspaper. For snow conditions, call 303–879–7300 or *Colorado Ski Country, USA,* 303–831–SNOW. Contact the *Steamboat Chamber Resort Association,* Box 774408, Steamboat Springs, CO 80477; 303–879–0880.

SEASONAL EVENTS. There is almost always something special going on in cowboy country. Three- and six-day *Billy Kidd Race Camps* are scheduled throughout the winter. In mid-**January** the most unusual ski area event happens—the *Cowboy Downhill;* top rodeo riders from the Pro Rodeo Tour come up from Denver's annual National Western Stock Show and try their skill at ski competition. The oldest continuous *Winter Carnival* in the west takes place for a week in early **February** with a fun mixture of cowboys and skiers, plus hot-air balloons. *Junior National Championships* are the end of February, the *National Masters Championships* in **March;** spring officially arrives in early **April** with the Steamboat *Spring Stampede.*

In summer the *Whitman Open Horse Show,* at Whitman School on Strawberry Park Rd., and the *10K Run for the Arts* start off in **June.** From the end of June through **July** arts activities are scheduled at the *Depot Arts Center,* 13th and Stockbridge Rd.,; *rodeos* are a regular event every Friday and Saturday evening throughout the summer, Howelsen Hill Rodeo Grounds, downtown Steamboat Springs; buffalo barbecue prior to the rodeo; the Chamber has additional information, 879–0880. A different kind of rodeo is the *hot-air balloon rodeo* in mid-July. *Golf Tourneys* and *fly-fishing seminars* take place during the summer, check local listings for dates and times. At the end of **August** is the *Rabbit Ears Bicycle Hillclimb Classic,* and **Labor Day** weekend features the *Vintage Auto Race* at EagleRidge. Santa always arrives at Christmas for the kids, and each week from the end of **December** there is a torchlight parade down the mountain, put on by the Ski School.

PARTICIPANT SPORTS. Ever since Carl Howelsen, "The Flying Norseman," came to Steamboat with long boards strapped to his feet and showed the townsfolks how to jump off hills with them, **skiing** has been a passion. Mount Werner contains 2,500 acres of skiable terrain with 1,551 acres groomed, served by 20 lifts, including an eight-passenger gondola. There are enough beginner, intermediate, and expert areas to satisfy most skiers. Instruction is available in racing, freestyle, powder (when there is six inches or more of new snow), mogul analysis, video review; call 879–6111. Rentals available at local ski shops. Recreational NASTAR races are held daily except Monday and the electronic Marlboro Ski Challenge is set for timed runs. Anyone can ski at 1 P.M. with Billy Kidd, the famous Olympian who makes his home in Steamboat as Director of Skiing; any day he is in town, except Sunday. 879–6111.

Skiing for the townies generally is at Howelsen Hill; located on the southside of the Yampa River in old town Steamboat Springs. It was built in 1915 by Carl Howelsen, the Norwegian ski jumper who eventually made his home here. A poma lift serves 30-, 50-, 70-, and 90-meter ski jumps, a beginner and an expert run; also night skiing is popular (at least among the kids).

Cross-country is avidly pursued in Steamboat. Besides ski touring from the Scandinavian Lodge, the *Ski Touring Center* maintains 12 miles of trails; guided tours on Rabbit Ears Pass, moonlight tours by appointment; lessons; call 879–8180. Other lodges that offer cross-country skiing are Bear Pole Ranch, Dutch Creek Guest Ranch, Elk River Guest Ranch, Glen Eden, Home Ranch, Post Ranch, Red Barn Ranch, and Vista Verde Guest Ranch. Anyone can ski here—it's open forest land.

Ski powder by **snow cat;** contact the *Steamboat Powder Cats,* 879–5188. **Dog sledding** is nearby at *Dog Sled Adventures,* 879–5280. **Ice fishing** is from Steamboat and Dumont lakes; license required, call 879–1870 for information. **Ice skating** is at Howelsen Hill in town, open to the public at no charge. Rent skates at Ski Haus, 1450 Lincoln; 879–0385. **Sledding** is also popular at Howelsen Hill for young children only; call 879–4300.

Sleigh rides go from *All Seasons Ranch,* 879–2606; *Double Runner Ranch,* 879–6459; *El Rancho,* 879–9988; *Red Barn Ranch,* 879–4580; *Vista Verde Guest Ranch,* 879–3858. In summer, the teams take hayrides out. **Snowshoeing** expeditions head out from Elk River, Red Barn, Vista Verde, and Post ranches. **Snowmobiles** can be rented at Dutch Creek, Elk River, Post, and Red Barn ranches.

Enjoy **hot mineral pools** any time of year in town at the public pool and at the *Steamboat Springs Health & Recreation Association,* 879–1828. Year-round early morning **balloon rides** are available through four hot-air balloon companies—*Balloon Colorado,* 879–4932, *Balloons Over Steamboat,* 879–3298, *Balloon the Rockies,* 879–7313, and *Pegasus Balloon Tours,* 879–7529.

In summer, visitors head off in all directions to hike, backpack, fish, and take part in all those wonderful mountain activities. The Routt National Forest (Mount Zirkel Wilderness Area is within the forest) surrounding the town of Steamboat has many **hiking** trails; stop by the *Chamber Resort Office,* 625 S. Lincoln St., or the *Forest Service Supervisor's Office,* 57 10th St., for maps and information.

The *Dock at Steamboat Lake* has **party boat** rentals, **fishing,** and **sailing** rentals; call 879–7019 for details. For fishing instruction, *Carl Creel/Outdoor Adventures* will help you out; equipment not furnished; 879–0199. *Andy Popejoy Outfitter,* 276–3321, and *Straightline Products Guide Service,* 879–7568 are outfitters who take **horsepacking** and **hiking fish** expeditions. Many of the guest ranches offer one-to-five day fishing expeditions and fishing clinics; the Resort Association central reservations can give details, 303–879–0740. Most of the same outfitters and ranchers are prepared to take out **hunters** in the fall for deer and elk.

Half-day to five-day **raft** trips are available through *Adventure Bound,* 879–1100; *Buggywhips Fish and Float Service,* 879–8033; *Colorado Adventures,* 879–2039; *Wild West River Riders,* 879–6215.

Tennis courts are found for their respective guests at Glen Eden Ranch, Lodge at Sky Valley, Overlook Hotel, Scandinavian Lodge, the Sheraton, and in the town parks; **volleyball** buffs should head for the Lodge at Sky Valley, and the town park at Howelsen Hill.

Llama trekking is becoming increasingly popular in the Rockies; the *Home Ranch* just outside Steamboat operates day and overnight treks with the South American pack animals doing the work; call Peter Nichol at 303–879–1780 for information and reservations. Home Ranch also has horsepacking trips.

Golfers can play at the nine-hole *Steamboat Golf Course,* five miles west of town, 879–4295, or the 18-hole *Robert Trent Jones, Jr., par 72* semiprivate Sheraton Golf Club. Open to the public on a non-reservation basis, greens fees are $32 including required carts, call 879–1391.

HISTORIC SITES AND OTHER LANDMARKS AND ACTIVITIES.

Fish Creek Falls is dramatic and accessible from town. It is a popular hiking area around here, but becomes more strenuous as the trail heads up behind the falls. (It's said the waterfall on Coors Beer cans is Fish Creek.) Fish Creek Road starts at Oak and Fourth streets at the east end of town and has a trail for the handicapped; follow the road to the end.

Plan a day for *Steamboat Lake State Park.* Drive up the Elk River Road, Highway 129, to Hahn's Peak, a small town originally settled in the local gold rush; 1,500 acres make up Steamboat and Pearl lakes, ideal for fishing, boating, waterskiing, sailing; trailheads nearby lead into *Mount Zirkel Wilderness* and the *Routt National Forest.* The town of Clark, halfway between Steamboat and Hahn's Peak, is a popular jumping-off spot for the wilderness area.

A drive about 20 miles east on US 40 brings you to *Rabbit Ears Pass,* and you'll see how the pass got its name; its been a landmark for the Indians, as well as modern-day travelers. Dumont lake on the east side of the pass is stocked with rainbow and brook trout; see "Camping," above.

Open only in the summer, the rugged road over Buffalo Pass leads to the Continental Divide—25 miles and two and one-half hours away. Above the town of Steamboat is an old onyx quarry with a sweeping view of the Flat Top Wilderness Area, Steamboat, and Sleeping Giant Mountain; take Blackmer Drive six miles, allow an hour.

An antique guns and memorabilia display can be viewed in the county courthouse, 136 Sixth St.; 879–1710. *Tread of Pioneers Museum,* Fifth and Oak in town, is an "Old West" museum; call 879–2214 for hours.

Explore the area from the air. *Steamboat Aviation* takes charter flights over the Routt National Forest, Steamboat Lake, and the ski area; instruction also available. Call at the Steamboat Airport, 879–1204.

From mid-June to Labor Day weekend, the gondola operates from the base of the ski area to the mid mountain Thunderhead Restaurant; it's a spectacular view, and you can ride or walk down. Call for times and current prices 879–6111.

The springs for which the area is famous are accessible by cross-country skis, dog sled, or powder cats in winter, by foot or car in summer. Actually, there are over 100 springs in the area; call 879–7568 for details and directions. Some, like the ones at the public Health and Recreation Center and in the park, are right in town.

CHILDREN'S ACTIVITIES. Kids "ski free" was started at the Steamboat Ski Area and they have made a high art of it. The Ski Corporation even publishes a newsletter for children called *Skids,* which lists all the special activities and rates for kids of all ages. *Skids Club* is an après-ski spot for kids and teens, open winter daily 2–7 P.M.; located in Gondola Square. The *Kids Ski Free Program* stipulates that children 12 and under can ski free with parents who purchase a five-or-more-day lift ticket and who are staying a minimum of five nights at a participating Steamboat Chamber/Resort Association lodging property. Children also stay free in the same room with their parents and will have free ski rentals when their parents rent skis for the same period of time. The offer is not valid during

the Christmas/New Year's holiday. Call Steamboat Ski Corporation for more details, 303–879–6111.

In addition, the *Nursery* accommodates children 6 months to 6 years of age; day supervision with games, crafts, movies. $25 a day, second child $14 a day, plus $4 for lunch for kids over 2; $18 a half-day, $12 for second child. The *Kiddie Corral Ski School* is for young skiers 3 to 5 years of age who are toilet trained. Lunch, lift privileges, and lessons $34 a day; $25 a half-day; $90 for three days; $145 for 5 days. Ground Floor, Gondola Building, 879–6111, ext. 216.

For kids 6 to 15, the ski school has lessons. Group lessons are two hours, $16; all day for $34; for details call 879–6111, ext. 222.

Kids seem to be the only ones who have energy for night skiing; take them to Howelsen Hill in town; Tues.–Fri. 6–9 P.M.

Off the slopes, children will enjoy the Hydro Tube and swimming at the *Steamboat Health & Recreation,* Lincoln Street in town, 897–1828.

If you want to leave junior at home while you party, many lodges provide a list of qualified babysitters; inquire at the front desk or call the Chamber/Resort Association for a list; 879–0880.

In summer, there are a number of camps in the area; while the adults look after themselves, the kids are involved in their own supervised activities. *Bear Pole Ranch* has two sessions for 9 to 18 years olds and 17 to 22 year olds; 303–879–0576. *Elk River Guest Ranch* has wilderness camping June-September; 303–879–3843. *Scandinavian Lodge* holds soccer camps in June for ages 9 to 13; 303–879–0517. For dance, theater, horseback riding, music, contact the *Stephens College/Perry Mansfield School and Camp,* 303–879–1060.

SHOPPING. Because Steamboat Springs is a real town, there are shops for tourists and residents alike, and you can find almost anything you are looking for. The shops at Ski Time Square, Gondola Square, Torian Plum Square, and other centers at the ski area itself cater to the tourist crowd and feature more gift and boutique items.

Ski area shops worth stopping in are *Bare Skin Leather,* Gondola Square, and *Dark Horse,* 1890 Mt. Werner Rd., for leather apparel and accessories; *Aristo's,* 1850 Mount Werner Rd., for handmade sweaters and tapestries; the *Shirt Stop,* 1860 Mount Werner Rd., for fashion tops of all sorts. A large array of home furnishings and decorating consultation is at *Dianna's Furniture Galleries,* Torian Plum Square; for the largest selection of après-ski boots, stuffed animals, and other toys visit the *Elephant's Trunk* in Torian Plum Plaza. Everything in the way of ski clothes and sports gear can be found at the *Inside Edge,* 903 Lincoln Ave.; *Ptarmigan Inn,* 2304 Apres Ski Way; *Sports Stalker,* 36900 Steamboat Village Circle; *Werner's Storm Hut* in Gondola Square; *Clock Tower Sports,* in Clock Tower Square; *Village Center Ski Rentals,* 2500 Village Dr.; and *Terry Sport* in Torian Plum Plaza.

In town on Lincoln Ave. is the famous *F.M. Light;* at least, it's famous by the time you arrive in town by automobile—there must be five miles of roadside signs, like the old burma-shave ads, telling visitors to visit the store. Most of them do. It carries all things western, including a selection of cowboy hats to suit all heads. Across Lincoln Avenue is *Cowboy's Mercantile,* 1104 Lincoln, to rival the Light Co. Within a few blocks are several shops for gift, housewares, designer accessories—*The Front Page,* 442 Lincoln; *Ericksons Interiors,* 729 Oak; *The Homesteader,* 117 8th St. Arts and crafts are rampant in the *Artisan's Market,* 442 Lincoln; *Emily Ingram Galleries,* Lincoln St., between the ski area and town, featuring originals by Colorado artists; *Curtis Zabel,* 39510 Routt County Rd. 44; *Mountain Haus,* 130 Ninth; *Steamboat Art Company,* 810 Lincoln Ave.; and *Fat Chance Antiques,* 12th and Lincoln. Secondhand Rose would be happy in *Maude's Mercantile,* 116 Ninth.

Sports stores downtown include *Inside Edge,* 903 Lincoln Ave., and *Straightline Outdoor Sports,* 744 Lincoln.

DINING OUT. There are several restaurants **on the ski mountain.** At the top of the gondola is the midmountain *Thunderhead* with the usual ski-time cafeteria food. The best deal is to hop the gondola early, have the special skiers breakfast at Thunderhead, and you'll be skiing while the crowd is still riding the lifts. Also a pleasant lunch spot is the casual, sit-down *Stoker Bar* on the first level.

On the second level is *Hazie's* for fine dining; open for lunch and on specific evenings for dinner. Reservations suggested, 879–6111. A large, outdoor barbecue deck is on the third level.

Rendezvous Saddle Restaurant in the Priest Creek area has seating for 600 inside and outdoors; included inside is the sit-down dining room, *Ragnar's,* noted for its fine food and Norwegian specialties; make reservations during February and March, 879–6111.

There are approximately 50 restaurants and bars in Steamboat Springs. Unless otherwise noted, all accept credit cards.

Expensive restaurants have entrées ranging $13–$16; *Moderate,* $9–$12; *Inexpensive,* under $9.

At or Near the Base

Cipriani's. *Expensive.* In the Thunderhead Lodge, 35215 Mt. Werner Way; 879–2220. Features northern Italian cuisine. Good wine list. Reservations recommended.

Mattie Silk's. *Expensive.* In Ski Times Square, 1890 Mount Werner Rd.; 879–2441. A delightful, split-level restaurant featuring veal, pork, duck, and lamb in a candle-lit atmosphere. Fifty imported beers. Children's menu. Reservations suggested.

Remington's. *Expensive.* In the Sheraton, 2200 Village Inn Court; 879–2220. Overlooking the Headwall of the ski area. Children's menu available. Open winters only; reservations recommended.

Dos Amigos. *Moderate.* 1910 Mount Werner Rd.; 879–4270. An old-time hangout in Steamboat. Good Mexican food and lots of activity. Dinner only. Children's menu.

The Tugboat. *Inexpensive.* 1860 Mount Werner Rd.; 879–9990. Another local favorite. Noisy, western atmosphere serving American burgers and beer. Open for three meals.

In and Around Town

L'Apogee. *Expensive.* 810 Lincoln St.; 879–1919. Probably the spendiest place in town, it is classic French. Blackboard menu, fresh vegetables, extensive wine list. Reservations recommended.

Brandywine. *Expensive.* 57½ Eighth St.; 879–9939. In a Victorian setting, beef, seafood, and good after-dinner drinks are served. Reservations needed during February and March. Children's menu.

The Coral Grill. *Expensive.* In Sundance Plaza on Angler Dr. off Hwy. 40; 879–6858. The specialty is Maine lobster, swordfish, salmon—all seafood in fact. Oyster bar and good sushi.

The Cove. *Moderate.* 709 Lincoln Ave.; 879–7720. Cantonese food and exotic drinks.

Mazzola's. *Moderate.* 440 S. Lincoln Ave.; 879–2405. Italian dishes, pizza, salad bar. Lunch weekdays, dinner daily, children's menu.

Melon's. *Moderate.* 903 Lincoln Ave.; 879–1225. Seafood, vegetarian meals, steaks, fresh fruit drinks. Lunch and dinner.

Pine Grove. *Moderate.* 1465 Pine Grove Rd.; 879–1190. Contemporary western atmosphere in a converted barn. American menu and children's menu. Award winner. Lunch and dinner in summer. Dinner only in winter.

The River Bend. *Moderate.* Five miles west of town, across from the golf course, 26795 Routt County Rd. 40; 879–1615. American menu featuring barbecued ribs. Free transportation for four or more. Children's menu. Lunch and dinner.

Blue Bayou Cafe. *Inexpensive.* 912 Lincoln Ave.; 879–8282. Specializes in Cajun food; has small tables, fresh flowers.

Cantina. *Inexpensive.* 818 Lincoln Ave.; 879–0826. Mexican food and pizza. Crowded with locals for breakfast; good margaritas in the evening.

The Shack *Inexpensive.* 740 Lincoln Ave.; 879–9975. Good for a quick breakfast or lunch. No credit cards.

Sidestep. *Inexpensive.* 738 Lincoln Ave.; 879–9933. Burgers and Mexican food. Breakfast, lunch, and dinner. No credit cards.

NIGHTLIFE. Join the *Steamboat Stompers* for square dancing the first and third Friday of the month, 8 P.M. at the Community Center, Lincoln Ave; 879–5837 for details. Once a week *Vista Verde Ranch,* 31100 Routt County Rd. 64, Clark, hosts square dancing; 879–3858.

Much of the late-night action is at the ski area. The *Tugboat,* 1860 Mount Werner Rd., is lively into the wee hours, often live entertainment. *Hershey's Bar* in the Clock Tower has a DJ spinning disco tunes; mostly a young crowd. *The Inferno* in Gondola Square has live bands after skiing and late night. A little more conservative is the *Conservatory* in Thunderhead Lodge; comfortable lounge, entertainment. *The Hatch* in the newly renovated Harbor Hotel has good country/western bands. *Glen Eden Ranch* 54737 Routt County Rd. 129, Clark; 879–3906. Pleasant lounge with western music.

Bowlers can head to *Sno Bowl II* just west of town; call 879–9840 for a lane. Three movie theaters have first run films. The *Steamboat Arts Council* holds dance concerts, melodramas, other local talent displays throughout the year; call 879–4434.

HINTS FOR THE HANDICAPPED. Ski instruction by appointment for the blind and some physically disabled; contact Vern Greco, Steamboat Ski School, 2305 Mount Werner Circle, Steamboat Springs, CO 80487; 303–879–6111.

SNOWMASS

The wide open valley that is Snowmass is no longer Aspen's stepsister, "Snowmass-at-Aspen," but has its own distinct personality. Snowmass is a premier, top-drawer year-round resort.

This valley was rich in pastures and a haven for Hereford cattle ranches in the 1880s. The railroad at Woody Creek was close for transport to Denver's slaughter houses and mining activity down the road at Aspen drew families to homestead the pristine valley. Not without hardships, the Ute Indians made a last-ditch stand against the whites by burning the forest land; today any Snowmass skier knows that area as the "Big Burn."

Ranching continued, even as mining gave out. There are still descendents of those original ranching families in the Snowmass area: the Anderson Ranch houses an arts center and the Hoaglund Barn is quarters for the Alpine Bank.

Bill Janss of Sun Valley fame saw the Snowmass valley and realized the potential for skiing. He bought up over 3,400 acres and made an agreement with the Aspen Skiing Company to take control and create the ultimate in ski areas. In December 1967, Snowmass-at-Aspen was born. Originally, the plans called for 26,000 tourists and residents in 7,480 units, but public concern over growth caused the master plan to be revised.

Today, 7,500 people can be accommodated in seven lodges and 22 condominium complexes, 95 percent of which are adjacent to the slopes for ski-in, ski-out convenience. Aspen Skiing Company still owns and operates the Snowmass Ski Area. The resort is modern, planned, and efficient.

You'd better have deep pockets, though, if you plan to vacation here—Snowmass is a class act and charges class-act prices but you can save up to 40 percent on lodging during early December, most of January, and April; summer rates are even less.

PRACTICAL INFORMATION FOR SNOWMASS

HOW TO GET THERE. Snowmass is in the White River National Forest, 200 miles southwest of Denver.

By air. All major airlines fly into Denver's Stapleton International Airport; connect via *United Express* (800–241–6522, 800–525–1143, 303–398–3746) or *Continental Express* (800–525–0280) to the Snowmass/Aspen Airport. Both carriers have up to 25 daily flights in pressurized 50- and 84-passenger planes. Nonstop flights from Chicago, Dallas, Los Angeles, Long Beach, and San Francisco on *United Express* operate into Aspen from mid-December to the end of March. In-flight concierge service provides resort information. There are charter flights from major cities and, in winter, flights into nearby Grand Junction. Both airports have connecting ground transportation, taxis, limousines, and rental cars (see "By Car" below). For further information, contact the Resort Association (303–923–2000).

By bus. *Trailways* has daily schedules to the Snowmass/Aspen Airport and into Aspen from Denver and from Grand Junction; call 303–292–2291.

By train. *Amtrak*'s California Zephyr stops eastbound at 2:50 P.M. and westbound at 2:10 P.M. in an extravagantly scenic route from Denver across the Rockies. Advance arrangements should be made for connecting ground transportation from Glenwood Springs to Snowmass through Amtrak or your travel agent. *Mellow Yellow* taxi service has the route, 303–925 2282. Call Amtrak at 800–421–8320 or in Denver at 303–893–3911.

By car. West on I-70 from Denver to Glenwood Springs, then Hwy. 82 to Snowmass, 200 miles. From Grand Junction it is 128 miles east on I-70 to Glenwood, Hwy. 82; 10 miles west of Aspen on Hwy. 82, 6 miles west of the Snowmass/Aspen Airport. In summer the drive over Independence Pass is breathtaking but not for the faint of heart; take I-70 west from Denver to US 91 through Leadville to Twin Lakes and Hwy. 82 over the pass. Rental cars available at airports: see *Practical Information for Denver;* at Grand Junction airport, there are *Avis* (800–331–1212), *Budget* (800–527–0700), *Hertz* (800–654–3131).

ACCOMMODATIONS. Contact Central Reservations at Box 5566, Snowmass Village, CO 81615, or call 800–332–3245 outside Colorado, 800–237–3146 in Colorado, locally 923–2010, for accommodations in one of the 7 lodges or 22 condo complexes in the Village. In addition, there are nearly 8,000 pillows in Aspen, 12 miles down valley (*see* Aspen, above).

A sampling of what's available follows. All properties are ski-in, ski-out, with the exception of the Snowmass Club, which is three miles away on the golf course; a free shuttle service runs between the mountain and the club.

Expensive

Crestwood. Box 5460, Snowmass Village; 303–923–2450. Attractive condominium complex with one- to three-bedroom units featuring fireplaces and private balconies with barbecues. Heated pool. One-bedrooms run around $197 a night, double occupancy.

Snowmass Club. Drawer G-2, 0239 Snowmass Club Circle, Snowmass Village; 303–923–5600. Ski lodge and villas at base of Snowmass Mountain ski area. Spacious rooms and condominium units with private balconies. Restaurant, bar, lounge. Indoor and outdoor tennis courts; championship golf course; squash and racquetball courts; indoor and outdoor pools; health club; cross-country skiing. Over $200 for a one-bedroom (double occupancy); $175 for a double hotel room.

Woodrun Place. 0425 Wood Rd., Box 6027, Snowmass Village, 303–923–5392. Luxurious premier condominium accommodations, with all the amenities. $260 per night for a one-bedroom, double occupancy.

Moderate

Stonebridge Inn. Box 5008, Snowmass Village; 303–923–2420. Rooms, with restaurant and lounge. Around $115 for one-room, double occupancy.

Timberline. Box I-2, Snowmass Village; 303–923–4000. Condominium units with rustic Western atmosphere. For rate information, call 800–922–4001.

Inexpensive

Pokolodi Lodge. Box B-2, Snowmass Village; 303–923–4310. Family-oriented lodge on hillside, 50 yards from ski lift. Pool and Jacuzzi. Restaurants nearby. $110 for a double room.

SNOWMASS

Snowmass Inn. 303–923–4202. Comfortable accommodations. $108 for a double room.

CAMPING. In Basalt, 18 miles north on Highway 82, there is a *KOA* campground for RVs; 303–927–3532. For additional campgrounds, see Aspen listing.

HOW TO GET AROUND. Intervillage bus service is available at no charge throughout the day and during ski season between the day-skier parking lot and Fanny Hill quad lift; check the Transportation Department at 923–3779 for specific times.

The *Roaring Fork Transit Agency* offers daily bus service between Snowmass and Aspen, with many stops in between. It costs $1.50 and runs from early morning to late at night. *Aspen Skiing Company* runs free shuttle buses between Snowmass, Buttermilk, and Aspen, from 8 A.M. to 4:45 P.M. for skiers; schedules are posted at the Snowmass Bus Stop and the Information Booth, or call 925–8484, 923–2085, or 923–2000.

Aspen Limousine (925–2400), *High Mountain Taxi* (925–TAXI), and *Mellow Yellow Taxi* (925–2282) offer services.

TOURIST INFORMATION. The information booth in the Mall at Snowmass, 923–5400, is a world of details on anything you want to know, open 8 A.M.–6 P.M. from Thanksgiving to early April and mid-June to Labor Day.

For snow conditions, call 303–925–1221. Aspen radio KSNO 1260 AM, 104 FM, or KSPN 97.7 FM keep you informed of local happenings; pick up a copy of the *Aspen Times,* the *Snowmass Sun,* or one of the several Aspen and Snowmass magazines for more in-depth Aspen and Snowmass activities. The local cable channel always has the latest info and weather. The resort address and phone numbers: Box 5566, Snowmass Village, CO 81615; 303–923–2000; or 800–237–3146; outside Colorado call 800–332–3245.

SEASONAL EVENTS. January is time for the winter celebrations—in Aspen and Snowmass it's *Winterskol,* featuring hot-air balloon races, telemark cross-country uphill/downhill race series, torchlight parade, and the Mad Hatter's Ball Mardi Gras mania is everywhere on Fat Tuesday (day before Lent). The *Snowmass/Ute Series 30K Touring Race* is mid-**March** and Banana Season is in early **April** when everyone goes bananas in the warm sunshine.

Summer gets underway with the *Aspen/Snowmass Food & Wine Classic* in mid-**June** and the *Aspen Music Festival* starts the end of June and continues until the end of August. *Ballet West* holds dance classes during **July** and the *Hot-Air Balloon Festival* gets off the ground in mid-July. The *Suicide Hill Challenge* 5K and 10K races are mid-July, and the *Fanny Buster Mountain Bike Race* is the end of July. **August** is the time for the *Arts and Crafts Fair,* and *Snowmass Children's Festival of Performing Arts.* The Arts Center Workshop at Anderson Ranch continues all summer as does the *Snowmass Repertory Theater* performances. *Rodeos* are scheduled throughout the summer on Wednesday evenings. *Oktoberfest* at the end of **September** brings a taste of Bavaria.

PARTICIPANT SPORTS. Snowmass was envisioned as a **ski** resort and that is still the most important season, although each summer the number of visitors grows.

It is a terrific "cruising" mountain and no Snowmass skier would dare return home without running the "Big Burn." Fourteen chairlifts serve 1,582 acres, and a new expert area of 120 acres in Hanging Valley has upped the amount of difficult terrain in this largely intermediate mountain. Snowmass Ski School: 923–2085. Rentals at sports shops.

Learn more about plant and animal adaptations to winter by joining a **snowshoe tour.** Groups trek through the snow to see the winter outdoors in a way few have ever experienced. Skiers or nonskiers and children over 10 welcome; wear warm clothing and flat-heeled boots. Reserve at least a day in advance through the Information Booth, 923–5400. Tours include guide, equipment, and instruction.

Over 80 kilometers of maintained **cross-country** trails linking the Snowmass Club Touring Center and Owl Creek Trail to Aspen's Buttermilk Mountain are free. The Aspen/Snowmass Nordic Center designed the system and the town governments groom the trails; for more information call 925–4790. Rentals, tours, and lessons at the Touring Center at the Snowmass Club, 923–3148.

The largest full-time working **dog sled** kennel in the world is in Snowmass. Visitors can take a half-day or full day dog sled ride pulled by 13 huskies from *Krabloonik Kennels* and then top it off with a gourmet game meal in Krabloonik Restaurant's hand-hewn log cabin. Advance reservations required; call 923–4342 for sled rides, 923–3953 for the restaurant.

Snowmobiles are available to rent in the Maroon Creek Valley at *T-Lazy-7 Ranch,* 925–4614. **Horse-drawn sleighs** whisk guests to a secluded mountain cabin for a barbecue and western entertainment; departures at 5:30 and 8 P.M. Reserve in advance at the Information Booth in the Mall, or call 923–3075.

If you want to get above it all, take a **hot-air balloon ride** in the morning; includes complimentary champagne upon landing. Call *Unicorn Balloon Company,* 925–5752, for information and reservations.

For other activities, there's **swimming** in one of 47 outdoor heated pools and hot tubs in the Village for guest use. Those staying in the Snowmass Club have use of the full-service athletic club and indoor tennis courts, and they can have a Personal Fitness Profile done to improve their athletic performance and eating habits.

Summer Sports

In summer, Snowmass has facilities for **volleyball, children's playground, pools,** and **therapy spas.** For information, call 923–2000.

Ten-speed **bicycles** can be rented from *Aspen Sports,* Snowmass Center, 923–3566. For the ultimate, contact *Blazing Pedals,* 923–4544 for "downhill" bicycle tours. You are provided with specially designed mountain bikes, safety equipment, a guide, and transportation to the top of the Continental Divide, Maroon Bells, or other high spots. Then you coast downhill at your own speed. Cost is $38 for adults.

An extensive network of **hiking** trails surround Snowmass. Go on your own or take a guided hike or gourmet picnic hike, even an overnight camping trip. Call 923–3649 for information.

Jeep tours take guests to some of the most spectacular and photographed scenery in Colorado; rates $38 for adults, $33 for children 12 and under. Call *Blazing Trails,* 923–4544. Another kind of ride is available through *Pioneer Springs Ranch:* **horseback rides** for one hour or all day, breakfast and supper rides, hayrides, and overnight pack trips. Contact the Information Booth at 923–5400, Pioneer Springs Ranch, 923–4252, or *Snowmass Stables,* 303–923–3075.

White-water rafting can be exciting on roaring rapids, or try a calm ride in the warm sunshine. Guided trips on the Colorado, Roaring Fork, or Arkansas rivers; prices $30–$58. OK for children six and over. Contact *Snowmass Whitewater* at 923–4544.

Indoors, there is **paddle tennis,** a European-style "parcours" physical conditioning course, and the full-service athletic club in the Snowmass Club. Two indoor **tennis courts** are for use by club members. Eleven **outdoor courts** are open to the public; call 923–5600.

The *Snowmass Club* **Golf** *Links* is reputed to be a tough 18-hole championship course, with 6,817 yards of narrow and well-trapped fairways; call 923–5600 for tee times.

HISTORIC SITES AND OTHER LANDMARKS. Just take off and drive to the much photographed landmark *Maroon Bells,* Maroon Bells Rd. off Highway 82, or *Ashcroft Ghost Town,* Castle Creek Rd., off Highway 82. An hour away is the semighost town of *Redstone* and the historic, castlelike Redstone Inn; directions from the Information Booth in the Mall. The *Aspen Historical Society,* in Aspen, presents an excellent history of the area's colorful past (see Aspen section, below). *Hallam Lake Wildlife Sanctuary* offers special summer courses; call 303–925–5756.

In Old Snowmass visit John Denver's experimental *Windstar Foundation;* take Highway 82 west, turn left at the Conoco station, two miles to the fork, and take the left fork for about a mile. Windstar is a non-profit organization, the basic philosophy of which is that our planet has all the resources we need to sustain ourselves and, as such, Windstar is an ecological and personal development center. Programs develop alternative energy resources, organic gardening techniques (especially critical at the high altitude and harsh environment of the Rockies), personal development workshops, aquaculture, Volunteers for Peace seminars. Public is invited; please call in advance. Every Friday of the year hour-and-a-half guided tours start at 3 P.M.; free. *St. Benedict Monastery* is found by taking the right fork; services are open to the public, there's a gift shop and an egg-producing center; call 927–3213 for egg information, 927–3311 for general information.

Drive beyond the monastery for a few more miles to *Cow Camp;* from here there are trailheads for *Capital Peak, Williams* and *Hardscrabble lakes*—some of the most beautiful vistas in the area.

CHILDREN'S ACTIVITIES. Summer programs for youngsters include *The Little Red School House* (2½ to 5 years; 923–3756); *Sunbunnies Adventure Camp* (ages 3–12, infants 3 and under upon request); meals, crafts, activities, weekly themes; 923–4620. **Western riding lessons** (5 and older, *Snowmass Stables,* 923–3075). A list of babysitters is available at the Information Booth on the Mall.

At *John Denver's Windstar* is a unique children's program for ages 5 to 16; contact the Windstar Foundation 923–2145 or 927–4777.

Winter **ski** programs include *Snowmass Snowbunnies* for 1½–3-year-olds and for 3–5-year-olds; includes ski instruction for the 3–5-year-olds, snow games, ski films, arts and crafts. Daily, 8:30 A.M.–4 P.M. and weekly rates and evening babysitters; call 923–4620. In Recreation Building one level below the Mall.

Children's ski classes are for 5–12-year-olds; meet at the *Ski School Youth Center* at 9:30; lessons, special races, and picnic; call 923–4873. *Big Burn Bears* day care/ski school program is for 3–6-year-olds; ski instruction and indoor activities; 8:30 A.M.–4:30 P.M. daily. The *Youth Program* is for children 7–12 and operates 10 A.M.–3:30 P.M. daily. *First Time on Skis* beginner specials for kids 6–12 and teens offer programs from two hours to three days. Call 925–4444.

A teen program for 13–19-year-olds is exclusive at the Ski School. Grouped by ability, students are led by an instructor through lessons, videotaping, racing, picnics, and after-ski activities; call 923–4873.

SHOPPING. Snowmass Village is a shopper's paradise and it won't take long to part with your money. Gold snowflakes and one-of-a-kind jewelry are found at *Bright and Shiny Things,* 60 Village Sq.; *Snowmass Jewelers,* 48 Village Sq. *Hillis of Snowmass,* 20 Village Sq., carries the finest in furs for men and women. Gifts, linens, accessories are in *Collections, Emmy's Art Gallery, Inside Outfitter,* all at Snowmass Village. Men's and women's apparel is carried in *Hung Up on Hang Ups,* 45 Village Sq. Sport and ski clothes and equipment are found in *Gene Taylor's,* 0055 Road 5; *Aspen Sport,* Snowmass Center; *Sport Kaelin,* 50 Village Sq.; kids sportswear and fashion are found in *Short Sport,* Crossroads/Ellesse, 45 Village Sq. The basics of life, such as food and drink, can also be found—Snowmass Center has a variety of shops, a liquor store and a post office.

DINING OUT. On the mountain are four restaurants. *Sam's Knob* cafeteria includes a deli; upstairs is a sit-down restaurant, *CeCe's Point of View.* The *Ullrhof,* at the base of the Big Burn, has undergone a face-lift and expansion, serves usual skier fare, as does *Elk Camp* cafeteria. *High Alpine* is a higher quality cafeteria with an elegant sit-down restaurant. *Gwyn's* is reasonable value for the high-quality food, large portions, and fine wine list.

Expensive restaurants have entrées ranging $15–$25; *Moderate,* around $10; *Inexpensive,* $5–$9. Nearly all accept credit cards, but call to be sure.

Chez Grandmére. *Expensive.* 0016 Kearns Rd.; 923–2570. Exclusive establishment that has room for only 34 at its once-nightly seating. Price fixed, five-course meal, $35.

Four Corners. *Expensive.* In the Snowmass Club; 923–5600. Known for game specialties. Members and club guests only.

Krabloonik. *Expensive.* 923–3953. At the dog kennels (see "Participant Sports," above). In spectacular setting and with homespun atmosphere, serving gourmet game cuisine. Ski in for lunch; dinner reservations required.

La Piñata. *Moderate.* 65 Daly Lane; 923–2153. Good Mexican food and margaritas.

Pippin's Steak & Lobster. *Moderate.* In the Hotel Wildwood, 40 Elbert Lane; 923–3550. Elegant dining, with wonderful views and a harpist.

Shavanos. *Moderate.* 20 Village Sq.; 923–4292. New American and Continental food overlooking Snowmass Mall.

Timberline Restaurant. *Moderate.* In Timberline Condominiums; 923–4004. Affordable family dining, nightly specials.

The Tower Restaurant. *Moderate.* On the Mall; 923–4650. Serves pasta, seafood, steaks—a lot of food for the money.

Mountain Dragon. *Inexpensive.* Snowmass Mall; 923–3576. Mandarin and Szechuan cuisines with panoramic views of the valley.

Pour La France. *Inexpensive.* 0016 Kearns Rd.; 923–5990. For soups, salads, pastries, specialty coffee drinks. Takeout service available.

Sno'Beach Cafe. *Inexpensive.* 45 Village Mall; 923–2597. Features cheese omelets, soups, salads, quiches, and sandwiches.

Stew Pot. *Inexpensive.* 15 Village Mall; 923–2263. Homemade soups, stews, sandwiches, bread, and salads.

NIGHTLIFE. Snowmass is more sedate than its neighbor down the valley. For heavy nightlife and the singles scene, head for Aspen. But "downtown" Snowmass Village isn't entirely quiet. The après-ski crowd heads for *Timber Mill,* 105 Village Sq., for live music till 5:30 P.M. or so. The *Tower Magic Bar* puts on a spontaneous magic show seven nights a week. The *Piano Bar* in the *Snowmass Club,* 0239 Snowmass Club Circle, is quietly elegant, members only.

The *Repertory Theatre* performs six weeks in winter and six weeks in summer. For tickets contact the Snowmass Resort Association or the ticket hotline: 923–2618.

HINTS FOR THE HANDICAPPED. Advance arrangements for blind skiers and those with some physical disabilities can be made through the ski school, 303–923–2085; also inquire about special parking.

ASPEN

Aspen is the grande dame of Rocky Mountain ski resorts, rivaled only by Sun Valley in the Sawtooth Mountains of Idaho for glamor and glitz. Aspen is mecca to skiers in winter and to music lovers in summer.

It has long been a haven for film stars. Folks the likes of Jimmy Buffet, John Denver, Jill St. John, Leon and Jill Uris, and Goldie Hawn call Aspen home at least part of the year.

The first silver prospectors staked their claims in 1879. By the 1880s Aspen had become one of the biggest silver towns in the west. In 1892 it was served by two railroads, had a fancy hospital, a court house, opera house, a first-class hotel, six newspapers, and nearly 12,000 people. Repeal of the Sherman Silver Act in 1893, however, instantly made Aspen destitute. By the 1930s only 600 people lived in the town, but the ski industry began to stir about this time. That industry blossomed after World War II to what we see today. The creation of the Aspen Institute for Humanistic Studies in 1949 set the stage for the emergence of a summer resort dedicated to intellectual and cultural pursuits.

The turn-of-the- century Victorian mining town atmosphere has been preserved, updated, and painted. The modern mansions on the hills surrounding the colorful town just add to the feeling of "upscale." Aspen mountain, called "Ajax" by the long-time skiers, juts up from downtown and the setting couldn't be any more perfect if it were a movie set.

PRACTICAL INFORMATION FOR ASPEN

HOW TO GET THERE. Aspen is in White River National Forest, 205 miles from Denver.

By air. *Continental Express* (800–525–0280 or 303–398–3000) and *United Express* (800–241–6522, 800–525–1143, or 303–398–3746) fly from Denver to the Aspen/Snowmass airport, four miles from town. Nonstop flights from Chicago, Dallas, Los Angeles, Long Beach, and San Francisco on *United Express* operate mid-December–end of March. In-flight concierge service provides resort information. Taxis are available between the airport and town lodging. Limos are also available for the ride from Denver's Stapleton Airport to Aspen. *Trailways* (303–925–1234) and Aspen Limousine and Bus Service (303–925–2400) both provide service between Denver and Aspen and Grand Junction and Aspen.

By train. *Amtrak* services Glenwood Springs (40 miles from Aspen) daily from Chicago via Denver and San Francisco via Grand Junction. For full details call toll free 800–872–7245. Also make advance reservations through Amtrak or your travel agent to book a *Mellow Yellow Taxi* (303–925–2282) or *High Mountain Taxi* (303–925–8294) for a special rate between Glenwood Springs and the Aspen area.

By car. It is 220 miles from Denver via I–70 to Glenwood Springs, then Hwy. 82 into Aspen. From Colorado Springs 260 miles via Hwy. 24 to 9 to I–70 and Hwy. 82 from Glenwood to Aspen. Grand Junction take I–70 East to Glenwood and Hwy. 82 to Aspen, 140 miles. For a spectacularly scenic drive in summer, exit from I–70 at US 91 for Leadville (before Glenwood Springs), take the turnoff at Twin Lakes onto US 82 and drive over Independence Pass to Aspen; if you're afraid of heights, don't look down.

ACCOMMODATIONS. Contact the *Aspen Resort Association,* 700 S. Aspen St., Aspen, CO 81611, call nationwide 800–262–7736; in Colorado 800–421–7145 or 303–925–9000. There's a lodge for every taste and nearly every pocketbook.

Lodging in town is within a maximum of an eight-block walk to the base of Aspen Mountain; also the free shuttle runs regularly through town to the mountain and to Buttermilk, Snowmass, and Aspen Highlands. Many hotels have shuttle service to and from ski areas and the airport. The listings here will give an idea of the range of lodgings available. Prices given below are a night per person, based on double occupancy.

Expensive

Aspen Club Lodge & Condominiums. 709 E. Durant; 303–925–6760, 800–882–2582 nationwide, 800–443–2582 in Colorado. Next door to Aspen Mountain and the Silver Queen gondola; amenities include airport shuttle, concierge service, 24-hour front desk, pool, sauna, health club privileges at Aspen Club. Restaurant and bar open daily. $142–$188 for a room up to $808 for a four-bedroom condo.

Aspen Mountain Townhouses. 623 S. Monarch St.; 920–3724. At base of Lift 1A, three-bedroom units with Jacuzzi, washer/dryer, three levels with fireplace; skylights, greenhouse windows, no smoking. $350–$450 per unit.

Aspen Ski Lodge. 101 West Main St.; 303–925–3434. One- and two-bedroom units with outdoor decks. Some with kitchenettes, fireplaces,

Jacuzzis. Heated outdoor pool and hot tub. Year-round health club privileges, gourmet breakfast. Small and intimate; $142–$270 for a room.

The Gant. 610 West End; 303–925–5000. One- to four-bedroom units in this condominium resort. Two heated pools, whirlpools, saunas. Five outdoor tennis courts. $200–$480.

The Hotel Jerome. 330 E. Main St.; 303–920–1000. Newly renovated in the Victorian style in its elegant 27 rooms; airport courtesy shuttle. Rooms $185–$210; suites $290–$350.

Moderate

Brass Bed Inn. 926 E. Durant St.; 925–3622. Friendly inn with brass beds, puffy down comforters, full breakfast, Jacuzzi, kitchenettes. Room $60–$90 a night; studio $100; one three-bedroom unit $250 a night.

Lift One Condominiums. 131 East Durant; 303–925–1670 or 800–543–8001. Full-service condominiums at base of Aspen Mountain. One- to three-bedroom units. Pool, sauna, Jacuzzi. Convenient to restaurants and nightspots. $168–$315.

Limelight Lodge. 228 East Cooper; 303–925–3025, or 800–433–0832 (in Colorado). Lounge, heated pool, sauna. Golf, tennis, horseback riding nearby. Popular with young ski crowd, complimentary breakfast, close to everything. $88–$122 per room.

St. Moritz Lodge. 334 West Hyman; 303–925–3220. 1930s lodge with European flavor. Apartments, rooms with private baths, dorm rooms with shared baths. Fireplace lobby; TV lounge; library and game rooms, après-ski refreshments, but no restaurant. Heated pool, sauna, Jacuzzi. $25 for dorm room; $98 a night hotel room; one- to five-bedroom apartments run $150–$490.

Inexpensive

Alpine Lodge. 1240 E. Hwy. 82; 925–7351. Bavarian style, home-cooked meals; optional full breakfast and dinner. Gather in lounge for cards, music. Rooms $30–$40; cottage $50.

Little Red Ski Haus. 118 E. Cooper Ave.; 303–925–3333. Friendly Victorian house, 21 rooms with and without private baths; 1890s decor, two blocks from lifts. Dorm rooms $22–$27; hotel room $72–$78.

CAMPING. While you cannot park and stay in your RV or camper overnight on the streets of Aspen, there are several campgrounds in close proximity. All on a first-come, first-serve basis. *Difficult Campground* is four miles southeast of Aspen at the base of Independence Pass. Water, toilets, hiking trails. Five-day limit, fee. *Lincoln Gulch* is ten miles southeast of Aspen, part way up Independence Pass. Water, toilets, good fishing in Roaring Fork River, rock climbing. Five-day limit, no fee. *Weller Campground* is in the same area, has water, toilets, and five-day limit; no fee. *Lost Man* is 16 miles from Aspen, nearly atop Independence Pass. Water, toilets, fishing in nearby reservoir. Five-day limit, no fee. It gets cold at 12,000 feet, even on summer nights, so come prepared. *Maroon Lake* is 11 miles southwest of Aspen on Maroon Creek Road, near Aspen Highlands. Water, toilets, picnic tables, fishing, hiking trails. Two-day limit, fee. *Silver Bar, Silver Bell,* and *Silver Queen* are all along Maroon Creek Road and have woodsy settings, good fishing, water, and toilets. Three-five day limit, no fees.

HOW TO GET AROUND. There is free bus service around town and to the ski areas of Aspen Mountain (in town), Buttermilk, Aspen Highlands, and Snowmass. Taxi (*Mellow Yellow,* 303–925–2282, or *High Mountain,* 303–925–5245) and horsedrawn sleighs from The Mall are other means. Aspen is compact enough to walk nearly everywhere and the center of town is a pedestrian mall, with no vehicular traffic permitted. Unless you're staying at a remote lodge or a friend's house, you won't need a car.

TOURIST INFORMATION. Local radio stations KSNO and KSPN bring the latest weather and news; the cable TV station features just about anything you'll ever want to know about Aspen activities if you just tune in long enough. Telephone for snow conditions 925–1221. The *Aspen Times* and several local city magazines cover activities and events. Visit the *Aspen Visitors Center* in the Wheeler Opera House, 328 E. Hyman Ave., for current listings and outfitters, or call 303–925–1940. The *Aspen Resort Association* can be reached at 700 S. Aspen St., Aspen 81611; 303–925–9000 or 800–421–7145 in Colorado. The *Aspen Skiing Company* administrates three mountains—Aspen, Buttermilk, and Snowmass; Box 1248, Aspen 81612; 303–925–1220.

SEASONAL EVENTS. *Winterskol* is the **January** carnival. The *Harpers Bazaar Ski/Fitness Forum* is the end of the month. *Subaru Aspen Winternational* features the top amateur racers in world competition on Aspen Mountain each **March.** The annual Aspen/Snowmass Banana Season in **April** offers parties, contests, and other special events, plus discounted lodging and lift tickets.

Throughout the **summer** there's the *Aspen Music Festival.* The *Wine Classic* is held in **June;** guests participate in a three-day event, attending lectures and tastings with a pastry bake-off on the last day. The world-famous *Design Conference* is also in June. *Ballet/Aspen Summer Dance Festival* performs throughout **July** and **August.** The *Humanistic Institute* schedules lectures during August. The *Aspen Writers Conference* is in early July. The *Aspen Community Theater* performs at the Wheeler Opera House; *Aspen Arts Festival* and *FilmFest* feature programs of special exhibitions throughout **September.** For information, call Aspen Resort Association, 925–1940.

PARTICIPANT SPORTS. Eight chairlifts, including the six-passenger, high-speed Silver Queen gondola, take **skiers** to more than 625 acres of varied terrain on Aspen Mountain. Buttermilk is a good mountain for learning to ski, with 35 percent easiest trails. Good intermediate runs are found on the Tiehack section on the side of Buttermilk and is a favorite area for locals to ski on powder days. Snowmass is part of the Aspen Skiing Company, see "Snowmass," above. Aspen Highlands is the fourth mountain in the area, but is not part of the Aspen Skiing Company—see "Aspen Highlands," below.

You can buy a three- or four-area lift ticket at reduced prices. A six-coupon book allows you to ski all four mountains over a seven-day period, for instance; a similar book of tickets is available for Aspen Skiing Company's three mountains; call them at 303–925–1220 for information and rates. Rentals at local ski shops at the base of Aspen and Buttermilk mountains. Credit cards are accepted for ski schools, rentals, and lifts.

There are guided **cross-country** tours on the Tenth Mountain Trail, a hut-to-hut European-type experience. Moonlight dinner tours and cross-country lessons are available. Check *Aspen Touring Center,* Box 2432, Aspen, CO 81612; 303–925–7625 or the *Tenth Mt. Trail Hut System,* 303–925–5775. A system of well-equipped shelters on the *Alfred A. Braun Hut System* connects Aspen with Crested Butte. Call 303–925–7162 for costs. Ski rentals are available from *Ute Mountaineer,* 925–2849, or *Snowmass Club Touring Center,* 303–923–3148.

In season there are deep-powder **snowcat** tours (call Aspen Skiing Company, 303–925–1220), as well as guided out-of-bounds skiing for powder freaks. Cost is $150 per person, including lunch, gondola ride to the summit, and a guide.

Snowshoe rentals are available from *Ute Mountaineer,* 925–2849; in fact, all kinds of touring equipment can be rented there.

There are also **sleigh rides, ice skating, ice hockey,** and **paddle tennis;** in nearby health clubs there is **indoor tennis, swimming, racquetball, squash, flyfishing;** call the *Aspen Resort Association* for details, 925–1940.

In summer there is **backpacking** and **hiking.** Trailheads are at Maroon Lake, Silver Queen, Difficulty Creek, Lincoln Gulch, Lost Man campgrounds (see "camping," above), Ashcroft and along Hunter Creek. Book and sport shops have guidebooks and maps, or go to the Forest Service, 315 N. Seventh. **Bicycling** is enjoyable along the paved bike paths; rentals at *Aspen Sports,* 408 E. Cooper Ave., 925–6331. **Biplane** rides are from the *Aspen Barnstorming Co.,* 303–925–3331. **Horseback riding** is available from *Heatherbed Stables* (925–6987), *T Lazy 7* (925–7040). **River rafting** and **kayaking** available on the Colorado, Roaring Fork, and Arkansas rivers from *Blazing Paddles* (925–5651) and *River Rats* (925–7648), *Colorado Riff Raft,* (303–925–5405). **Soar** with *Gliders of Aspen* (925–3418). Public **tennis courts** are at *Iselin Park,* southwest of town, call 925–9220 for reservations; tennis is also available at the *Aspen Club* (925–8900) and *Grand Champions* (920–1533) year-round. *Aspen Tennis Festival* is held at the Aspen Club in August; other tennis tournaments take place during the summer. *Silver Queen Gondola* takes sightseers to the top of Aspen Mountain, end of June to early September. *Aspen Golf Course* is a 7,125 yard championship 18-hole course; pro shop, carts, driving range, PGA instruction (925–2145). Bob Johnson's *Hockey School* runs the end of July to early August.

HISTORICAL SITES AND OTHER LANDMARKS. Historical sites include the refurbished *Wheeler Opera House,* built by Jerome Wheeler, president of Macy's department store at the turn of the century. Today it hosts cultural events year-round and the summer opera theater in conjunction with the Aspen Music Festival. The *Hotel Jerome,* 330 E. Main St., is another Wheeler edifice, a good example of Victorian architecture during the silver mining heydays; recently renovated. The Victorian-furnished *Stallard House Museum,* 620 W. Bleeker, 925–3721, might be worth a visit. Open seven afternoons during summer and winter seasons.

In summer, drive to Aspen over 12,000-foot-high Independence Pass. It is not for the faint-hearted but it is one of the most spectacular drives anywhere in the state. Closed in winter. Also in summer, visit the Maroon Bells, famous landmark of the area, seen in nearly every poster shot of the Aspen area. There are trails around the lake and farther on. Catch the bus at Aspen Highlands parking lot, since no cars are allowed. Closed in winter.

An hour's drive to the semighost town of Redstone and the historic *Redstone Inn* is a step back in time. Go to *Marble* over rough roads to see the marble quarries (the Lincoln Memorial in Washington D.C. is made from Marble marble). The long, rough drive over Kebler Pass to Crested Butte takes you through the largest stand of Aspen trees in the world.

The *Smuggler Mine,* northeast side of Aspen, is open for tours year-round. It was from this mine that the largest silver nugget ever mined was found—it weighed over a ton, but had to be cut down to 1,800 pounds to be excavated; call 303–925–7159 for reservations.

CHILDREN'S ACTIVITIES. Aspen Mountain has no child-care or children's ski-school facilities, but several in-town nursery services are available; 925–1940 for information. *Aspen Sprouts* day care takes 1 to 5 year olds, located at the Aspen Airport Business Center; 920–1055. Buttermilk Mountain operates the *Powder Pandas Ski School* for ages 3 to 5. Beginner to advanced instruction, rental equipment, private ski hill, lunch and snacks. Write to Box 223, Woody Creek, CO 81656; 303–925–6336. Also, see Snowmass section for children's programs there.

Preschool story hour is Tuesday mornings at the *Pitkin County Library,* 120 E. Main St.; school-age children have story hour Tuesday afternoons. A children's film program is held here Friday afternoons beginning in January to early March; call 925–7124. Teens will enjoy hockey or figure skating at the *Aspen Ice Gardens,* open seven days a week; 925–7485 (winter only).

The *Aspen Center for Environmental Studies* at the Hallam Lake Wildlife Sanctuary (925–5756) offers guided walks and snowshoe hikes Mon.-Fri. and Wednesday evening slide shows; animals and educational displays.

SHOPPING. This list could be endless. Whatever you would like to buy, you'll find in Aspen. **Boutique fashions** are found in *Elli of Aspen,* 101 S. Mill; *Geraniums 'n Sunshine,* 520 E. Durant, *Peaches en Regalia;* 205 S. Mill; *Rita St. John,* 209 S. Galena; *Baggage Claim,* 307 S. Galena; *Chestnut Run,* 309 S. Galena. Look for **ethnic clothing** and **gifts** in *Uriah Heep's,* 303 E. Hopkins Ave.; *Siri and Peters,* 408 S. Hunter; *Scandinavian Design,* 607 E. Cooper. **Western wear** is popular in *Smith's,* 601 E. Hopkins Ave.; *Tom Mix Inc.,* 410 E. Hyman Ave.; *Fast Eddie's,* 533 E. Hopkins Ave. Unusual **accessories** in *Byrne-Getz Gallery,* 520 E. Durant Ave. **Specialty** and **gift shops** include *For Your Eyes Only* (glasses, goggles), 422 E. Hyman Ave.; *Patricia Moore,* 610 E. Hyman Ave.; *Swiss Gift Shop,* 425 E. Cooper Ave.; **Junior fashions** are featured in *Junior Mountain Sports,* 555 E. Durant Ave.; *Kindersport,* Mills St. Plaza; *Kid's Bazaar,* 517 E. Hopkins; and *Think Toys,* 401 E. Hyman. **Ski** and **sports wear** and **equipment** from *Aspen Ski Mart,* 412 S. Spring; *Ute Mountaineer,* 308 S. Mill; *Aspen Sports,* 408 E. Cooper Ave.; *Aspen Mountain,* 611 E. Durant Ave.; *L'Equipe,* 427 E. Hyman Ave.; *McDonough's,* 419 E. Cooper Ave.; *Molterer,* 520 E. Cooper Ave.; *Sport Kaelin,* 414 E. Cooper Ave.; *Hub of Aspen,* 315 E. Hyman; *Pomeroy's,* 614 E. Durant Ave.; *Sabbatini,* 434 E. Cooper Ave.; *Sports Stalker,* 428 E. Hyman Ave.; and *Silver Queen Sports* in the Gondola Building.

DINING OUT. On Aspen Mountain the mountaintop *Sundeck* offers the usual ski fare, indoor and outdoor seating. *Bonnie's Restaurant* is midmountain in Tourtelotte Park serving good ole American food inside and out. The outdoor deck is THE place to meet and to be seen. *Ruthie's,* near Ruthie's Run, has cafeteria-style service; also try *Coyote Grill.*

On Buttermilk Mountain, *Cafe Suzanne,* located at the bottom of Lift 3, features French country food, outdoor tables, wine, and beer. *The Cliffhouse,* located at the top of Lifts 5 and 2, features cafeteria-style dining and a special sit-down dining area called "Little Switzerland." *The Main Buttermilk Restaurant,* located at the bottom of Lift 1, features cafeteria-style dining and sundeck. *Racer's Edge,* at the bottom of Lift 4 at Tiehack, features cafeteria-style dining and a sundeck.

In town, there are over 100 restaurants to choose from, most of them excellent and most of the prices comparable to New York or San Francisco. *Expensive* restaurants run around $18–$30 for entrées; *Moderate,* $12–$18; *Inexpensive,* under $12. All restaurants listed take MasterCard and Visa unless otherwise noted.

Abetone Ristorante. *Expensive.* 620 E. Hyman Ave.; 925–9022. Northern Italian dinners. Seafood and vegetarian dishes. Reservations encouraged.

Charlemagne. *Expensive.* 400 W. Main; 925–5200. Fine French food.

Maurice's. *Expensive.* 700 Ute Ave.; 925–7822. Continental and French cuisine.

Parlour Car. *Expensive.* 615 W. Hopkins Ave.; 925–3810. French cuisine in a restored railroad car. Reservations necessary.

Ute City Banque. *Expensive.* 501 E. Hyman Ave.; 925–4373. An eclectic variety of dishes for lunch and dinner. Reservations encouraged.

Chart House. *Moderate.* 219 E. Durant Ave.; 925–3525. For steaks and salad bar.

Copper Kettle. *Moderate.* 535 E. Dean Ave.; 925–3151. A different country's cuisine is featured each night. The restaurant is decorated with paintings and the wine cellar. Advance reservations necessary.

Crystal Palace. *Moderate.* 300 E. Hyman Ave.; 925–1455. Epitome of Victorianism, with dinner and shows twice a night. Do make advance reservations.

Guido's Swiss Inn. *Moderate.* 403 S. Galena St.; 925–7222. Aspen's classic fondue specialist. Patio dining; open daily. Reservations required for dinner.

Poppie's Bistro Café. *Moderate.* 834 W. Hallam; 925–2333. For quail, fish, beef dishes.

Home Plate. *Inexpensive.* 333 E. Durant Ave.; 925–1986. For meals in a home-cooked style.

Marika's. *Inexpensive.* 205 S. Mill St.; 925–6633. Greek food prepared by owners; takeout available. No reservations.

Mother Lode. *Inexpensive.* 314 E. Hyman Ave.; 925–7700. Italian food in surroundings of brick walls, with music.

Skier's Chalet Steak House. *Inexpensive.* 710 S. Aspen; 925–3381. Prime rib and steaks.

Takah Sushi. *Inexpensive.* 420 E. Hyman; 925–8588. Complete sushi bar and menu. Reviewed as the finest between Malibu and Manhattan. Takeout available; reservations suggested.

NIGHTLIFE. This offers another amazing choice of activities. If anyone can both ski and party, there are rewards. Among the best known is *Andre's* disco (glimpses of movie moguls are possible here), 312 S. Galena.

The *Tippler Oyster Bar* is a must after skiing and later at night, 535 E. Dean Ave. *Little Nells* at the bottom of Aspen Mountain is lively; open winter only, 611 E. Durant Ave. The *Paragon,* 419 E. Hyman Ave., blares disco music till the wee hours; *Little Annie's,* 517 E. Hyman Ave., and *O'Leary's Pub,* 521 E. Hyman, are favorite locals' spots. The *Hotel Jerome Bar,* 330 East Main St., is a popular late-night gathering spot.

For those of a more cultural bent, an old favorite for dinner theater is the *Crystal Palace,* an elegant red velvet Victorian restaurant where waitpersons present zany Broadway revues; reserve dinner and show, 925–1455. Next door is *Grand Finale* with a delightful show of Broadway and Hollywood tunes; reservations for dinner and show at 920–1488. There are also four movie theaters in town. See also "Seasonal Events."

HINTS FOR THE HANDICAPPED. For ski programs for visually impaired, contact BOLD, 533 E. Main St, Aspen, CO 81611; 303–925–8922. Instruction is at Buttermilk and Snowmass Mountains. Special lift ticket rates and free equipment. See also "Snowmass."

ASPEN HIGHLANDS

One of the few privately owned resorts in Colorado, the Highlands was started in 1957. Primarily, it is a winter resort and the skiing and the ski facilities haven't changed much over the years. On a good powder day, Highlands is a place a lot of local powder hounds head for. It is uncrowded, has long, steep runs, and is as unpretentious as neighboring Aspen (one mile away) is pretentious. An affordable area, Highlands is popular with families and students.

PRACTICAL INFORMATION FOR ASPEN HIGHLANDS

HOW TO GET THERE. By air. Denver is the major gateway year-round, and Grand Junction becomes a minor one during the winter ski season. (See *Practical Information for Denver* and *Practical Information for the Areas Beyond Denver.*) From Denver two commuter airlines fly to the Aspen/Snowmass Airport: *United Express* (800–241–6522, 800–525–1143, or 303–398–3746) and *Continental Express* (800–525–0280). Both carriers have up to 25 flights daily in pressurized 50- and 80-passenger aircraft. There are charter flights from major cities and, in winter, flights into nearby Grand Junction. Nonstop flights on *United Express* from Chicago, Dallas, Los Angeles, Long Beach, and San Francisco fly from mid-December to the end of March. Taxis from the airport will take you to your lodge, generally about a 10–15 minute drive. From Grand Junction airport there is connecting transportation into Aspen (*see* By car, below).

By bus. *Trailways* has daily schedules to the Snowmass/Aspen Airport and Aspen from Denver and from Grand Junction; call 303–292–2291.

By train. *Amtrak's* California Zephyr stops in Glenwood Springs eastbound about 2:50 P.M. and westbound at 2:10 P.M. in an extravagantly scenic route across the Rockies. Advance arrangements should be made for connecting ground transportation from Glenwood Springs to Aspen Highlands through Amtrak (800–421–8320 or 303–893–3911), or your travel agent. It is a $55 taxi ride per person without advance reservations from Glenwood to Aspen; call *Mellow Yellow,* 925–2282.

By car. Take I–70 west from Denver to Glenwood Springs, Highway 82 for 43 miles to Maroon Creek Road (between the Aspen Airport and the town of Aspen), right for a mile and a half. From Grand Junction it's 128 miles; take I–70 east to Glenwood Springs, then Highway 82. From Colorado Springs it is 231 miles via State Highway 24 to 9 to I–70 to Highway 82. Rental cars are available at Grand Junction airport. There are *Avis,* 800–331–1212, *Budget,* 800–527–0700, *Hertz,* 800–654–3131.

ACCOMMODATIONS. Most people opt for one of the 10,000 pillows in nearby Aspen (see above). A new, luxury hotel has been planned at the base of Highlands Mountain. Construction is uncertain. Call Aspen Resort Association for reservations, 303–925–9000.

HOW TO GET AROUND. Free buses leave from Rubey Park, Durant Street, and Galena Street in Aspen, every 15 minutes for the Highlands base area parking lot. In summer, they are scheduled every 30 minutes. Twenty-one-passenger minibuses serve small groups by reservation, as well as Snowmass guests on Tuesdays and Thursdays; Contact the *Snowmass Lodge* for times and pickup points.

PARTICIPANT SPORTS. Skiing is the name of the game, both downhill and cross-country. Nine chair and two poma lifts serve 21 miles of trails, bowls, and glades; Loges Lift is the highest chairlift in Colorado, providing a sweeping view of the Maroon Bells. *Telemark* classes and *snowboard* instruction are available through the ski school. The *Silver Series* races are held every other weekend starting in mid-January in conjunction with Hunter Mountain, NY, Mt. Ste. Anne in Quebec and Innsbruck, Austria. A four-area lift ticket is valid for Highlands, Aspen Mountain, Buttermilk, and Snowmass. Rentals and repair at the base ski shop; call 925–5300. The *Star Test,* available daily, is a way to match ability to national skiing standards and other skiers around the country. The *Ski Patrol Deck Jump* over a 54-foot-wide picnic deck is a favorite several times a week at Cloud 9 Restaurant. *Ski Clubs* of 25 or more can build their own wine and cheese party; call Skier Services at 925–5300.

Hiking, backpacking, and **tennis** are the mainstay of summer activities. See "Aspen," above.

CHILDREN'S ACTIVITIES. In ski season, children can get a three-day ski-school package for $120, a five-day package for $170. Snowpuppies are ages 3–6, and for $45 a day they get ski lessons, lifts, and lunch. Highlands advises this is *not* a babysitting service, but a "learn to ski experience." Lift tickets only for kids 12 and under are $16 a day; multiday rates available.

DINING OUT. On the mountain the *Merry-Go-Round Restaurant* and *Cloud 9* provide good ski fare. On spring days the outdoor barbecue can't be resisted. The base lodge cafeteria is open for breakfast and lunch.

NIGHTLIFE. Most action is in the town of Aspen, a mile away. See above. Some of the best après-ski music of any ski area anywhere is at *Schwanie's* in the base lodge, until 6 P.M.

HINTS FOR THE HANDICAPPED. Special arrangements can be made for handicapped skiers by contacting the Aspen Highlands Ski School director, Bob Smith, Box T, Aspen, CO 81612, or calling 303–925–5300.

CRESTED BUTTE

Unlike the other Colorado mining towns, Crested Butte never really died. Amax Mining Company gets a good deal of molybdenum from the area, sparking classic confrontations between mining officials and environmentalists. This rather remote town, in the Gunnison Valley, has been listed as a National Historic District. Crested Butte's weatherbeaten buildings reflect the price of survival in the harsh mountain winters. Behind the 1880s facades are gourmet restaurants, shops, art galleries. The ambience is Victorian without the cutesyness of Aspen or Breckenridge.

The ski area is two miles up the road at Mount Crested Butte. Here the condos are modern with a view of the Elk Mountain Range and Raggeds Wilderness Area unmatched anywhere in the Rockies. The ski area is actually the back side of Aspen Mountain and hardy cross-country skiers make their way across the summit in winter; hikers do so in summer. A dirt road between Aspen and Crested Butte is only open in summer, and even then it can be an arduous drive.

Crested Butte is affordable and anti-glitz. It attracts students from nearby Western State College in Gunnison, singles and families from the southeast and Texas. It is strictly a destination area, luring those with enough money to take a ski or summer vacation, but who are price conscious as well. Bargain hunters can do well here.

PRACTICAL INFORMATION FOR CRESTED BUTTE

HOW TO GET THERE. Crested Butte is in the Gunnison National Forest, 230 miles southwest of Denver.

By air. The closest gateway is Gunnison, 30 miles down valley in west central Colorado. Direct flights on major airlines from major gateways have made Crested Butte an easy destination, while retaining its "off the beaten path" ambience.

During ski season, *United Airlines* has three flights a week from Chicago, *American Airlines* has daily service from Dallas, and *Delta* has twice weekly flights from Salt Lake City, connecting with flights from the West Coast. Contact any of these airlines at 800–525–4220. *Braniff* has charter flights through *Adventure Tours* out of Dallas. *Continental Express* and *United Express* serve Gunnison year-round from Denver, making connections from all major gateways.

From Gunnison Airport **taxis** (349–5749) and **limousines** (349–5874) operate daily schedules to Crested Butte; rental cars are also available at the airport in *Budget,* 303–641–4403; *Hertz,* 303–641–2881; *Great American Rental Cars,* 303–641–1391. Pickup at the *Trailways Bus Terminal* requires arrangement in advance; call the ski area at 303–349–2333.

By bus. *Trailways* runs from Denver, Colorado Springs, and Grand Junction to Gunnison, 30 miles from the area.

By car. Crested Butte is not on the "main Thoroughfare" of I–70 resorts found just west of Denver. It is a five-hour drive from Denver via US 285,

US 50 over Monarch Pass, and CO 135. From Grand Junction it is 160 miles on US 50 and CO 135.

ACCOMMODATIONS. Call Crested Butte Central Reservations from outside Colorado at 800–525–4220, or within Colorado call 800–332–5875. There are 6,000 pillows in numerous condominium complexes and lodges between the town of Crested Butte and the ski area of Mt. Crested Butte.

Expensive

Crested Mountain Condos. 21 Emmons Rd.; 303–349–7555. Located on warming house hill, each unit has a whirlpool in the master bath, fireplace, TV, phone, washer/dryer, and use of an indoor heated pool and health club. $190 a night for a two-bedroom condo. $290 a night for three bedrooms.

Grand Butte Hotel. 500 Gothic Country Rd., Mt. Crested Butte; 349–7561, 800–441–2781 in Colorado, 800–341–5437 outside Colorado. This $45-million hotel is one of the most elegant in the Rockies, with fine pottery, pink Italian marble, and original paintings as part of the decor. 209 rooms, 52 suites plus a presidential suite, all with kitchenettes, cable TV, whirlpools, 24-hour front desk, sports shops, indoor pool, sauna, three restaurants, three lounges, 20 yards from lifts. Rooms $100–$160; suites $150–$225; nightly presidential suite $525. Packages include free lift tickets.

The Penthouse. 21 Emmons Rd., Mt. Crested Butte; 349–7555. Atop the Conference Center, there are a few studios, one-, two- and three-bedroom units; ski-in, ski-out. Studios $142 a night; one-bedrooms $187; two-bedrooms $217; three-bedrooms $365.

Moderate

Skyland Resort & Country Club. 385 Country Club Drive, Crested Butte; 349–6129. Good for summer. Located three miles south of Mt. Crested Butte, this is a self-contained resort with lodges, free shuttle to ski area, pool, whirlpools, raquetball, tennis, restaurant and lounge, conference facilities; 18-hole championship golf course, close to cross-country ski touring. One-bedroom units $65–$80 nightly.

Three Seasons. 701 Gothic Rd., Mt. Crested Butte; 349–2448. 900 yards from slopes, shuttle bus, units with kitchens, fireplaces, indoor pool, hot tub, sauna; grocery and liquor store. One-bedroom $115 a night; two-bedroom $168; three-bedroom $203.

Inexpensive

Christiana Bed & Breakfast. 621 Maroon St., Crested Butte; 349–5326. Comfy and homey, this is a delightful inn serving full breakfast. Double or queen room $53 a night; two double beds $60; double plus bunk beds $65.

Elk Mountain Lodge. 129 Gothic Ave.; Crested Butte. 303–349–5114. Rustic, historical building, three blocks from shuttle. Rooms on first floor $55 a night; second floor $65; third floor $75.

CAMPING FACILITIES. Facilities are all first-come, first-serve. Seven miles north of Crested Butte is *Avery Peak Campground,* off County Road 317 at 9,600 feet. No trailers over 16 feet, piped and stream water, pit toilets, and tables; 14-day limit. *Gothic Campground* is nearby, no trailers and 14-day limit. Southeast of Crested Butte about eight miles is *Cement Creek* at 9,000 ft. Tank and stream water, no trailers over 32 feet; 14-day limit with fee. *Lake Irwin Campground* is six miles west of town at 10,200 feet. No trailers over 32 feet. Pit toilets, piped and lake water, fishing, and boating; 14-day limit. For general information on these four, call 303–641–0471. Another 12 miles farther west is *Lost Lake* with similar facilities; call 303–527–4131. Several other U.S. Forest Service campgrounds are near Almont and Gunnison.

HOW TO GET AROUND. The *Mountain Express* resort shuttle operates at no charge every half hour from 7 A.M. to midnight every day between the town of Crested Butte and the mountain, three miles away. Call 349–5616 or 349–6298. Many visitors hire rental cars during their stay for more flexibility.

TOURIST INFORMATION. For snow conditions call 303–349–2323, or *Colorado Ski Country, USA,* 303–831–SNOW. for general information (between 9 A.M. and 4 P.M.) call 303–349–2211. The *Crested Butte Chronicle* and the *Crested Butte Pilot* carry all the local news. Mount Crested Butte has its own weekly paper, *The Mountain Sun.* Gunnison radio stations KGUC 98.7FM and KVLE 102FM will fill you in on news and music. Contact the resort at Box A, Mount Crested Butte, CO 81225; 303–349–2211 or 2333. Summer information outlet at Highway 135 and Elk Ave.; in winter, at Old Town Hall Bldg., Elk and Second.

SEASONAL EVENTS. January or early **February** sees *Snowboard championships;* a unique nordic race, the *BOLS Alley Loop* goes through town each February; in **March** the *American Airlines Celebrity Cup* features film stars to raise money for charity; the infamous Al Johnson Uphill-Downhill Nordic Race is in late March or early **April;** winter is "flushed out" in April with Flauschink celebrations.

In summer, **4th of July** is celebrated with the *Gothic/Crested Butte Marathon; Wildflower Festival* is held in July. Probably the most colorful weekend is the last weekend in July when the *Aerial Weekend* finds the sky filled with hot air balloons, hang gliders, sky divers, stunt planes, and other aerial paraphernalia. *Dos Rios Golf Open* is in nearby Gunnison in early **August;** also in early August is the *Festival of the Arts.* The town's main street is closed to vehicular traffic and more than 100 artists display their work; the restaurants and town shops are also open with special bargains. Mid-August is *Windsurfing Championships* at Blue Mesa. *Summer Shakespeare* goes through August. The *Mountain Man Rendezvous,* a gathering of rugged types who live in a pre-1845 era for a weekend, is usually mid-August. *Fat Tire Bike Week* (fat tires are bicycles with fat, heavy-duty tires made to withstand the rough, dirt and gravel mountain roads) is mid-**September,** with races, tours over Pearl Pass to Aspen.

PARTICIPANT SPORTS. The Telemark Turn is said to have been rediscovered and perfected here, making Crested Butte famous for its extensive and excellent **cross-country ski** programs. As the self-styled "Telemark Capital of the World," there is instruction of same at the *Nordic Adventure/Touring Center*—$20 for a two-hour group lesson; $60 for a two-hour private lesson. There are 9-miles of groomed track and 100 miles of backcountry trails in the Elk Mountains. For information on cross-country guided tours, cookouts, and overnights call the Ski Touring Center and at 303–349–2250 (also for advance bookings). The downtown *Nordic Ski Center* at Second Street near the bus stop and the Bench ski track rents skis, gives lessons and provides guides; a track system is planned. Call 349–5439 or 349–5363 for information.

Eleven lifts take **Alpine skiers** into 420 acres of mostly beginner and intermediate terrain plus 390 acres of what had been "outer limits" extreme expert skiing. Rentals: 349–2240 and local ski shops. NASTAR and fun races are scheduled; **ice skating** at the new *Treasury Center* ice rink (call 349–2333) and **broomball** available, 349–2211. Arrangements can be made nearby for **sleigh rides** (call 349–2211), **racquetball,** at Skyland Resort, 349–6131. **Ice fishing** at Blue Mesa Reservoir; call U.S. Forest Service 641–0471. For a special treat, hop on a **snowmobile** and head for isolated Irwin Ranch for lunch or dinner, 12 miles from Crested Butte (call Resort Sports, 349–6193); for lodging packages at Irwin Ranch, call 800–255–9574 in Colorado or 800–221–5228 nationwide. Guided **snowmobile** trips and **dog sledding** are available through *Action* Adventures, 349–2211 or 349–6792; prices, $20–$74.

Summer Sports

Summer finds the typical mountain activities of **rafting, kayaking, hiking, windsurfing,** and, of course, **fat-tire bicycling.** Call Chamber of Commerce, 349–6438 for information.

Outdoor tennis is available at the public courts in Crested Butte Town Park, south side of Hwy. 135—free and no reservations; The Plaza at Woodcreek has two courts for their guests, reserve by calling 349–2130. Indoor tennis is available at Skyland Resort, call 349–6131 for court time and check fee; the Grand Butte Hotel has courts, call 349–7561. Fine **fishing** is found in Irwin, Emerald, Meridian, and Taylor lakes and Spring Creek Reservoir. The new *Skyland Resort and Country Club* has a sprawling 18-hole Robert Trent Jones II golf course. It has been named by the Society of Golf Course Architects as one of the top one percent in the U.S. Weekly clinics are available at $735 all inclusive (lessons, meals, lodging, greens and cart fees); contact John Jacobs Golf School, 349–6129. Golf packages are available through the Grand Butte Hotel at Skyland Golf Course starting at $50 per person; call 349–7561 or 800–441–2781 in Colorado, 800–341–5437 outside Colorado.

River rafting on the Gunnison, Taylor, and Arkansas rivers or Lake Fork is available through C.B. Rafting, 349–7423. **Hot air ballooning** goes up year-round with Big Horn Balloon Company, 349–6335. Fantasy Ranch provides custom **horseback rides,** from an hour to a three-day excursion; 349–5425 or 349–5355.

Ride the Silver Queen cabin chair to the top of the mountain, end of June through Labor Day. Time to hike, enjoy the view between 10 A.M. and 2 P.M. $6 adults, $2 children under 12 with an adult. Call 349–2266 or 349–2333.

HISTORIC AND OTHER SITES. For the hardy and adventurous get off the ski area trails and head for the backcountry. Trails start west of town off the Kebler Pass Road and east of town up Brush Creek and Cement Creek; from above the ski area to Gothic or across Pearl Pass to Aspen.

Pick up a copy of the pamphlet *Walking Tour of Crested Butte* with historic notes on the buildings, lodges, churches, even cemeteries. The entire town of Crested Butte is a living museum. Available at Chamber of Commerce. Check out the Rocky Mountain Biological Laboratory in Gothic, all but a ghost town except for the lab, just seven miles north of Crested Butte.

The Gunnison Chamber of Commerce and Columbia Savings Bank put out a pamphlet of 20 circle tour trips in the Gunnison area; write the Chamber at Box 36, Gunnison, CO 81230 or call 303–641–1501.

CHILDREN'S ACTIVITIES. *Buttetopia* is the ski and day care center for the little ones located in the Whetstone Building, call 303–349–2209 for reservations. *No-ski Buttetopia Nursery & Day Care* is for 6 months–6-year-olds, 8:30 A.M.–4:30 P.M. daily; $30 a day includes lunch; half-day is $20.

ABC-On-Skis is a beginner's skiing program for 3–6-year-olds. Full day is 8:30 A.M.–4:30 P.M., $35 with lunch, nursery care, ski equipment, and two hours of lessons; no lifts used. Rates for children 7–12 in *Butte Busters* ski school are $32 a day with supervised lunch. A full-day Never-Ever lesson using Peachtree Lift is $32. During Christmas week, children ski free with the Christmas Present Package; call Crested Butte Mountain Resort, 800–525–4220.

SHOPPING. Galleries of shopping arcades have been created in renovated buildings in the town of Crested Butte; at Mount Crested Butte the *Treasury Center* at the base of Keystone Lift is the newest retail shopping area. There are dozens of the usual T-shirt stores at the base area. Ardent shoppers can find jewelry in *Ice Mountain,* 311 Sixth, and *Zacchariah Zypp,* 301 Elk Ave.; kid's stuff in *Pooh's Corner,* 302 Elk Ave.; and second-hand stuff in *Rags to Riches,* 303 Elk Ave. *Handworks,* 432 Elk Ave., carries gifts, crafts, Colorado wildflower seeds, jams, and jellies. Sports gear can be found at *Alpineer/Bicycles etc.,* Bullion King Building, *Flatiron Sports* at the base area, and in *Crested Butte Grocery.*

DINING OUT. *Expensive* entrées, $13–$20; *Moderate,* $8–$12; *Inexpensive,* under $8. Visa and MasterCard accepted unless otherwise specified.

On the mountain, early risers can hop on Keystone Lift for the first run of the day and ski down to *Bubba's* in the *Paradise Warming House* for breakfast; this full-service sit-down restaurant also features Sunday brunch; groups of 25 or more may reserve for private functions. Sleigh-ride dinners ($30 per person) snowmobile dinners ($49 per person) end up here; call 349–2211 or, for groups, 349–2225. The *Rafters cafeteria* at the base, 349–2298, and *Paradise Warming House,* 349–2274, serve the usual mountain fare.

Penelope's. *Expensive.* 120 Elk Ave.; 349–5178. A long time favorite (especially for Sunday brunch), this is a cheery, sunny restaurant with plenty of ferns and antiques.

Moderate

Artichoke. 433 Emmons St., Mt. Crested Butte; 349–5400. Specializes in steaks, chops, with sides of mushrooms and, of course, artichokes.

Casey's. In the Manor Lodge at Mt. Crested Butte; 349–5365. Steaks, chicken, pasta; ski video during happy hour, live entertainment weekends; lively, good meeting place.

Gulf Coast Grill. 621 Gothic Rd.; 349–6942. For serious seafood lovers, fresh seafood flown in three times a week.

Jeremiah's. In the Lodge at Crested Mountain Village, 21 Emmons St.; 349–7555. Traditional American fare, especially steak. Breakfast also served.

Slogar's. 517 Second Ave.; 349–5765. Chicken, steaks served family-style, generous helpings, Victorian atmosphere. Reservations.

Spaghetti Slope. 500 Gothic Country Rd., in the Grand Butte Hotel; 349–7561. Italian cuisine, upbeat contemporary Italian decor.

Inexpensive

Cafe Creole. 7 Emmons Loop; 349–5276. This New Orleans streetcar is at the ski area base next to the bus stop. Gumbo, Creole, Cajun burgers, and stuffed baked potatoes; open 8 A.M.–8 P.M.

Donita's Cantina. 332 Elk St.; 349–6674. Serves what is allegedly the biggest portions of the best Mexican food in the Rockies. No reservations, come after 9 P.M. for shortest wait.

Karolina's Kitchen. 127 Elk Ave.; 349–6756. He-man sandwiches, chili, kielbasi, salads; lunch and dinner.

The Tincup Cafe and Bakery. Crested Mountain Village in Mt. Crested Butte; 349–7555. Slopeside, hearty breakfasts, lunches, family-style dinners; chicken and ribs.

Wooden Nickel. 222 Elk Ave.; 349–6350. A good ole American bar with a rah-rah college atmosphere; a local favorite. Steamed clams, giant sandwiches, soups, steaks, and prime rib.

NIGHTLIFE. Casey's. In the Manor Lodge, Mt. Crested Butte; 349–5365. Ski and sports videos, live entertainment, tourists and locals alike meet here.

Donita's Cantina. 332 Elk St.; 349–6674. $4 liter of margaritas on certain nights; local hangout.

Kochevar's. 127 Elk Ave.; 349–6745. Live music with local clientele.

Rafters Nightclub. At the base area in the Gothic Building; 349–2298. Has live bands nightly except Mondays playing a variety of music–country/western, big band sounds, rhythm 'n' blues. College students.

The Crested Butte Mountain Theatre performs year round; 132 Elk Ave.; 349–5685. The **Crested Butte Society** sponsors activities for artists, dancers, and musicians, and community workshops foster the arts; 349–6355.

HINTS FOR THE HANDICAPPED. Ski instruction is by prior appointment for blind and some physically disabled; contact Robel Staubhaar, Ski School, Box A, Mount Crested Butte, CO 81225; 303–349–2252.

TELLURIDE

This tiny Victorian gem lies at the end of a box canyon in a remote southwestern Colorado valley in the spectacular San Juan Mountains. A typical story in this part of the country, Telluride sprang to life as a bustling mining camp: gold and silver miners thronged the streets and the exuberant red-light district—Popcorn Alley—was famous for miles around. The name Telluride comes from the rare, lustrous crystalline element tellurium, found in a compound with gold or silver.

Following the goldrush, Telluride slumbered for over half a century. Young people seeking an alternative life-style migrated to this remote town in the 1960s and early '70s and saw the charm of the elegant Victorian buildings; they stayed, renovated the houses, and carefully preserved the amalgam of gothic and Victorian. These young, counterculture people also grew up, cut their hair, opened businesses, married, and are having children. In short, they are the solid citizens of Telluride, those environmentally concerned town council leaders. Today, Telluride is registered as a National Historic District; it is a low-key, self-contained, dramatic mountain hideaway with one main street and a two-block walk from the backcountry and the surrounding 14,000-foot peaks. Telluridians have no plans for resort glitz, now or in the future.

In the last few years Telluride has become more accessible with the new airport. However, it is still a good bargain and attracts vacationers primarily from the west and southwest. Due to numerous summer festivals, summer touring is as popular as the winter skiing.

PRACTICAL INFORMATION FOR TELLURIDE

HOW TO GET THERE. Telluride is located in the Uncompahgre National Forest, 325 miles southwest of Denver.

By air. Telluride's regional airport is the highest commercial airport in the country, at 9,085 feet. Just five miles from town, it has brought a remote resort a bit closer. However, expect frequent weather delays or reroutings. *Mesa Airlines* (800–233–9292) and *Continental Express* (800–525–0280) have daily flights from Denver and Phoenix, Mesa from Albuquerque, Farmington and Durango. Montrose, Durango, or Grand Junction also are gateways to Telluride. *America West* (800–247–5692) flies from Phoenix, Austin, and all major southwest cities daily to Grand Junction and Durango. *United Express* (800–525–1143 outside Colorado or 800–821–7126 in Colorado) provides daily service to Montrose, 65 miles from Telluride. Continental Express and United Express connect with major airlines at Denver's Stapleton Airport. Jet charter service from *U.S. Sports Adventures* brings skiers from San Jose and Long Beach, CA, to Montrose from mid-Dec. to mid-Mar. Call Telluride Central Reservations for reservations and information, 800–525–3455 or, in Colorado, 303–728–4432.

Telluride Transit (728–3856) meets all flights with 24-hour advance reservations in Montrose, Grand Junction, and Durango. From Telluride Airport it is $5 per person to town. *Telluride Taxi,* 728–3275, is $4.50 per person to town.

By bus. *Rocky Mountain Stage* (303–259–2366) serves Montrose and Durango from Grand Junction, Albuquerque, Cortez, Salt Lake City, Phoenix, Los Angeles, Flagstaff, and Pueblo; Telluride Transit provides ground transportation to Telluride with 24-hour advance reservations. Montrose to Telluride is $15 per person; Durango to Telluride $35; Grand Junction to Telluride $30. In the town of Telluride, a free shuttle bus runs regularly.

By car. Telluride is 330 miles from Denver on US 285, 50, CO 62, and 145. Durango is 125 miles south via CO 145, 62, US 789, and 550. Montrose is 65 miles north via US 789, 550, CO 62, and 145. Grand Junction is 127 miles north via US 789, 550, CO 62, and 145. Car rental agencies at Montrose, Cortez, Durango, Grand Junction, and excepting *Avis* and *National,* at the Telluride Airport are *Budget* (800–527–0700 or 303–728–4642); *Hertz* (800–654–3131 or 800–728–3057), *Avis* (800–331–1212), and *National* (800–328–4567).

ACCOMMODATIONS. Telluride Central Reservations, Box 1009, Telluride, CO 81435, 800–525–3455; in Colorado 303–728–4431, handles lodging information and reservations for all properties in town. With only ten lodges totaling 3,200 pillows, the area fills quickly during holiday periods. There are two base areas for lifts in town, while the Mountain Village and the Meadows base areas are accessible by shuttle bus from Telluride.

Expensive

LuLu City Condos. 182½ S. Mahoney Dr.; 728–4387. All units are close to lifts; and all have phones, TV, hot tubs, steam showers, and saunas; $105 per night for a one-bedroom condo. A seven-night, six-day package is $593, regular season.

Riverside. 460 S. Pine; 800–233–9292 or 728–3970. A seven-night, six-day package is $548, regular season; one-bedroom $90–$175 a night, two-bedroom $120–$230, three-bedroom $140–$260.

RiverWatch Condos. On the San Miguel River (no street address); 800–233–9292, or 728–3970. Walking distance of lifts. Two super-luxury units available with Jacuzzi hot tub; $500 a night.

Moderate

Boomerang Lodge and **Boomerang Village.** 154 Tomboy; 800–538–7754 nationwide, in Colorado 800–835–7433 or 728–4405. Close to Coonskin Lift. A seven-night, six-day package is $432–$471; nightly rates are one-bedroom $110–$195, two-bedroom $170–$265.

Manitou Lodge & River Houses. 333 S. Fir; 800–852–0015 or 728–4311. On the lift side of the San Miguel River, close to Oak Street and Coonskin lifts. Decorated with turn-of-the-century antiques, après-ski wine and cheese. Studio $60–$110 a night, queen-size room $95, a seven-night stay is $85 a night; two-bedroom $115–210. Rates include breakfast.

Ore Station Lodge. 260 S. Aspen; 728–4311. In town; studio to 3-bedroom condos furnished in antiques and oak furniture, $80 per night per person; seven-night, six-day package is $501 regular season.

Inexpensive

Coonskin Inn. 333 S. Davis St.; 728–3181. The unpretentious lodge is 300 feet from the Coonskin Lift and, by skiing down Telluride Trail, you can ski to your door at the end of the day. Hot tubs, small rooms, breakfast in the lobby, 24-hour front desk, $60 per night, double occupancy, seven-night, six-day package for $373.

Johnstone Inn or **Dahl House.** 403 W. Colorado; 728–3316. Victorian bed-and-breakfast houses, three blocks from Coonskin Lift; $35/night per person, double occupancy. A seven-night, six-day package is $278.

New Sheridan Hotel. 231 W. Colorado Blvd.; 728–4351. Smack in the middle of town, this is a Victorian beauty built in 1895 and renovated in 1977. William Jennings Bryan spoke here in 1902. Access to free ski shuttle, lifts are six blocks away; a room with queen-size bed and private bath is $45 a night, per person, double occupancy. A seven-night, six-day package is $320.

CAMPING. No reservations at any of the following. Two blocks east of town by the San Miguel River is the *Telluride Town Park and Public Campground;* shady, pleasant, can walk to town; $5 fee, maximum six people or two cars. *Cayton Campground* is 20 miles south of Telluride on CO 145; stream nearby for fishing, good hiking; U.S. Forest Service, 14-day limit, fee. *Matterhorn* is 10 miles south on CO 145; 14-day limit with fee. *Priest Gulch* is in the same area, has well water, is near a stream; hiking, fishing; 14-day limit, fee. Eight miles southwest on CO 145 is *Sunshine Campground;* it's high so bring warm sleeping bags; good hiking; 14-day limit, U.S. Forest Service, fee.

HOW TO GET AROUND. *Telluride Transit* is a free shuttle bus making the loop from town to the mountain on irregular trips to the Coonskin, Mountain Village, and Meadow lifts; a free bus circulates in town during ski season and summer festivals, 728–4105. Taxis are available by calling 728–3275. From one end of town to the other is no more than a 10-minute walk. The Oak Street base and Coonskin base areas are only a few blocks from town.

TOURIST INFORMATION. For snow conditions call 303–728–3614 or *Colorado Ski Country USA,* 303–831–SNOW. For road conditions call 728–3931; or in Montrose, 249–9363; weather 728–3856. Tune in to KOTO 91.7 FM for local news and activities. Telluride Cablevision gives daily weather and activity reports. The *Telluride Times* and *Telluride Mountain Journal* are weekly papers. *Telluride Magazine,* found in most lodge rooms, is full of tourist information and articles on local happenings. You can contact *Telluride Ski Resort* at Box 307, Telluride, CO 81435; 303–728–3856 or the *Telluride Chamber Resort Association,* Box 653, Telluride, CO 81435; 303–728–3041.

SEASONAL EVENTS. The *Invitational Governor's Cup* is in mid-**January**—fun if you follow politicos. Late January is the *Sonoma County Wineries SkiFest* for those who like to ski and go to wine tastings. **February** brings the *Best Skiers in the Rockies* Race. *Spring Fling* heralds spring's arrival at the end of **March.** Summer is full of festivals and artsy events. **May** starts off with *Mountainfilm Festival;* mid-**June** is the *Wine Festival* and *Invitational Hot Air Balloon Rally* over Telluride's peaks; the *Bluegrass and Country Music Festival* in mid-June is one of the biggest musical events in the west. **July** Fourth is celebrated by family fun in the Town Park and a *Fireman's Bar-B-Que;* the end of July is the *Dance Festival and Workshop,* a weekend of jazz entertainment and workshops; **August** finds the *Chamber Music Festival* performing at the Opera House several weekends; the *Wild Mushroom Fair* is the end of August; the *International Film Festival* is a gala affair the end of August and early **September;** Hang gliding's premier event happens each September. *Colorfest* activities take place during September and **October** throughout the southwest, with Telluride an important stop in a circle tour of Dolores, Durango, Silverton, and Ouray. The Telluride Academy offers *Master Classes in the Sacred Arts* (Byzantine icon painting, sacred music of the sufis, medieval stained glass painting), a jazz camp, wilderness camp, and adult classes in massage, gourmet mountaineering, and local history. Program information is available by writing Box 2255, Telluride, CO 81435, or calling 303–728–5311. Self-guided walking tours are available by checking with the Chamber Resort Association, 728–3041.

PARTICIPANT SPORTS. Skiers have the choice of three distinct areas on 660 acres, served by nine chairlifts and one poma lift. The Front Face, which is what people first see, is justifiably terrifying; Gorrono Basin is good for intermediates and beginners, and The Meadows for beginners and never-ever skiers; mostly an intermediate mountain. Despite its reputation as a tough mountain, Telluride is 54 percent intermediate terrain. The two-plus-mile high-speed quad serving Sunshine Peak in only 11 minutes is the world's longest detachable quad chairlift.

The *Nordic Center* guides, 728–3404, introduce **cross-country** skiers to the backcountry with picnics, lessons; 10K and 17K ski tracks. Trail fee is $4; equipment rental available, $9 a day. Telemark lessons available on the mountain for $18. Inquire about guided tours through Central Reservations, 728–4431, or outside Colorado 800–525–3455. For those who like to ski tour the back country on their own, call 728–3856 for information on trails from the town Park, to Lizard Head Pass, Sunshine, and Wilson mesas. The *San Juan Hut System* is a route following old mining roads and across a mesa, designed for intermediate Nordic skiers; $12 per person per night at the huts. For reservations and information, write Box 1663, Telluride, CO 81435, or call 303–728–6935. Family discounts available.

Heli-skiing is available, even for the not-so-fantastic skier; contact *Heli-Trax,* 728–4909, and find the hidden basins of the San Juan Mountains. Four to seven runs for $275–$335 a day. **Ice skating** is available on the town pond, skating parties every Wednesday evening with a bonfire and music; rentals from *Olympic Sports* at $3 adults/$2 children, 226 W. Colorado Ave.; 728–3501.

Snowmobiling packages by the day or multiple days start at 10 A.M. daily, tours cover about 50 miles; $70 per adult, less with your own machine. Reserve by calling 325–4444, 800–358–5577 in Colorado, or 800–327–5080 nationwide.

Mountain-climbing courses and guide services are available from *Beyond the Abyss,* 303–728–3705, June through September; and *Fantasy Ridge Mountain Guides* for winter ice climbing, 303–728–3456; and Antoine Savelli, 728–3705.

In summer, chairlift rides are available from town, ascending 10,500 ft. up the mountain; start mid-June; $4 adults, $2 children, 11 A.M.–4 P.M. Thursday through Sunday. Barbecue on top of mountain.

Bear Creek Horses southwest of Telluride, 303–728–4431, offers chuck-wagon dinners, hayrides, trail rides, and pack trips (reserve two weeks in advance for pack trips). *D&E Outfitters* in town offer sleigh rides, hayrides, cookouts, sightseeing trail rides, 303–728–3200.

Guided **fishing** trips are available from *Olympic Sports,* 728–4477, and *Far Flung Adventures,* 728–3895; kids can fish in the town pond, no charge.

Rent **mountain bikes** (those klunkers with the fat tires) from *Telluride Sports* (728–3501) to pedal on old mining roads throughout the San Juans, including Bridal Veil Falls. Four-wheeling is available over Imogene, Ophir, or Black Bear passes, the mining ruins of Tomboy and the Dallas Divide.

Canard **Jeep Tours** (728–3664) and *San Juan Jeep Tours* (728–3208) take summer guests to Ouray, over Ophir, Imogene, and Black Bear passes.

Telluride Academy (666 W. Colorado Ave.; 728–4628) conducts one- and two-week classes on outdoor sports, mushrooming, French, local history, and other eclectic subjects.

Hot-air balloons lift off every morning; call the Chamber Resort for the company names, 728–3041. From $75–$150.

The 18-hole, championship *Mountain Village Golf Course* is situated at 9,100–9,400 ft. and opens the summer of 1989.

Raft the San Miguel or Dolores rivers, or learn to **kayak** with *Far Flung Adventures* (728–3895).

HISTORIC SITES AND LANDMARKS. Telluride was incorporated as the town of Columbia in 1878. It later changed its name to Telluride, growing into a rough and wild mining camp. There is still ample evidence of its tough past. This is where Butch Cassidy robbed his first bank. The ski area opened in 1972 and the first music festivals took place in the summer of 1973. Drive south on CO 145 about 17 miles to Lizard Head Pass—with a little imagination you'll see how it got its name. The pass itself is a huge mountain meadow surrounded by rugged peaks; from here there are trails to the mountain, but you should be in good physical condition; the peak of Lizard Head is for mountain climbers.

For the brave or those with four-wheel drive, head south from town for a few miles and turn at the sign for Ophir. Named after King Solomon's Mines, it is now a ghost town. Lurching over Ophir Pass makes you wonder what drove those early miners to choose life in remote mountain locations. You'll end up near Red Mountain, west of Silverton.

East of town, at the end of the San Miguel River Canyon, is *Bridal Veil Falls* cascading 300 feet down the mountain. Part of the way up is the old power plant that used to generate electricity for the miners; it's a tough hike or four-wheel drive to the plant.

Each September the town puts on a tour of Telluride's finest historic and contemporary homes; for information call 728–3041. A self-guided tour of the restored Victorian buildings is possible just by reading some of the historical plaques. Check out the *Galloping Goose* next to the Court House. It is a motor car that ran on rails to carry passengers, freight, and mail with a one-man crew, designed to help save the faltering Rio Grande Southern Railroad in the 1930s and 40s.

Visit the nearby Orvis Hot Springs, off Hwy. 550, 1.3 miles south of Ridgeway, nine miles north of Ouray. Hot mineral ponds $5 per person, $30 per night for rooms; 626–5324.

CHILDREN'S ACTIVITIES. Children 2 months to 12 years old are cared for at the *Meadows Childcare Center* and the *Mountain Village Nursery* during ski season. The program includes organized play, story reading, learning concepts; $28 a day with lunch; $6 an hour; call 728–4424. For 5–12 year olds ready to ski, the rates are $42 a day, $52 with rentals. Check Snowcare for 3–4-year-olds ready to ski.

Lift tickets for children 4 and under are free with the purchase of an adult ticket; tickets for kids 5–12 are $13 (1988 adult lift ticket prices were $28 a day).

Underdawg for Kids, 121 W. Colorado Ave., is an ice cream parlor with video games, and other kid entertainment. The *Teen Center,* at Columbia and Townsend, has special programs once a week throughout the year and is open to visitors.

SHOPPING. For books and maps check out *Between the Covers,* 224 W. Colorado Ave., and the *City Hall,* 135 W. Columbia—especially for town maps and information. Most sports stores carry topographical maps. *Zia Sun,* 210 W. Colorado, carries jewelry, stuffed animals and fine gifts; *Les Ware's Studio & Gallery,* 208 S. Fir, features wood carvings and watercolors. *Breuer's,* 213 W. Colorado, carries Indonesian and South American artifacts, imported clothing, and textiles; for clothing, head for *Trapping and Toggery,* 109 E. Colorado, *Examiner,* 232 W. Colorado, or *Ritzy Teeze,* 136 E. Colorado. Sporting goods and apparel are sold in *Olympic Rentals,* 105 S. Davis, *Telluride Sports,* 226 W. Colorado; *Paragon Sports,* 119 W. Colorado; *Summit,* 307 W. Pacific; antiques and "new used" in *Old Claims Trading Post;* the *free box* on S. Pine between Columbia and Colorado always has used clothing, ski equipment, books, and household appliances, free for the giving or taking. Art galleries are numerous. *Rose's Victorian Market* (one of two grocery stores in town) is a "boutique" market, featuring foods packaged by the store's owner, and gourmet items not usually found in a small, remote town; 666 W. Colorado at the edge of town.

DINING OUT. At the mountain: *Cassidy's* at the Coonskin Lift is good for lunch and après-ski. The *Plunge Restaurant* at the top of Lift 9 is a cozy little place featuring pizza and beer. For a leisurely and delicious lunch, go to the *Cactus Café* in the Mountain Village, just below Lifts 3 and 4. The *Prospector Restaurant* at the base of Lift 1 is a full-service cafeteria and bar with a large outdoor deck and tent.

In town there is a good choice of eateries. *Expensive* restaurants have entrées ranging $15–$19; *Moderate,* $9–$14; *Inexpensive,* under $8. Most accept credit cards, and reservations should be made at the better restaurants during high season.

Expensive

Julian's. In the New Sheridan Hotel, 231 W. Colorado; 728–3839. *Gourmet Magazine* has called it one of the finest resort restaurants; features northern Italian cuisine, breakfast, lunch, and dinner; credit cards, closed Tuesdays.

La Marmotte. 150 W. San Juan; 728–6232. An authentic brick-and-wood French restaurant, featuring fresh fish, veal, and Raclette.

Silverglade. 115 W. Colorado, 728–4943. Specializes in mesquite-broiled fresh fish, quail, shrimp—California style; the garlic bread comes with hunks of garlic cloves; credit cards.

Moderate

Excelsior Café. 200 W. Colorado; 728–4250. Marvelous upscale breakfasts and lunches; soups, fondues, espresso, fine wine by the glass.

Floradora Saloon. 103 W. Colorado; 728–3888. Extensive lunch and dinner menus featuring charbroiled hamburgers and salad bar; open late, credit cards.

Pandora's Box. 101 E. Colorado; 728–5137. Good variety for lunch and dinner with enormous salad and soup bar; credit cards.

Sofio's Mexican Café. 110 E. Colorado; 728–4882. Has an extensive menu for breakfast and dinner, excellent food, and margaritas; credit cards.

T-Ride Country Club. 333 W. Colorado; 728–6344. This is a cook-your-own-over-a-charcoal-fire affair, featuring steaks, chicken, and shish kabob; children's plate.

Inexpensive

Baked in Telluride. 127 S. Fir; 728–4705. Sandwiches, salads, fresh baked pastries.

The Deli Downstairs & Mini-Mart. 217 W. Colorado; 728–4004. Has deli sandwiches, groceries, sundries; open until midnight daily.

The Underdawg. 121 W. Colorado, 728–4790. Features hot dogs and burgers; a video game center for kids; open until 11 P.M.

NIGHTLIFE. While visitors may not be overwhelmed by the choices, there are enough evening activities to keep most busy during their stay. *Fly Me to the Moon Saloon,* 132 E. Colorado Ave., features lively live music, a dance floor, pool, and munchies, 3 P.M.–2 A.M. The historic *Sheridan Bar,* 225 W. Colorado Ave., has scheduled live entertainment, also until 2 A.M. *Leimgruber's Bierstube and Restaurant,* 573 W. Pacific, is *the* place to be after skiing. Twenty kinds of beer, wine and spirits, and the noisiest ski crowd this side of The Plunge. Good German sausage plate for lunch, too. *O'Bannon's Irish Pub,* 121 S. Fir, is noisy, fun, lots of food and *grog. Roma Bar & Café,* 133 E. Colorado, has pizza and entertainment.

The *Nugget Theatre* puts on melodramas, plays, and movies; there's also a movie theater in *Sheridan Opera House,* 110 N. Oak. *Mountain Splendor,* 200 E. Colorado, puts on a multimedia presentation of the San Juan Mountain wildlife, birds, and flowers.

HINTS FOR THE HANDICAPPED. Skiing is free, contact the Ski School for details, 303–728–3856.

PURGATORY

Durango, in southwest Colorado, has long been a summer tourist destination. Purgatory Ski Area came to life in 1965, and the winter season has increased in importance since then. This area will come of age in the mid-1990s with the completion of the master development plan.

Durango was named after Durango in Mexico; its past is rich with Spanish history. Spanish prospectors came through in 1765 and 1776; at that time the river upon which Durango is located was already named Rio de las Animas, River of Lost Souls. Durango was located by fiat of the Denver and Rio Grande Railroad in 1880, when the company decided to locate the railroad depot a few miles below the existing Animas City. By the end of that year the town already had 500 buildings and a population of about 3,000.

Today, Durango still takes its heritage from both the Spanish and the Native American, more than the North American, experience. It is surrounded by wilderness areas, close to the New Mexico border, yet it is a substantial town of over 16,000 permanent population, many of them ranchers, college faculty, artists, and small business owners. It is a Registered National Historical Landmark—not cutsey like Aspen or Breckenridge, not weather-beaten quaint like Crested Butte, but quite livable in a real-life way.

PRACTICAL INFORMATION FOR PURGATORY

HOW TO GET THERE. Purgatory is located in the San Juan National Forest, 340 miles southwest of Denver, 25 miles north of Durango.

By air. La Plata Airport, 20 miles south of Durango and 45 miles south of Purgatory, is the gateway to Purgatory. Direct flights are scheduled from Denver, Dallas/Ft. Worth, Houston, Albuquerque, Phoenix, and Tucson on *America West, Mesa Airlines,* and *United Express* and *Continental Express.* Common fare rates are available from Denver to Durango in conjunction with package tours; charter flights also go into La Plata. The *Air Shuttle* operates between the airport, Durango, and the ski area, $5 to Durango, $10 to Purgatory. Call 259–LIFT for schedule. Rental cars available, see below.

By bus. *Trailways* has regular service to Durango, 303–247–1581. *The Lift* regularly runs between Durango and Purgatory, $5 round-trip. Call 259–LIFT. Charters are available by contacting Purgatory/Durango Central Reservations, 800–525–0892 out of state, 800–358–3400 in Colorado.

By car. From Denver to Purgatory is a 340-mile drive via US 285, US 150, and US 550 in the southwest corner of the state. From Grand Junction it is 150 miles south on US 50 and US 550. Flagstaff, Arizona, is 319 miles to the south, Albuquerque is 212 miles via Highway 44 to US 550; Phoenix 456 miles. Durango, the major town in the region, is 25 miles south on US 550. Rental cars available at La Plata Airport: *Avis* (800–331–1212); *National* (800–328–4567).

ACCOMMODATIONS. At Purgatory, there are 700 pillows with up to 2,500 pillows planned by 1993. In Durango, there are over 10,000 pillows with prices for all pocketbooks. Midway between the ski area and town is a fine resort in its own right, **Tamarron.** Accommodations are deluxe, there are 13,000 square feet of conference facilities, a separate small ski area, fine golf course, summer and winter activities, two gourmet restaurants. Call 800–525–5420 or in Colorado 303–247–8801. Address is Box 3131, Durango, CO 81301. There is a free shuttle to Purgatory and into Durango. Two-bedroom units cost around $208 a night.

Durango Reservations, Box 3418, Durango, CO 81301, 800–525–9090 or in Colorado 303–259–4142, represents Best Western and condominium properties in town and at the ski area. Purgatory/Durango Central Reservations, 534 Main Ave., Durango, CO 81301, 800–358–3400 in Colorado and 800–525–0892 out of state, represents the majority of lodging both in town and at Purgatory. Following is a sample of what's available.

Expensive

Cascade Village. 50827 Highway 550 North; 303–259–3500. A mile north of Purgatory. $165 a night for a two-bedroom unit.

Eolus Condominiums. Box 666, Durango; 303–247–9000. Slopeside lodging. A two-bedroom condo goes for $220 a night. Summer rates are 50 percent less.

Village Center. Box 666, Durango; 303–247–9000. Slope-side two-bedrooms $220 a night; summer rates 50 percent less.

Moderate

Angel Haus. Box 666, Durango, at base of Purgatory Mt.; 303–247–8090. Reasonably priced condominiums: one-bedroom $125; two-bedroom $165.

Best Western General Palmer House. 567 Main St., Durango; 303–247–4747. Historic 19th-century house with Victorian decor. Restaurant and bar. $45–55 a night for a double.

Best Western Lodge at Purgatory. 49617 U.S. Highway 550, Durango; 303–247–9669. Western-style lodge; restaurant and lounge. Double rooms $80 a night.

Purgatory Townhouse. 303–247–0026. Studio condos with two sofa-beds for $65 a night.

Strater Hotel. 699 Main Ave.; 303–247–4431. Built in 1882 and authentically restored, this is an outstanding facility. Double room for $55–$60 a night.

Inexpensive

Alpine North Motel. 3515 Main Ave.; 303–247–4042. $26 a night.

Durango Hostel. 543 E. Second Ave.; 303–247–9905. One block from the train depot, with 40 dorm rooms and cooking facilities.

Pino Nuche Pu Ra Sa. Box 347, Ignacio; 303–563–4531. 25 minutes south of Durango on CO 172. This is a motel and visitor center with restaurant, pool, and meeting rooms run by the Southern Ute Tribe. The name means "gathering place of the Pine River Indians."

CAMPING. No reservations, but call district ranger 259–0195 for information. Turn right off US 550 onto Cascade Highway to *Purgatory Campground.* Drinking water, 14-day limit, fee; U.S. Forest Service. *Junction Creek* is six miles north of Durango on Junction Creek Road; U.S. Forest Service, restrooms, water, 14-day limit; fee. *Hermosa Meadows Camper Park* is ten miles north of town; full trailer and tent facilities, laundry, groceries, propane; commercial and fee-charging. *Cottonwood Camper Park,* within walking distance of town to the west, is also commercial; showers, restrooms, tent spaces, daily or weekly fees. *Jaycee Memorial Campground* is in town, west of Las Animas River. *Vallecito Lake* is 20 miles northeast of Durango via Highway 160 to Bayfield; drinking water, 14-day limit, fee, U.S. Forest Service-operated.

HOW TO GET AROUND. Major car rental agencies are at the Durango airport (see "How to Get There," above) and many visitors opt for the convenience of their own vehicle. A shuttle service operates regularly to and from Purgatory and within Durango on all major arteries. Tamarron runs a regular, free shuttle between the resort, Purgatory, and town.

TOURIST INFORMATION. The Purgatory/Durango Central Reservations system is set up as a one-stop shopping call. PDCR can book the narrow-gauge railroad, reserve a car, room, ski rentals, arrange lift tickets and ski lessons, and give information on the Purgatory/Durango area and what discounts are available. Call outside of Colorado 800–525–0892; in state 800–358–3400. Listen to KDGO 1240 AM, KDUR 91.9 FM, KIUP 930 AM, KRSJ 100.5 FM for local weather, news, and activities. The *Durango Herald* is a good daily newspaper for regional news.

For road and weather conditions call 303–247–0312; snow conditions 800–525–0892, locally 247–9000. The *Durango Chamber of Commerce* has current information and literature; 2301 Main Street by the locomotive, 303–247–0312.

Purgatory's address and phone are: Box 666, Durango, CO 81302; 303–247–9000.

SEASONAL EVENTS. *Snowdown Winter Carnival* is celebrated late **January** through early **February;** mid-**March** sees *Wolverton Days* cross-country championships, and *Sunburst Festival* welcomes spring skiing. **Memorial Day** generally opens the summer season at Purgatory; while ski resorts farther north are still in operation (see Keystone) this "sun-belt" resort gets an early start on summer. **July** through **September** there is a regular *Twilight Concert Series* with classical and jazz at Purgatory's mountain restaurants. **Labor Day** weekend always sees special tournaments and competitions at the mountain; *Colorfest* is scheduled to coincide with the changing of the Aspen trees in the high country, usually at the end of September or the first of **October**—cultural and culinary events are part of the celebration.

Southwest Colorado has excellent *deer* and *elk hunting,* and the resorts and hotels cater to that crowd in **late fall.**

PARTICIPANT SPORTS. The Durango Chamber of Commerce can give current listings of all outfitters and activities. In winter, *Purgatory Ski Resort's* nine chairlifts take **skiers** up to 10,822 feet and 630 acres of skiing terrain. The mountain is known for its intermediate terrain, but The Legends has 150 acres of extreme expert terrain, highlighted by glade skiing and over 2,000-feet elevation. The view alone of the La Plata Mountains, Wilson Mountain Range, Lizardhead, and Grizzly is worth the trip.

For beginners, Columbine Station is it. Seven acres strictly set aside as a beginner area has its own chairlift. As encouragement, Purgatory gives a free, half-day beginner lesson to anyone who purchases a day or multiday lift ticket. For information on lessons and rentals call the central reservations number. (See "Tourist Information," above.)

Purgatory Ski Touring Center maintains nine miles of trails across US 550 from the entrance to Purgatory Village. Lessons, rentals, telemark clinics are available; a trail ticket is $3. Contact directors Tony Forrest and Ken Emrick, 247–9000.

For real excitement, book a day with *Telluride Helitrax* and head for 500 square miles of untracked powder in the San Juans; intermediate to expert skiing. Day heli-skiing begins at $60 for one run or $210 for all day (four runs). Group rates available, prices subject to change. Gourmet lunch and beverages included in the full day. Extended heli-ski packages available and scenic flights for nonskiers. Contact Purgatory Ski Area at 303–247–9000, ext. 140. *Rent-a-Snowmobile* does just that in winter, *Rent-a-Jeep* in summer; 3600 Main Avenue, Durango; 259–1252. *Black Thunder* also rents **snowmobiles,** contact Purgatory or Cascade Village for reservations. **Sno-Cat tours,** nearby **ice fishing, ice skating, tennis, tubing, sleigh rides** can be arranged. Call the Chamber of Commerce 247–8900.

The San Juan National Forest, nearby Weminuche Wilderness, and Rio Grande National Forest are popular and beautiful **hiking** and **backpacking** areas in summer. Stop in at the office of the supervisor for the national forest in the GSA Building, 710 Camino Del Rio, Durango, to buy maps of trails.

Oar and **paddle** trips on the Animas, Dolores, and San Juan rivers and Rio Grande can be booked through *Colorado River Tours,* 339 E. 13th St., Durango 81301; 303–259–0708 (April–September) or *Wild Goose River Tours,* 8 Pine Tree Lane, Durango; 303–247–0224. **Fishing** is good on Vallecito, Lemon, Navajo, and Piedra lakes and in streams in the wilderness areas. Check local sporting goods shops for details and licenses.

The Court Club in Durango, is open year-round with racquetball, handball, basketball, weight training, steam, sauna, pool, restaurant, and juice bar; open to the public; 1600 Florida St., 259–2579.

HISTORIC SITES AND OTHER SITES OF INTEREST. Drive the *Million Dollar Highway* north from Purgatory over Red Mountain Pass to Ouray. Named in 1922 when it cost over a million dollars to upgrade three miles from wagon to automobile use. Tricky driving in winter.

At Purgatory in summer take the *scenic chairlift ride* at lift 4 for nature hikes; walk or ride down, no charge. The *Alpine Slide* runs under lift 4, fun for kids of all ages, $3.50 a ride.

Ride the *Durango and Silverton Narrow Gauge Railroad* between Durango and Silverton. In operation since 1882, this is the railroad Durango was built for. Originally used to haul silver out of the mines, it's strictly for the tourists today; advance reservations needed. The station is at 479 Main Avenue, Durango, CO 81301; 247–2733.

The largest collection of cliff-dwelling ruins in the world are of the Anasazi in *Mesa Verde National Park,* 45 miles west of Durango—definitely worth the trip. Camping, lodging, restaurants, and tours at the site; some trails but backcountry use is restricted; only the Spruce Tree House is open in winter—a dramatic and quiet time to visit Mesa Verde. See the chapter on "Southern Colorado."

In Durango, the Animas School Museum is a collection of the town's past; the Great Western Museum has an extensive collection of Durango antiques and Indian artifacts. Fort Lewis College has an excellent Center of Southwest Studies with Native American artifacts; by appointment only. The central business district adjacent to the train depot contains the town's oldest buildings and Victorian homes.

CHILDREN'S ACTIVITIES. Call 247–9000 at Purgatory Ski Resort for information. The *Teddy Bear Camp* operates during ski season for children 2 months to 6 years of age. Day-care is $23 a day, $13 a half-day, lunch included. The ski school is $33 a day, $16 a half-day with lunch and ski lessons; skis and boots are available with the program; children should be provided with adequate warm clothes, goggles, and sunscreen.

Older children go into ski school, $27 a day with lunch and lift ticket; lift tickets (12 and under) are $8 a day (adult tickets are $22), and a season's pass for children 12 and under is only $25.

SHOPPING. The $9 million *Village Center* is the central point of the mountain base. Sports clothes and equipment are found in *Purgatory Sports* and *Gold Medal Sports;* the *High Country Emporium* is for gifts and spirits. There's also a chocolate factory, two photography shops, and an art gallery, ski storage and rental, information, and repair are all found here, plus two restaurants. In Kendall Mountain Condominiums, you'll

find a T-shirt shop, leather goods, Native Indian retail outlet, and a cookies and ice cream shop.

For a wide choice of shopping, head for Durango. You can find everything from ranchers' coveralls (the *Stockman,* 110 E. Fifth, or *Graden's Department store,* 777 Main Ave.), to imported clothing at *Stuart's,* 713 Main Ave., as well as groceries, hardware, camping supplies. The *Main Mall,* 835 Main Ave., often enclosed shopping in small, imaginative stores. *Town Plaza Shopping Center,* has large department stores and other service outlets.

DINING OUT. With over 30 restaurants in Durango and a half-dozen at the mountain, plus the restaurants at Tamarron, one need not go hungry. **At the mountain,** *Farquarht's North* in the Village serves lunch, dinner, and drinks at moderate prices. *Powderhouse* is midmountain next to *Pitchfork* with outdoor barbecues and home-style favorites; *Dante's* is midmountain by Chair 5, with cafeteria, sit-down dining, a greenhouse, and *Dante's Den and Lounge. Sterling's* is in the Village Center, geared toward family-style cafeteria, with outdoor sun deck and lounge. *Doe's Deli* and the *New York Bakery* are also in the Center.

Expensive restaurants have entrées running $15–$25; *Moderate,* $9–$15; *Inexpensive,* below $9. All restaurants listed take Visa and MasterCard unless otherwise noted.

The Ore House. *Expensive.* 147 Sixth; 247–5707. One of the oldest restaurants in town, rustic and casual with extensive wine selection. No reservations.

The Palace. *Expensive.* 1 Depot Pl; 247–2018. Victorian decor with a wide variety of entrées; mesquite grill. Live music weekdays 4–7 P.M.

Sweeney's Grubstake. *Expensive to Moderate.* 1644 County Rd. 203, at the north end of town; 247–5236. Serves steaks, seafood, and huge salads.

The Atrium. *Moderate.* 21382 Highway 160; 385–4834. Basic American fare.

Francisco's. *Moderate.* 619 Main Ave.; 247–4098. For Mexican food, steaks, and seafood. Children's menu available.

Katie O'Brien's. *Moderate.* 152 E. Sixth; 247–9083. Steak and seafood in a Victorian atmosphere.

Lost Pelican. *Moderate.* 658 Main Ave.; 247–8502. Fresh seafood, salad bar, and beef dishes; with happy hour in *The Nest.*

New York Bakery. *Moderate.* 750 Main Ave.; 259–1007. Also in Village Center at Purgatory Ski Resort. Although known for their scrumptious desserts, they have a full menu as well; good for fast breakfasts.

Father Murphy's. *Inexpensive.* 636 Main Ave.; 259–0334. Pub atmosphere, serving pasta, burgers, and soups. No credit cards.

Griego's Taco House. *Inexpensive.* 1400 E. Second Ave.; 247–3127. No credit cards.

Hoop's Hickory House. *Inexpensive.* 3690 Main Ave.; 259–5666. Pit-smoke barbecue and burgers.

Mr. Rosewater. *Inexpensive.* 552 Main Ave.; 247–8788. A deli with sandwiches, soups, imported wine, and beer; breakfast and lunch; catering available.

Olde Tymer's. *Inexpensive.* 1000 Main; 259–2990. Casual surroundings, with menu of burgers, soups, pasta.

Pronto's. *Inexpensive.* 160 E. Sixth; 247–1510. For Italian food.

NIGHTLIFE. Yes, there is life after skiing, at least if you go into Durango. *The Sundowner,* 3777 Main Ave., features country and western music, both après-ski and after dining; popular with the older crowd. The *Diamond Belle Saloon,* 699 Main Ave., an historic Durango landmark, is right out of the Old West—those swinging barroom doors have been swinging for over a century; elegant Victorian atmosphere, ragtime piano. *The Old Muldoon,* 561 Main Ave., is for popcorn and to meet singles. *Sundance,* 602 Second Ave., features country and western dancing, live music, and a Western flavor—you'll feel comfortable in your cowboy hat and boots. *Sixth Street Parlour,* 110 W. Sixth, has contemporary live sounds. Another gathering spot with no planned entertainment is the *Ore House,* 147 Sixth.

There are even nighttime activities that do not have to do with drinking. Bowl at *Durango Bowl,* 760 Camino del Rio, 259–1012, see a movie, or attend the two live theaters—*Abbey,* year-round (128 E Sixth; 247–2626), and *Diamond Circle* in summer (699 Main Ave.; 247–4431).

HINTS FOR THE HANDICAPPED. Purgatory Ski Area has a new and active program for handicapped skiers. Equipment, instruction, and learn-to-ski scholarships are available by contacting the Durango/Purgatory Handicapped Sports Association, Cathy Craig, Box 666, Durango, CO 81302, 303–247–9000. Professional instruction for virtually any handicap.

OTHER RESORTS

Here are a few ski/summer resorts which are coming into their own as destination areas.

Monarch Ski Resort

Monarch lies in south central Colorado, 157 miles southwest of Denver via US Hwy. 185 and US Hwy. 50, 120 miles west of Colorado Springs via CO. Hwy. 115 and US Hwy. 50 just two miles from the summit of Monarch Pass. The annual snowfall of over 350 inches provides skiing in the worst of years. Day skiers from the Colorado Springs area and groups from the Midwest make up most of the clientele. Monarch is only an hour and a half east of Crested Butte Resort, and it is possible to ski both areas if you have your own transportation. Gunnison Airport (see "Crested Butte") is 47 miles away and, with prior notice, there is a pickup service.

Four chairlifts serve 650 acres with an incredible amount of varied terrain, from groomed runs to ungroomed bump and tree skiing. Expansion plans would more than triple the existing ski boundaries. From Skywalker Run, on top of the Continental Divide, you can see five mountain ranges and four wilderness areas. In the natural amphitheater, you can always face the sun. A "ski count-down" card gives skiers $1 off the lift ticket price each time, making the 19th day free.

A day lodge with cafeteria and dining room, ski school, ski and rental shop, day-care center and children's ski school, Nordic ski center with groomed ski tracks and NASTAR races round out the resort facilities. Contact Monarch Ski Resort, US Hwy. 50, Garfield, CO 81227; 303–539–3573 or 800–332–3668; outside Colorado call 800–525–9390.

Three miles down the pass is the Monarch Lodge, set alongside the south fork of the Arkansas River in the Sawatch mountain range. The lodge has a bar, restaurant, pool, sauna, tennis and racquetball courts, gift shop, and the Garfield post office. It is simple and basic—the way skiing was in the "old days." Stay at the lodge and ski free. Contact Monarch Lodge, 303–539–2581, 800–332–3668, or, outside Colorado, 800–525–9390. The lodge is under the same ownership as the ski area.

Hot springs, restaurants, and other accommodations are a half-hour away in the nearby towns of Salida and Poncha Springs.

In summer there is rafting, hiking, horseback riding, fishing, jeep tours, and tennis.

Silver Creek

The wide-open pasture land of Middle Park is only 80 miles northwest of Denver on Hwy. 40 (just beyond Winter Park), but because the Continental Divide lies between, this area has remained remote and less developed than other more accessible Colorado valleys. Silver Creek is in the sunny Fraser Valley, the ragged edge of the Divide looming to the east. Cattle, buffalo, and elk still graze in the lush mountain pastures surrounding the resort.

Silver Creek Ski area offers skiers five lifts and over 200 acres of mostly beginner and intermediate terrain. The Silver Creek Nordic Center has 25K of groomed cross-country trails. Sterling Center, at the base of the ski area, provides skier services, a restaurant, lounge, rentals, ski school, and child care. Silver Creek is one of the few western ski areas built on private land. Other winter activities are ice skating and sleigh rides.

In summer the activity list includes tennis, golf, horseback riding, white-water rafting, mountain biking, hiking, fishing, sailing; Rocky Mountain National Park is 20 miles to the north.

The 342-room Inn at Silver Creek has three restaurants, two nightclubs, and several shops, plus the 21,000-sq.-ft. Convention Center. The Silver Creek Athletic Club is available year-round with heated indoor-outdoor pool, whirlpools, sauna, racquetball courts, weight room, and tanning salon. Mountainside Condominiums (800–223–7677 or, in Colorado, 800–331–9788) offer five- and seven-night packages, beginning at $40 per person per day for one bedroom with spa and lift tickets.

For more information, call Silver Creek Resort, Box 4001, Silver Creek, CO 80446; call 800–526–0590 or 303–887–2131.

Ski Sunlight

Ski Sunlight is a sleeper, located next to Glenwood Springs between two of Colorado's most famous resorts—Aspen and Vail. Its niche is in providing an affordable family vacation and group facilities. Glenwood Springs boasts the world's largest hot springs pool and you can buy "Ski & Swim" packages starting at $34 per person.

Thirty runs are on 300 acres of terrain with surprising variety; lift tickets are reasonably priced, while kids under 5 ski free with an adult. At slopeside are 75 rooms in two inns while nearby Glenwood Springs offers some 1,300 rooms. Campgrounds offer hookups. Other activities include bowling, ice skating, horseback riding, sleigh rides, snowmobiling, sledding, and tubing. Great hiking in summer. Sunlight has 24K of cross-country trails; $3 a day for adults, $2 for children under 12 and Golden Agers over 60.

Glenwood Springs is served by *Amtrak* (see Aspen or Snowmass sections above).

NORTHWEST COLORADO

by
CURTIS W. CASEWIT

There is still more to Colorado than the resorts and the urban areas. This chapter covers the parks and forests and towns (other than the resort towns described in the preceding chapter) that make up the northwest section of the state: Rocky Mountain National Park; farther west, the Roaring Fork Valley (with the historical gold town of Leadville and Glenwood Springs, noted for its hot mineral baths); still farther west, the Western Slope (with the little town of Rifle and the Colorado National Monument at the southwest edge of Grand Junction); and finally the northwest corner with the Dinosaur National Monument and one of the world's largest collections of fossilized dinosaur bones.

EXPLORING NORTHWEST COLORADO

Perhaps the most memorable area in which to begin your exploration of the northwestern part of the state is the Rocky Mountain National Park and the charming towns that surround it: Estes Park, Granby, and Grand Lake.

The town of Estes Park has long been one of Colorado's most important summer tourist centers, complete with an outstanding dinner theater at the historic Stanley Hotel. Elkhorn Avenue boasts a great number of interesting shops, art galleries, and artisans. At night, you can dine at every type of restaurant; accommodations include cabins, motels, inns, bed-and-breakfasts, and the superbly restored Stanley Hotel.

Although the mountain village has a permanent population of just a few thousand, each summer it hosts more than two million visitors thanks to the surrounding mountains and the famous Rocky Mountain National Park.

Rocky Mountain National Park

The resort town of Estes Park is "base camp" for each year's 2½ million-plus visitors to the Rocky Mountain National Park. The National Park's 266,943 acres (or 414 square miles) straddle the Continental Divide.

Both entrances to the park, Estes Park and Grand Lake, have complete visitors' centers. Here you can get detailed maps and information on outings, activities, backcountry permits, camping, and a free movie about the park. (Backpackers must register here.) Nature walks and talks by park rangers offer personalized educational and wildlife experiences for the whole family. The Rocky Mountain National Park programs begin in early June and extend into September. There are also some self-guided trails.

To acquaint yourself with the area, take a day or more to drive its very safe and well-maintained roads. The main route is via Trail Ridge Road, which connects Estes Park with Grand Lake and Grandby. The famous highway rises and descends, curves and straightens, or turns into serpentines for many hours and miles. It is the longest continuous such paved mountain road in North America. At several points, the route reaches and stays at 12,000-foot levels. Yet the driving is quite manageable for flat-landers.

Trail Ridge is open only after it has been cleared of snow, usually from June through Labor Day. You need no special tires or mountain driving expertise. Caution is necessary for the 11 miles you're above timberline, in a world of dwarfed, wind-carved trees and alpine tundra jeweled with miniature flowers. American elk and mule deer sometimes graze in the upper meadows. From the lookout at the highway's topmost point, at 12,183 feet, the vistas weave in all directions. Frozen lakes, formed by the slow sculpturing of the ice, gleam at the foot of glacial moraines. From near the summit you can see Iceberg Lake with its ever-present glacial surface. Dress warmly for this drive.

Visit the Alpine Visitor Center, just beyond Fall River Pass. The exhibits will help you understand some of the things you have seen along the way. The entire highway is, in fact, lined with unforgettable sights: Jackstraw Mountain, where huge trees burned in an 1872 forest fire still lie like bleached bones; the Never Summer Mountains with their eternal snows; and Moraine Park, where an ancient glacier began to form the area. Most park entrances have booths that rent cassettes and cassette players to give you an expertly self-guided tour of the entire area.

Another route through the park is the original Fall River Road, built in 1920. Because of the steep grades and many switchbacks, this road is not open to trailers and motorized vans.

If you have an extra hour, you may also wish to explore Bear Lake Road, just nine miles long. It begins at the Moraine Park Visitors' Center, and ends at Bear Lake, one of the most spectacular sights at the park. The

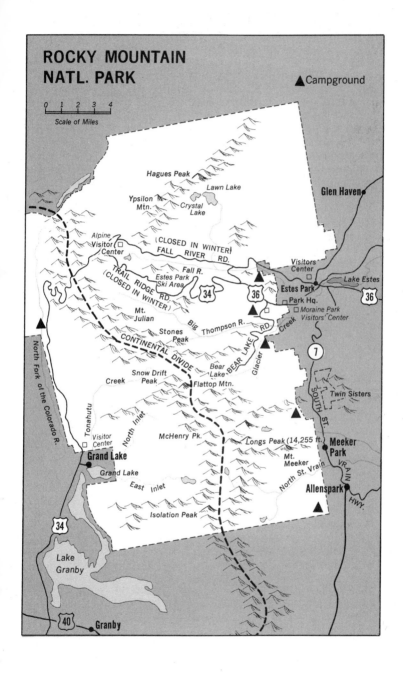

ROCKY MOUNTAIN
NATL. PARK

▲ Campground

0 1 2 3 4
Scale of Miles

Hagues Peak
Lawn Lake
Ypsilon Mtn.
Crystal Lake

Glen Haven

Alpine Visitor Center

(CLOSED IN WINTER)
FALL RIVER RD.

Visitors' Center

Fall R.
TRAIL RIDGE RD.
(CLOSED IN WINTER)
Estes Park Ski Area

34

36

Estes Park

Lake Estes

36

Park Hq.

Moraine Park Visitors' Center

Mt. Julian

Big Thompson R.

Stones Peak

CONTINENTAL DIVIDE

Snow Drift Peak

Creek

Bear Lake

BEAR LAKE RD.

Glacier Creek

Flattop Mtn.

7

SOUTH ST.

Twin Sisters

North Fork of the Colorado R.

Tonahutu

Visitor Center

North Inlet

McHenry Pk.

Grand Lake

Grand Lake

East Inlet

Isolation Peak

Longs Peak (14,255 ft.)

Mt. Meeker

North St. Vrain

Meeker Park

Allenspark

ST. VRAIN HWY.

34

Lake Granby

40 Granby

lake area offers a panorama of glaciers, mountain peaks, forests, and streams. Above Bear Lake lie several other beautiful lakes. Hiking trails connect you with Dream Lake.

A note on driving in the park: speed limits and traffic laws are enforced.

This national park is a mecca for fishing enthusiasts. Forty-four lakes and innumerable streams hold masses of German brown, brook, rainbow, and cutthroat trout. The fish may not be particularly big, but there will be plenty. (You need a Colorado license. Use of live bait is prohibited except under certain special conditions. Review special fishing regulations at park headquarters or at the nearest ranger station.)

Since hunting is forbidden here, all forms of wildlife abound. Herds of elk and deer browse the high plains and slopes near the top of Trail Ridge Road during summer. Above the treeline in the tundra area, you see the yellowbelly marmot and the tiny Pika. Beavers are easy to observe.

Horseback riders flock to the National Park Village Stables, on Hwy. 34 at the park entrance, and Hi Country Stables, in the park at Glacier Creek. Riding is restricted to certain trails within the park to protect the environment.

Below 9,000 feet or so you wander among forests of Englemann spruce, subalpine fir, and limber pine.

Granby, Grand Lake, Loveland

It is 62 curvy miles from Estes Park to the town of Granby, elevation 8,369 feet above sea level, on the western side of the divide. Allow yourself three hours for a leisurely drive along Trail Ridge Road, more if you can afford it. Three sizable lakes—Grand Lake, Shadow Mountain, and Granby Reservoir—make the Granby area a recreation center. The Colorado River and its tributaries provide trout fishing. The lakes have been stocked with kokanee salmon, among other species, and they provide fair angling as well as a unique sport—snagging with treble hooks—during the early winter spawning season. Since the kokanee die anyway after they spawn, snagging is permitted to avoid wasting a food resource. Granby is also in the center of the Middle Park area, noted for its dude and cattle ranches and lumbering.

The sleepy village of Grand Lake is a popular area for summer homes. The namesake lake, Colorado's largest natural body of water, and nearby Shadow Mountain Recreation Area have the nation's highest—two miles above sea level—chartered yacht club. Each summer, the group sponsors regattas and other boating events. In winter, the community of Grand Lake attracts snowmobilers.

Leave the Estes Park area east on US 34 through Big Thompson Canyon. The 20 mile drive is among the most scenic mountain passages in the state, passing craggy rock cliffs as it parallels the Big Thompson River.

Loveland on the flat land east of the canyon's mouth, is named for the man who built a railroad through the canyon in 1877. The town is known for its Cloverleaf Dog Track (spring and summers only) and for its Post Office; the latter remails thousands of Valentine greetings with a special Loveland "Sweetheart City" postmark.

The Roaring Fork Valley

The town of Leadville remains a historical center of this central Rockies area. The community of 4,000 people owes its existence to a gold boom in the 1860s and 1870s. By 1880, Leadville counted 30,000 citizens and became "the richest and roughest town in the world." English poet Oscar Wilde visited Leadville on his 1882 American tour. "I read the miners passages from the *Autobiography of Benvenuto Cellini,*" Wilde recalled, "and they seemed much delighted. I was reproved by my hearers for not having brought him with me. I explained that he had been dead for some little time, which elicited the inquiry, 'Who shot him?' "

The story of Leadville is largely the story of Horace Tabor. He came to the gold fields as a shopkeeper and put up a $17 grubstake for two miners in return for a one-third interest in whatever they found. The two men quickly stumbled onto the Matchless Mine, one of the richest silver veins ever uncovered. Tabor lavished his income from the mine—as much as $100,000 a month—on Leadville and Denver, financing opera houses, grand homes, and office buildings. He created Colorado's greatest scandal after he divorced his prim wife, Augusta, and married Elizabeth "Baby" Doe, a working-class woman 30 years his junior. Tabor was ruined when the value of silver plummeted in 1893. He died penniless in 1896. His last words to Baby Doe were "hang onto the Matchless." She did, in the vain hope it would again make millions. She died impoverished in Leadville during the cold winter of 1935. The complete Tabor story is told in the book, *Colorado Off The Beaten Path* (Globe-Pequot Press).

The Leadville tragedy is remembered in the American opera *The Ballad of Baby Doe,* which gave Beverly Sills one of her first roles with the New York Opera Company. The opera is a staple in the town of Central City.

The Matchless Cabin, one mile out of town on East Seventh Street, contains a small museum that tells the Tabor story to summer visitors. Tabor's original frame home at 116 East Fifth Street has been preserved. A small gift shop sells relics, including copies of old newspapers. Tabor's Opera House on Harrison Avenue has also been restored.

Leadville remains a magnet for geologists, the area having produced more than $700 million in silver, lead, and zinc. Molybdenum, a steelhardening element used for military and industrial hardware, is also found nearby.

The Leadville area boasts a nine-hole public golf course and many hiking trails. Several hundred lakes are close by, including Turquoise Lake, on the west edge of town, rimmed by bicycle trails.

Farther west is the renowned resort town of Aspen (see chapter on Ski and Summer Resorts).

Aspen was transformed from a near-dead mining town into a yearround cultural and recreational center by Walter Paepcke, chairman of the Container Corporation of America. In 1945, Paepcke and a group of associates "discovered" the hamlet and decided it was the perfect setting for "a community of peace . . . with opportunities for man's complete life. . . . "

West of Aspen on Colorado 82 along Maroon Creek, sightseers will discover the often-photographed Maroon Bells peaks. A glacial lake lies at the foot of the jagged, snow-topped mountain giants, the Bells. The area with its many hiking trails, is part of the Maroon Bells/Snowmass Wilderness.

Glenwood Springs

Colorado 82 continues from Aspen to Glenwood Springs, 40 miles northwest. Glenwood, as residents call it, sits in the White River National

Forest. The two million acres are renowned for all manner of open-air sport. The forest includes the Flat Tops Wilderness, a huge 117,800-acre plateau north of Glenwood Springs and Rifle, which extends into three counties. Allow a few hours for a hike to Hanging Lake and Spouting Rock, ten miles east of Glenwood Springs. The small lake was formed by erosion.

Glenwood Springs' location at the confluence of the Roaring Fork, Crystal, and Colorado rivers makes it one of the state's most popular river-rafting centers. Local guides are available for trips of all lengths and difficulties.

Glenwood's original attraction, the acclaimed hot springs mineral baths, are always open to the public. In the 1880s, silver baron Walter Devereaux decided to convert the springs used by the Utes to a health resort for the rich. He built the two-block-long swimming pool, intended for use only by guests of the posh adjacent Hotel Colorado. By the early 1900s, so many wealthy and famous people were coming to the spa that a rail siding was installed beside the hotel to hold their private railroad cars. Teddy Roosevelt made the hotel his summer White House in 1901 while bear hunting in the nearby hills.

The mineral baths and vapor caves are open all year, with trained personnel on hand. Locals say the water is a quick cure for visitors' aching muscles and stiff joints after days in the nearby wild.

From Glenwood, take Highways 82 and 133 to the year-round charmer of Redstone, with its historic Redstone Castle—a great place for cross-country skiing (free for everyone), stream fishing, dining, or weekend partying. The opulent manor is in the national register of historic places with three tours conducted daily.

The Western Slope

Western Colorado is known as "Standing Up Country." Towering pine forests are dwarfed by the large peaks.

In the rural town of Rifle, you enter the heart of energy country. The nearby oil, gas, and shale fields have attracted many workers.

The growth has yet to affect Rifle's popularity as a big game hunting center; each autumn, hordes of transient elk and the nation's largest herd of mule deer cross the region on their way to winter pastures.

South of here you will see Grand Mesa looming before you. Grand Mesa is one of the world's largest flat-top mountains with about 625 square miles of national forest. Deep canyons, waterfalls, abundant camp and picnic grounds, and more than 200 lakes and reservoirs give outdoor enthusiasts yet another place to linger.

Grand Junction

The 18,000-acre Colorado National Monument lies at the southwest edge of Grand Junction, the West Slope's commercial center. Follow the Rim Rock Drive, 2,000 feet above the Grand Valley.

The town of Grand Junction got its name from the Colorado and Gunnison rivers meeting here. Summer events range from horse shows and rodeos to drag racing and balloon rallies. Local points of interest include the downtown Museum of Western Colorado, which presents the region's geological and social history.

There are many tangible resources within a 250-mile radius of Grand Junction. Uranium, lead, zinc, and other minerals have been mined here for years. Grand Junction is also becoming a national energy center. The Book Cliff Mountains and Piceance Basin to the north hold some of the nation's recoverable shale oil—perhaps some three billion barrels, or enough to power the entire nation for almost a century. It will be many years before a significant amount of oil is produced from the rock, but pilot plants already function.

For a brief but interesting side trip, take US 50 southeast out of Grand Junction after making sure your gas tank is full. Nine miles up the highway is the tiny crossing called Whitewater. Turn right here onto State 141, and prepare to enter some of Colorado's wildest, loneliest canyon country, an area largely overlooked by most tourists. The highway, paved and well maintained, stretches through sagebrush flats and dry washes for 44 miles to Gateway, where it crosses the muddy, shallow Dolores River. For the next 37 miles to Uravan, the road borders first the Dolores, and then the San Miguel (pronounced San M'gill) rivers, leading past towering red sandstone cliffs polished by wind and sand into monolithic slabs, often into the shapes of ships and pyramids.

Back in 1881, gold-seekers found a soft yellow-orange ore near what is now Uravan. Its main use was for coloring pottery. In 1898, several tons of this ore were shipped to France, and Mme. Marie Curie used it in experiments that resulted in the extraction of radium. For the next 30 years, this region produced about half the world's radium supply. A mill was built at Uravan to process vanadium, a steel-hardener, from the same ores. During World War II, in the crash program to develop a nuclear bomb, the waste rock in the tailings piles at the Uravan mill was reprocessed to extract the suddenly precious uranium which had been thrown away. The mill, now operated by Union Carbide, extracts uranium from local mines, and vanadium has become just a by-product.

Nineteen miles past Uravan, take the right fork to State 141 for the 57 mile drive to Dove Creek. This apparent wasteland has a strange, lonely beauty of its own, but you'll be glad to reach civilization once more at Dove Creek, center of a prosperous pinto bean-growing area. The total distance from Grand Junction to Dove is 169 miles. Dove Creek was little more than a raw frontier town until farmers from the dust bowl in eastern Colorado came in to conquer the arid flats. Zane Grey, the author of Westerns, lived here for some years.

Northwest Corner

Dinosaur National Monument occupies Colorado's northwest corner. This area of about 325 square miles in Colorado and Utah contains one of the world's largest concentrations of fossilized dinosaur bones. The remains of brontosaurs and other species of prehistoric creatures have been removed from the shales and sandstones of an 80-acre tract within Dinosaur National Monument. Visitors may watch technicians expose and relief the bones of many kinds of dinosaurs and other prehistoric reptiles. There are now more than 2,000 fossilized bones on view as a permanent exhibit.

PRACTICAL INFORMATION
FOR NORTHWEST COLORADO

HOW TO GET THERE. (See also "How to Get There" in *Practical Information for Denver.*) **By air.** Grand Junction is the largest city in the northwest part of the state served by major airlines. *Continental Express* and *United Express* fly into Grand Junction and Aspen from Denver. *Continental Express, American,* and *Northwest* fly to Steamboat Springs. Leadville can be reached in most weather by private plane.

By bus. *Greyhound Trailways* services all of northwestern Colorado. In Denver, their phone number is 292–2291. Daily buses depart for many of the towns mentioned here, including year-round daily service to Estes Park.

By train. *Amtrak* serves Glenwood Springs and Grand Junction from Denver. You can also take the train to the little town of Fraser.

By car. Northwest Colorado is easily reached from Denver on good paved roads. Travel times may be longer in winter, when snow and ice sometimes accumulate on the highways. If you must drive under these conditions, remember to do so slowly and smoothly; sudden jerks of the steering wheel or slamming on the brakes may result in a slide. On some mountain highways you may need chains or snow tires.

Highway 36 from Boulder leads to Estes Park, where you can catch Highway 34, which heads east to Loveland and west over Trail Ridge Road toward Grand Lake and Granby. (Note: Trail Ridge Road is closed during the winter.)

To reach Glenwood Springs, Aspen, Rifle, and Grand Junction, take I-70 west from Denver. (The turnoff for Leadville is just after the town of Dillon. Take Highway 91 south if you plan to visit this mining town.) Your route will take you through the massive Eisenhower tunnel and across the Continental Divide, where you'll encounter some of the most beautiful scenery in the world. You'll also encounter steep roads, however, and its important to go easy on your car's brakes on some of the downhill sections. Many a driver has had to learn this the hard way!

For rental car information see *Practical Information for Denver.*

HOTELS AND MOTELS. Although the selection is not as great as in the major metropolitan areas or resorts, northwestern Colorado offers a good variety of accommodations. Here are a few of the best choices. Rates for double occupancy average as follows (though they may vary depending on the season): *Deluxe:* $80–$130, *Expensive:* $53–$79, *Moderate:* $32–$52, *Inexpensive:* $25–$31.

ESTES PARK

(Zip Code 80517)

Long's Peak Inn and Guest Ranch. *Deluxe.* South St. Vrain Highway; 6925 Colorado Hwy. 7; 303–586–2110. Charming chalets and lodge accommodations for 80 to 90 guests. Horses. Guided hikes. Restful, isolated. Scenic, brookside dining, rafting, own fishing, stables. Children's programs. Well managed. Highly recommended. Member of Colorado Dude and Guest Ranch Association. Closed in winter.

Stanley Hotel. *Deluxe.* 333 Wonderview Ave.; 303–586–3371 or 800–ROCKIES. Well-managed hotel with Victorian rooms, fine ambience. Tennis court, pool. Children's playground, restaurants, theater, nearby shops. Ideal for weddings and functions.

Holiday Inn. *Expensive.* 101 S. Vrain Hwy.; 303–586–2332. At highways 36 and Colorado 7. Large rooms, Olympic-size indoor pool, game area. Café and bar on premises. Favored by conventions.

Ponderosa Lodge. *Moderate.* 1820 Fall River Rd.; 586–4233. Overlooking river. Scenic and comfortable. Playground.

FORT COLLINS

(Zip Code 80521)

Holiday Inn. *Expensive.* 3836 E. Mulberry; 303–484–4660. At I-25 and Highway 14. Chain member with heated pool, restaurant, cocktail lounge, entertainment, beauty shop, minigolf.

Lamplighter. *Expensive.* 1809 N. College; 303–484–2764. A Best Western establishment. 40 units.

Ramada Inn. *Expensive.* 3709 E. Mulberry; 303–493–7800. Indoor pool. Coffee shop. Lower prices in winter.

Best Western University Motor Inn. *Moderate.* 914 S. College Ave.; 484–1984. Opposite Colorado State University, with heated pool, café.

Comfort Inn. *Moderate.* 1638 E. Mulberry St.; 484–2444. Nice rooms, heated pool, cable TV. Free coffee. Café nearby.

Days Inn. *Moderate.* 3625 E. Mulberry; 303–221–5490. Clean rooms. Color TV. Free Continental breakfast.

GLENWOOD SPRINGS

(Zip Code 81601)

Antlers Best Western. *Expensive.* 305 Laurel St.; 303–945–8535. Motel with 106 units, pool and (wading pool for the little ones), tennis, playground.

Hotel Colorado. *Expensive.* 526 Pine St.; 303–945–6511. Handsomely restored 120-room hotel. Once a retreat for such notables as William Howard Taft and Teddy Roosevelt. Suites, convention facilities. Near hot springs.

Hot Springs Lodge and Pool. *Expensive.* Box 308; 303–945–6751. Newly refurbished lodge, facing Glenwood Springs' famous hot springs pool. 107 rooms. Many amenities.

Holiday Inn. *Expensive to Moderate.* 51359 U.S. 6; 303–945–8551. Two miles west at I-70 exit. Chain member, with heated pool, saunas. Restaurant, bar, entertainment, dancing. Car needed.

Hotel Denver. *Moderate.* 402 7th St.; 303–945–6565. Popular with businesspeople. A historic hotel, recently completely renovated. Pets, restaurant, cocktail lounge. Across the river from Hot Springs Pool.

GRANBY

(Zip Code 80446)

El Monte. *Expensive.* Box 105, ¼ mile west on US 40; 303–887–3348. TV, heated pool, playground, pets limited. Café and cocktail lounge. A Best Western motor Inn.

Broken Arrow Motel. *Inexpensive.* Box 143, U.S. 40; 303–887–3532. Small establishment. No phones in rooms. Playground, outdoor picnic tables.

Thunderbird Motel. *Inexpensive.* Box 1111, U.S. 40; 303–887–2331. Small, comfortable motel accommodations. Commercial rates. Year-round.

GRAND JUNCTION

(Zip Code 81506)

Grand Junction Hilton. *Deluxe.* 743 Horizon Dr.; 303–241–8888. Off I-70. Golf, tennis, health spa. Convention hotel with gourmet restaurant.

Best Western Sandman. *Expensive.* 708 Horizon Dr.; 303–243–4150. Modern, with spacious grounds. Heated pool, restaurant, bar, free airport bus.

Holiday Inn. *Expensive.* 755 Horizon Dr.; 303–243–6790. Massive convention motel. Two cafés, free airport shuttle, dancing, golf.

Howard Johnson's Motor Lodge. *Expensive.* 752 Horizon Dr.; 303–243–5150. Cocktail lounge, tennis, laundry, heated pool, balconies, nearby café.

Rodeway Inn. *Expensive.* 2790 Crossroads; 303–241–8411. Pool, dancing, two restaurants. Near airport.

American Family Lodge. *Moderate to Inexpensive.* 721 Horizon Dr.; 303–243–6050. Three and a half miles north at I-70 airport exit. Attractive rooms, heated pool, playground, pets. Café opposite.

Frontier Motor Lodge. *Inexpensive.* 1940 North Ave.; 303–242–7620. Heated pool, movies, some suites. Near VA Hospital.

GRAND LAKE

(Zip Code 80447)

Riverside Guesthouses. *Expensive.* Box R Central; 303–627–3619. Fully carpeted log homes. Friendly owners.

GREELEY

(Zip Code 80631)

Holiday Inn. *Expensive.* 609 Eighth Ave.; 303–356–3000. At Eighth Avenue and Sixth Street; centrally located highrise. One hundred rooms with TV. Sauna, pool, golf privileges. Nightly entertainment.

Heritage Inn. *Moderate to Expensive.* U.S. Hwy. 85, Evans; 303–353–5900. Outdoor pool. Pleasant dining room with fireplace. Game room. Picnic facilities.

Greeley Inn. *Moderate.* 721 13th St.; 303–353–3216. Basic accommodations.

Inn Towne Motel. *Moderate.* 1803 Ninth St.; 303–353–0447. Comfortable motel. Free coffee, some kitchen units available. Café three blocks away.

Sundown Motel. *Moderate.* 2131 8th Ave.; 303–352–9261. Color TV and nearby dining facilities; homey atmosphere.

LEADVILLE

(Zip Code 80461)

Best Western Silver King Motor Inn. *Expensive to Moderate.* 2020 N. Poplar; 303–486–2610. Large, modern hotel with sauna, restaurant, and cocktail lounge, dancing. Pets OK. Rates are moderate most of the year, but go up during ski season. Gift shop, laundry, hiking trails, and horseback riding.

Timberline Motel. *Inexpensive.* 216 Harrison Ave.; 303–486–1876. Small but comfortable. Cable TV and ski packages.

LOVELAND

(Zip Code 80537)

Best Western Coach House Resort. *Moderate.* 5542 E. US 34; 303–667–7810. At I-25 and Highway 34. Large and new. Spacious units overlooking lake. Coffee shop. Cocktail lounge and disco dancing. Two swimming pools.

Dreamland Motel. *Moderate.* 617 E. Eisenhower; 303–667–2748. Clean motel on main thoroughfare. Free coffee. Pool.

King's Court. *Moderate.* 928 Lincoln St.; 303–667–4035. Small motel with heated pool, free coffee, nicely landscaped grounds. Café three blocks away. Centrally located.

RIFLE

(Zip Code 81650)

Econo Lodge. *Moderate.* At Highway 70, exit 90; 303–625–4320. Color TV.

Red River Inn. *Inexpensive.* 718 Taughenbaugh; 303–625–3050. Large motel with pool, across from restaurant.

BED-AND-BREAKFASTS AND DUDE RANCHES. Here and there in Colorado, you'll stumble upon accommodations that are homey, charming, and unique. The U.S. is fast catching on to Europe's B&Bs, and Colorado is no exception. Guest ranches, another lodging choice, are ideal for active people who really want to experience the beauty of Colorado's outdoors. Many of the best are listed below. Write also for these information booklets: *Bed and Breakfast Colorado,* Ltd., Box 6061, Boulder 80306, call 303–442–6664; and *Colorado Guest and Dude Ranch Association,* Box 300, Tabernash, Colorado 80478.

ESTES PARK

Deluxe to Expensive

Aspen Lodge Ranch Resort & Conference Center. Long's Peak Route, 80517; 303–586–8133. 36 lodge rooms and 24 cabins in aspen grove with lake, riding, hiking, pool, restaurant, lounge, and sports center with racquetball and saunas. Conference convention center is state's largest log structure.

Long's Peak Inn and Guest Ranch. Long's Peak Route 3A, 80517; 303–586–2110. Summertime ranch with stunning scenery, horses. Surrounded by mountains, the inn offers guided rides and hikes, cookouts. Van tours. Swimming pool, games for children, fishing. Evening entertainment includes square dancing. Well-run and relaxing.

GRANBY

Deluxe

C Lazy U Ranch. Box 378A, 80446; 303–887–3344. Off Highways 40 and 125. The state's most prestigious, versatile vacation center. American plan; includes horses, riding instruction, tennis, fishing, guided hiking, racquetball, whirlpool-sauna, cross-country skiing, Western evening entertainment. Scenic location.

LYONS

Moderate

Peaceful Valley Lodge and Guest Ranch. Star Route; 303–747–2881. Chalets and main lodge. Indoor swimming. Horseback rides in summer. Cross-country skiing in December and January. Under same ownership for many years. Square dancing. Convenient to Boulder.

HOT SPRINGS. In Glenwood Springs the following are open year-round: the *Hot Springs Lodge and Pool* is located one block off I-70 at exit 116; 945–6571; Denver phone 623–3400. Admission, $5.25, adults.

The *Vapor Cave Baths and Massage, Inc.* are a short walk east of the Hot Springs Pool; 945–5825. Vapor baths, facials, massage. Admission is separate from pool entrance fee.

CAMPING AND CABINS. Rustic accommodations of all types abound. For general camping information in the state, and for directories, write *KOA (Kampgrounds of America),* 30558, Billings, Montana, 59114; *Mistix* makes reservations for state parks. During the camping season, call 303–671–4500. A fee is charged. *National Park Service,* 12795 W. Alameda Pkwy., Box 25287, Denver 80225, call 303–969–2000 (for information on camping in national parks in the state); and *U.S. Forest Service,* 11177 W. Eighth Ave., Lakewood, 80225, call 303–236–9520 (for information on Forest Service sites). The following list contains some of the best campgrounds in or around towns. For other campground details, see Parks and Forests, below.

ESTES PARK

Estes Park Campground, five miles southwest of town on Colorado Highway 66; Box 3517, 80517; 303–586–4188. Wooded area ideal for tents and camping trailers. Reservations accepted.

Glen Haven is a pleasant little tourist hamlet that offers cabins for rent: *Inn of Glen Haven* is on Devil's Gulch Rd., Box 19, 80532; 303–586–3897. Open May–Sept. Situated in a deep valley seven miles northeast of Estes Park, on the North Fork of the Big Thompson River. Stop in Glen Haven's small café and grocery store.

Olive Ridge Campground; on Colorado Highway 7 about 15 miles south. Operated by the forest service.

FORT COLLINS

Ansel Watrous Campground, in Poudre Canyon. Operated by U.S. Forest Service.

Horsetooth Reservoir, three miles west. Numerous sites off U.S. 287. Fishing and boating are popular activities here. For reservations write Parks and Recreation Dept., 145 E. Mountain Ave., Fort Collins 80524; 303–221–6640.

GLENWOOD SPRINGS

Deep Lake, 26½ miles northwest on FR 600; 328–6388. 21 sites, no showers. Boating (no motors) and fishing. Pit toilets. No fee.

The Hideout, 1293 Road 117, 81601; 303–945–5621. Campgrounds, quiet in wooded area. Picnic tables, playground, restrooms, and showers. Also cabins.

Rock Gardens, 1308 County Rd. 129, 81601; 303–945–6737. Camper park located on the Colorado River two miles east of Hot Springs Pool. Offers river rafting.

GRAND JUNCTION

Highline Lake, 14 miles west. State recreation area with 25 campsites on 824 acres. Swimming, boating, waterskiing. To reserve sites phone 303–858–7208.

Island Acres, 15 miles east of town, near Palisades. State recreation area on the Colorado River. Buffalo herd. 32 campsites. For reservations call 303–464–7297.

LEADVILLE

Turquoise Lake Recreation Area, eight miles west of Leadville at Sixth Street stoplight. Operated by U.S. Forest Service. Elevation 9,800 ft. 49 sites, drinking water, boat ramp, access for large trailers.

LOVELAND

Barbour Ponds State Recreation Area, seven miles east of town; 669–1739. 60 campsites. Located in the shadow of Long's Peak. Barbour Ponds consists of 40 acres of land and 80 acres of water.

Boyd Lake State Recreation Area, one mile east; 303–699–1739. 200 sites, fishing, swimming, boating, water skiing; 80 sites, primitive camping.

RIFLE

Rifle Gap Falls, ten miles north; 303–625–1607. There are 70 campsites in this state recreation area, which offers a turquoise-blue reservoir and triple falls, water sports, fishing, and picnicking.

TOURIST INFORMATION for this part of the state can be obtained from the *Denver Metro Convention & Visitors Bureau* at 225 W. Colfax, Denver, 80202; 303–892–1112. Or write to the following *Chambers of Commerce: Estes Park:* 500 Big Thompson Ave., Box 3050, 80517, call 303–586–5431 or 800–621–5888; *Glenwood Springs:* 1102 Grand Ave., 81601, call 303–945–6589; *Grand Junction:* 360 Grand Ave., Box 1330, 81501, call 303–242–3214; *Loveland:* 114 E. Fifth St., Box 58, 80537, call 303–667–6311.

SEASONAL EVENTS. In **January** Grand Lake holds its *Winter Carnival,* with ice skating, snowmobiling, and parades. In **February,** it's Leadville's turn. Their *Winter Carnival* is held each weekend. The *Estes Park Hobby Show* opens in **April.** Late **May** brings the *Loveland to Estes Park Stanley Steamer Run.* In **June** Trail Ridge Road opens in Rocky Mountain National Park. Estes Park hosts its *Alpine Marathon.* Rodeos appear all over: Grand Junction has its *Colorado Stampede Rodeo* the third weekend. Glenwood Springs presents their *Auto Race and Car Show* at Hot Springs Lodge. **July** means rodeos and horse shows throughout the state, including the *National Arabian Horse Show* and *Rooftop Rodeo* at Estes Park (see "Spectator Sports," below). Grand Lake hosts *Western Week,* a *buffalo barbecue* with a parade and begins its summer *sailing regattas. Ballet Aspen,* a dance festival, brings international dance troupes and stars. In **August,** Grand Junction offers the *Intermountain Market Days;* stock-car races, and the *Rocky Mountain Open Golf Tournament;* Grand Lake continues its sailboat regatta. In **September** Glenwood Springs and Grand Junction have annual *Art Festivals* and *Aspencades*—trips into the mountains to see the colorful changes autumn brings to the aspens; *harvest festivals* are also common. On Labor Day, the *Garfield County Fair and Rodeo* takes place in Rifle. Estes Park has its *Aspenfest*—celebrations including a Scottish fest, arts and crafts show, folk dancing, magic acts. Also, Vail celebrates *Vailfest* (similar to Octoberfest). **October:** *Potato Day* in Glenwood Springs, the *Stone Age Fair* in Loveland, and the opening of the *big-game hunting* season.

Most of the state's major *ski areas* open in **November.** *Goose hunting* season opens. Leadville puts on a *Victorian Christmas Homes Tour* in early **December.**

SIGHTSEEING AND TOURS. Northwest Colorado draws visitors to explore the natural wonders of the "High Country" and the flavor of historic mining and pioneering towns of the Old West. See also "Museums and Historic Sites" and "Parks" sections for areas worth touring.

In the fall a number of *"Aspencades"* depart from various towns to view the spectacular colors of the changing leaves. Check with local chambers of commerce for exact dates and times (See "Tourist Information," above). *Jeep tours* are popular in various parts of the state as a way to enjoy the mountains and get into little-traveled areas in the manner more comfortable than on the back of a horse or by foot. Whitewater rafting is exciting in spring and summer. Again, local chambers of commerce can help in arrangements.

ESTES PARK

Estes Park Aerial Tramway carries passengers to the 8,896-foot summit of Prospect Mountain for an unmatched look at the community and surrounding mountains. Mid-May through mid-September. Located at 420 E. Riverside Dr.; 586–3675. Hiking trails and picnic area at top.

The Rocky Mountain National Park Rangers offer free guided hikes, lectures, and other programs. Inquire at the Park's Visitors' Center.

Rocky Mountain Park Tours takes group and private tours of Bear Lake and Trail Ridge Road in summer. 907 Moraine Ave.; 586–8687.

GLENWOOD SPRINGS

Tour the *Maroon Bells Wilderness* by bus. Summers only. Contact the Chamber of Commerce, 1102 Grand Ave., 945–6589.

GREELEY

Walking Tours of this town, 50 miles northeast of Denver, are provided by the Municipal Museum, 919 Seventh St.; 353–6123. Greeley began as a temperance colony, sponsored by the editor Horace Greeley.

LEADVILLE

Tour of the *U.S. Fish Hatchery* four miles south of town off US 24. Daily, 7:30 A.M.–4 P.M. 486–0189. Free. Hiking and cross-country ski trails nearby.

PARKS AND FORESTS. Much of Colorado is parkland. The magnificent scenery and opportunities for all manner of outdoor sport cannot be overstated. See also "Camping," above.

Rocky Mountain National Park is 266,943 acres of lakes, valleys, meadows, and mountains that straddle the Continental Divide. Plant life varies with elevation, climate, and soil conditions—from the pine and fir trees of the lower elevations, to berries and wildflowers, to the treeless, rolling terrain of the alpine tundra at the highest elevations. A visitor may spot elk or bighorn sheep (possibly at Sheep Lake in Horseshoe Park early in the morning), bears, martens, coyotes—although, in truth, these larger mammals are seldom seen, and you'll be much more likely to see chipmunks, squirrels, and varieties of birds and fish.

Headquarters of the park is at the town Estes Park; there is also an entrance at Grand Lake. *Trail Ridge Road* connects the two towns and is considered one of the great "highroads" of the world. It crosses the Continental Divide at 12,000 feet. Following an old Indian trail, this road (open summers only) offers a 50-mile drive through spectacular and always-changing terrain. At Rock Cut, for instance, you'll see one of the park's most awe-inspiring views. Nearby is Tundra Trail, which can give visitors the chance to learn about the unusual plants of the alpine tundra. Other roads in the park: *Fall River Road,* with steep grades and many switchbacks (not open to trailers and vans) and *Bear Lake Road,* nine miles from the Moraine Park Visitors' Center, ending at Bear Lake—with a panorama of glaciers, mountain peaks, forests, streams.

Ski Estes Park, ten miles west of Estes Park, is the hub of winter recreation in the park: ice skating, skiing, snowshoeing are all available.

In the southwest corner of the park, Shadow Mountain Recreation Area includes Lake Granby and Shadow Mountain Lake and offers camping, fishing, hunting, picnicking, horseback riding, and water sports.

The visitors centers in the park provide all kinds of information: maps, details on programs and camping, backcountry permits, etc. Visitors centers are located at: Estes Park; Grand Lake; just beyond Fall River Pass (the *Alpine Visitors Center*); at the beginning of Trail Ridge Road, Deer Ridge Junction (the *Moraine Park Visitors Center*).

The park is a favorite with fishing lovers. Lakes and streams are filled with German brown, brook, rainbow, and cutthroat trout. You will need a Colorado license. Use of live bait is prohibited under certain conditions. Information on special fishing regulations is available at park headquarters or ranger stations. Hunting is prohibited within the park. See also "Sports," below.

In the Rocky Mountain National Park campgrounds are first-come, first-serve, except for two (*Glacier Basin,* eight miles west of Estes Park on Bear Lake Rd., and *Moraine Park,* one mile west of Moraine Park Visitors Center off Bear Lake Rd.) where reservations may be made by mail or in person at the park or at the National Park regional office, 12795 W. Alameda Pkwy., Denver, 80225; 303–969–2000. No telephone reservations. Mail reservations are handled by Ticketron offices Box 2715, San Francisco, CA 94126.

You can get complete listings of campsites in the park, with maps and regulations, at any ranger station. See also "Camping," above.

A favorite way to see this park and surrounding country is on horseback. Estes Park calls itself the "horse capital of Colorado" and horses can be leased by the hour or day; you can ride with a guide or on your own. Some stables offer breakfast rides, fishing trips, and other outings. Full details available at the Estes Park Visitors' Center.

The White River National Forest covers more than two million acres and stretches from south of Aspen halfway to the town of Craig to the north. Glenwood Springs sits right in the middle of this wonderland and is a good base for exploration. One of the most beautiful spots within the forest is the 6-square-mile Maroon Bells-Snowmass Wilderness, near Aspen. Hike or ride horses among its many alpine lakes, or climb one of the peaks. Campsites are available, though they may fill up quickly in summer; no reservations. Also in the White River Forest is the *Flat Tops Wilderness,* about 20 miles from Glenwood. For information write: Old Federal Building, Box 984, Glenwood Springs, 81601; 303–945–2521.

Grand Mesa, Uncompaghre, and Gunnison National Forests make up a huge expanse of parkland, all under one headquarters. Grand Mesa boasts over 200 trout-filled lakes at an average elevation of over 10,000 feet. From Grand Junction, I-70 eastbound leads to DeBeque Canyon and the Plateau Creek, Colorado 65 turn-off to Grand Mesa.

Camping sites are abundant (no reservations), and boat and horse rentals are available. The *Powderhorn Ski Resort* is located within the forest as well (Box 370, Mesa 81643; 303–245–5343 or 800–233–9882). For information on these national forests, write 2250 Highway 50, Delta 81416.

Colorado National Monument is located at the Southwest edge of Grand Junction; follow Rim Rock Drive. Five-hundred-foot-high Independence Rock, Window Rock, and Red Canyon may be seen from lookouts along the 22-mile drive. Meadows of wildflowers and forests of juniper and pine surround the mountains. Wildlife, protected by the National Park Service, roams the area. Dinosaur beds have been excavated here during the past decade. Stratified ramparts carved by time create a gallery of strangely beautiful natural sculptures.

The visitors' center at park headquarters (off Highway 340, about four miles west of Grand Junction) will assist the traveler in the area. Nightly programs are given by rangers during the summer. Campsites with excellent facilities and picnic areas are available; no reservations. Well-marked trails beckon to hikers. For information write: Colorado National Monument, Fruita, CO 81521; 303–858–3617.

Dinosaur National Monument in the northwest corner of the state contains one of the world's most outstanding collections of dinosaur bones. Displayed in the quarry as they were found, there are over 2,000 bones on view. Visitors can watch as archaeologists expose the fossils; the setup permits an unusual chance to see these scientists at work.

Among the exceptional features of the monument are deep, narrow gorges with sheer, strangely carved, and delicately tinted sandstone cliffs. Lodore Canyon, cut by the meandering Green River, varies in depth from 1,000 to 3,300 feet.

A 31-mile paved road from the dinosaur headquarters leads north into the heart of the canyon country. Scenic overlooks and the two-mile-long trail at Harpers Corner provide spectacular views of the Green and Yampa rivers and their confluences at Steamboat Rock—over 2,500 feet below. Rather primitive camping sites are available; no reservations. For information write Box 210, Dinosaur 81601; 303–374–2216.

PARTICIPANT SPORTS. Hiking, river running, and backpacking are the most popular sports in northwest Colorado, supplemented of course by hunting and fishing (see below).

For **hiking** contact the National Forests and Parks listed above for general trail maps. The U.S. Geological Survey maps are ideal for hikers and can be found in most large backpacking stores.

Llama Hikes, Box 2777, Estes Park 80517; 303–586–5940. Organized pack trips with llamas. Meals and equipment provided.

The *Colorado Mountain School,* 351 Moraine Ave., Estes Park 80517; 303–586–5758. In summer teaches rock climbing techniques.

A list of **river running** companies in the area can be found below.

Adventure Bound, Box 125, Mack, 81525; 800–525–7084 (outside Colorado); 800–332–1400 (in state). Trips on Green River, the Yampa, the North Platte, and the Colorado.

Colorado Canyons Whitewater Expeditions, 1816 Orchard Place, Fort Collins, 80521; 303–493–4005. Rivers include Yampa, Green, North Platte, Arkansas, Poudre, Rio Chama, Talkeetna (Alaska). Trips range from one-half to five days.

Outrageous Adventures, Box 771631, Steamboat Springs, 80477; 303–879–3676; out of state, 800–872–3676. Rivers include Arkansas, North Platte, Colorado, Dolores. Trips are from two to three days long.

Wilderness Aware, 5104 Greenview Court, Fort Collins, 80525; 303–223–8924. The Dolores, N. Platte, Arkansas, Colorado, Rio Grande, Rio Chama, and Gunnison rivers. Trips one to ten days long.

ESTES PARK

Among Estes Park's sports features: the 18- and 9-hole **golf** courses, both challenging to play. The 18-hole course, *Estes Park Golf and Country Club,* is located just one mile from downtown on Highway 7 and has a pro shop, snack shop, driving range, rental bags, clubs, pull and electric carts, and all other equipment, 586–4431. The 9-hole *Lake Estes Golf Course,* located just east of the Visitor Center on Highway 34, is also next to the Big Thompson River and Lake Estes; 586–9871. Electric carts can be rented only at the 18-hole course.

At Lake Estes you will find rental **boats,** boat docks, tackle shop, snack shop, and other boating and fishing needs.

The district-owned **tennis** courts are available free both day and night. There are two lighted courts at night (small charge). Other courts are located in Stanley Park on Community Drive and for guests only at the Stanley Hotel.

The recreation district maintains many picnic areas along Lake Estes, Mary's Lake, and Stanley Park. Also available is a children's playground in Stanley Park near the tennis and **basketball** courts.

For **cross-country skiing,** try *Rocky Mountain Ski Tours,* 130 East Riverside Dr., 80517; 586–2114.

FORT COLLINS

For **swimming, water skiing,** and **boating,** there is *Horsetooth Reservoir* west of town. City Park, Mulberry at Sheldon, is a large park with lake, pool, **jogging** tracks, **ice skating** in winter. *Beaver Meadows,* west of town is a **cross-country ski** center. Contact them at Box 2167, 80522; 482–1845.

GLENWOOD SPRINGS

Cross-country skiing spots abound in the Glenwood area, with ski rentals available at many sports shops (check the *Yellow Pages*). Two particularly nice spots are *Four Mile Park,* in Ski Sunlight (945–7491) south of town, and the *Redstone Inn*—a bit of a drive, but worth it. **Tennis** is available at the *Glenwood Springs Raquet Club;* 2800 Midland Ave.; 945–6070. Of course, **swimming** is a must at the two-block-long mineral pool (see "Hot Springs," above). Children's pools are available here also.

GRAND JUNCTION

Golfing is popular, with links open most of the year. Play at the nine-hole *Lincoln Park,* east of 12th, between North and Gunnison Ave., 242–6394, or at *Tiara Rodo,* an 18-hole course at the base of Colorado National Monument—2063 S. Broadway, 242–9979. *Bookcliff Country Club* also has an 18-hole course: 2730 G Rd., 243–3323. **Tennis** is available at *Grand Junction Athletic Club,* which also has **raquetball:** 2515 Foresight Circle, 245–4100. Many parks have courts as well. **Ski** at nearby *Powderhorn,* Box 370, Mesa 81643, 245–5343 or 800–233–9882. **Watersports** at *Vega Dam* and *Highline Lake.*

GRAND LAKE

With three large lakes surrounding this charming little town, **boating** and **sailing** are the most popular activities in the area. The *Grand Lake*

Yacht Club is the highest registered yacht club in the world. Races are held most summer weekends. Boats may be rented at the *Trail Ridge Marina,* on Highway 34, 2½ miles south, 627–3586; *Sunrise Harbor,* on Shadow Mountain Lake, 627–3668; *Lake Kove Marina,* also on Shadow Mountain Lake, 627–3605; and at the *Gala Marina,* on the north shore of Lake Granby, 627–3220.

Hiking is also a favorite sport. Contact the Chamber of Commerce, 928 Grand Ave., Box 57, (U.S. 34 and 278), 80447, 627–3402, for trail maps. A **golf** course (18-hole) ringed by mountain peaks is open to the public. Phone 627–8226 for golf course information. In winter, **cross-country skiing** and **snowmobiling** are the rage. Rent equipment at *Grand Country Sports,* Box 238, 80447, 627–3981 or *Trail Ridge Marina* (see above).

GREELEY

Swimming is at three city parks (*Centennial Pool,* 23rd Ave., and Reservoir Rd.; *Island Grove,* at 14th Ave. and A St.; *Sunrise Pool,* at Fourth Ave. and 12th St.). Try also the *Greeley Recreation Center,* 353–6522, for swimming, weightlifting, and racquetball. **Golf** is at *Highland Hills,* at 23rd Street and 54th Ave.; 330–7327. **Tennis** is available at six different municipal parks: *Centennial Park,* 23rd Ave. and 22nd St.; *Farr Park,* 15th Ave. and 26th St.; and *Sherwood Park,* 29th Ave. and 13th St. No reservations required. Call Parks and Recreation Department, 353–6123, for more information. *Bittersweet Park* offers **jogging** tracks at 35th Avenue and 13th Street. Many **bike paths** circuit the town. **Fishing** is permitted in four municipal lakes.

LEADVILLE

Golf is available at the nine-hole *Mt. Massive Golf Course,* the highest in the world, 259 County Rd. 5, 486–2176. *Turquoise Lake* is rimmed by **bike** trails.

Mountain climbing doesn't have to be for experts. Two "14ers," as the peaks above 14,000 feet are called, are accessible to people with little experience. They are *Mt. Elbert* and *Mt. Massive.* Visit the Forest Service office for maps.

HUNTING AND FISHING. Colorado's northwestern corner boasts some of the best hunting and fishing in the state. The area is dotted with hundreds of lakes and streams in thousands of acres of forest lands. Deer, elk, and antelope are all abundant, and bighorn sheep, Rocky Mountain goats, and black bear are also present.

For anglers, there are rainbow, Mackinaw, cutthroat, and German brown trout; catfish, Kokanee salmon, crappie, perch. As in the rest of the state, licenses are required for both sports. License fees vary; most large sporting goods stores sell them. See *Facts at Your Fingertips* at the beginning of this book for addresses and phone numbers to use to obtain detailed license and season information.

Near *Rocky Mountain National Park,* anglers find some of the best fishing in the state. Grand Lake, Shadow Mountain Lake, and Lake Granby, all in the Shadow Mountain Recreation Area, offer up Kokanee salmon (snagging season is Oct. 1–Dec. 31), and Mackinaw, rainbow, German brown, and cutthroat trout are plentiful in the lakes and mountain streams. A particularly popular area is Trout Haven, one mile west of

Estes Park on US 36. Fishing is permitted within park boundaries, except at Bear Lake and where otherwise posted. No live bait or hunting is allowed in the park, although once outside park boundaries, you can hunt in the Shadow Mt. Recreation Area, west of Shadow Mt. Lake.

In the Fort Collins-Loveland area, *Boyd Lake State Recreation Area* has six lakes, including Horsetooth Reservoir. Crappie, walleye, and perch are abundant here. The area also boasts excellent duck hunting. "Colorado's Trout Route" is a circle drive through Poudre Canyon. The route begins 9 miles northwest of Fort Collins on Highway 287. The *Red Feather Lakes,* a chain of lakes along this road, are especially good for trout.

Glenwood Springs sits in the center of some of the western region's best hunting and fishing locales. The *White River National Forest* is excellent elk and deer country; Sweetwater Lake east of Glenwood through Glenwood Canyon is a prime spot for Kokanee, and both the Colorado and Roaring Fork rivers are popular for trout. Glenwood also serves as a good base for exploring the well-known Frying Pan River and the Ruedi Dam area, which can be reached from the town of Basalt southeast of Glenwood on Highway 82. The dam offers both shore fishing and trolling. Farther along Highway 82, near Leadville, are the Twin Lakes. Also good for fishing are Turquoise, Crystal, and Emerald lakes, Clear Creek, and the Arkansas River near Leadville. Leadville's U.S. Forest Service Office, 130 W. Fifth St. has maps and information.

West of Glenwood Springs, Rifle is a popular center for elk and deer hunting.

Grand Mesa National Forest is another first-rate elk locale in Colorado, and because of its 200 lakes also offers excellent fishing and waterfowl hunting. Bear also roam the wilderness areas along Grand Mesa.

For forest maps, write to the U.S. Forest Service, Rocky Mountain Regional Office, 11177 W. 8th Ave., Box 25127, Denver, CO 80225, 236–9431. This office has maps of all Colorado's forests.

SPECTATOR SPORTS. Some of the sporting events in northwest Colorado need not be played—they can be watched. See "Seasonal Events," above and contact local chambers of commerce for special events such as horse shows, rodeos, and sailing regattas.

In **Loveland** *dog racing* fans congregate at the Cloverleaf Kennel Club, four miles east of town on I-25 at US 34. Phone 667–6211. Post time 8 P.M. 13 races nightly, except Sundays, March–May. Must be 18 or over.

MUSEUMS AND HISTORIC SITES. When you're not absorbing the scenery or involved in your favorite sport, spend some time learning about the history and culture of this area.

ESTES PARK

The Estes Park Area Historical Museum, 200 Fourth St.; 586–6256. On Highway 36, next to rodeo grounds, it relates the history of the region through photos, artifacts, and documents. Open daily, Memorial Day through September.

The (modest) *MacGregor Ranch Museum,* a half-mile north of downtown on Devil's Gulch Road; 586–3749. Preserves the 100-year life of a working cattle ranch. MacGregor's first cabin and the 1896 farmhouse display tools, clothes, and other memorabilia of the owners and their times. Open Memorial Day through Labor Day, closed Mon.

FORT COLLINS

Fort Collins Museum, 200 Mathews; 221–6738. Locally oriented history, archaeology, and more. Tues.–Sat. 10 A.M.–5 P.M., Sun. noon–5 P.M. Free.

GLENWOOD SPRINGS

Frontier Historical Museum, 1001 Colorado Ave., 945–4448. Lifestyles museum includes display of implements for coal mining, polo, and military history. Other exhibits include the Doc Holiday exhibit, a 1930s clothing show, and a large collection of Ute Indian arrowheads. Thurs.–Sat., 1–4 P.M.

GRAND JUNCTION

Dinosaur Valley has paleontology exhibits at 4th and Main; 243–DINO. *Museum of Western Colorado,* Fourth Street and Ute; 242–0971. Science and natural history exhibits, firearm collection. *Cross Orchards,* a living history farm at 3079 F Road; 434–9158, has been preserved since 1909. Open for summer tours.

GREELEY

Centennial Village. 1475 A St., ext. 391; 353–6123. Museum depicts growth of the area 1860–1920 with restored school, fire station, Victorian home, etc. Landscaped grounds, guided tours. Open Mon.–Fri. Free.

The Greeley Municipal Museum, 919 Seventh St., 353–6123. Features exhibitions, demonstrations, lectures, and films that illustrate regional history. Open year-round Tues. through Sat., 9 A.M.–5 P.M.; closed holidays. Free.

The Meeker Home Museum. 1324 Ninth Ave.; 353–6123. 1870s two-story adobe house, home of Greeley-founder Nathan Cook Meeker, with personal belongings and furniture. Open Tues.–Sat., closed holidays.

LEADVILLE

Memories of this mining town's early days are preserved in the *Heritage Museum and Gallery,* Ninth St. and Harrison Ave.; 486–1878. Small fee. *The Healy House,* 912 Harrison Ave.; 486–0487, built in 1878, is restored and serves as a museum to illustrate the bonanza mining period. On the same grounds is the *Dexter Cabin,* which looks like a log cabin from the outside but is finished inside with fine woodwork and hardwood floors. Open daily, June to mid-October. Operated by Colorado Historical Society. Fee.

LONGMONT

Longmont Pioneer Museum, 375 Kimbark; 776–6050 (weekends; 776–6059). Artifacts relating to the settlement of the area. Mon.–Fri. 9 A.M.–5 P.M. Sat. 10 A.M.–4 P.M. Closed holidays. Free.

LOVELAND

Loveland Museum and Gallery. 503 N. Lincoln; 667–6070. Murals, farming history, old photos, rugs, tools—even an ancient dental lab. Tues.–Sat. 9 A.M.–5 P.M.

DINING OUT. For a full meal at a *Deluxe* restaurant (without drinks, tax, tip) expect to pay $30 and up; *Expensive* $17–$29; *Moderate* $11–$16; *Inexpensive* $6–$10. Major credit cards accepted unless noted otherwise.

ESTES PARK

Nicky's. *Expensive.* One and a half miles from downtown on U.S. 34; 586–5376. Locally popular beef restaurant.

Stanley Hotel. *Expensive.* 333 Wonderview Ave.; 586–6892. Charming and elegant. Good management. Outdoor porch dining in summer.

The Aspens. *Expensive to Moderate.* At Holiday Inn, 101 S. Vrain Ave.; 586–2123. Pleasantly lighted. Variety of dishes. Outstanding salad bar.

The Other Side Restaurant. *Moderate.* Highway 36 and Mary's Lake Road; 586–2171. Enjoy dining and a spectacular view of the Rocky Mtn. National Park. Offers fine dining and a family-minded café menu.

Coffee Bar Cafe. *Inexpensive.* 167 East Elkhorn Ave.; 303–586–3626. Well-established renovated café on main street. Open all year. Recently enlarged. No liquor.

La Casa. *Inexpensive.* 222 E. Elkhorn; 586–2807. Outstanding Mexican and Cajun food. Outdoor garden in summer. Open all year. Congenial.

FORT COLLINS

Nico's Catacombs. *Expensive.* 115 South College Ave.; 484–6029. A downtown gourmet restaurant. Long menu. Also lunches.

Spanish Manor. *Moderate.* 6324 S. College Ave.; 303–226–5986. Family-operated authentic Mexican restaurant. Food and decor offer a real flavor of the country.

Farmers Inn. *Inexpensive.* 2721 S. College Ave.; 223–5544. Great Mexican food and drinks.

GLENWOOD SPRINGS

Sopris. *Expensive.* Seven miles south on State 82; 945–7771. European cuisine.

Buffalo Valley Inn. *Moderate.* About three miles southeast on State 82; 945–5297. In a rustic western setting. Steaks and ribs.

Springs Restaurant and Lounge. *Moderate.* 722 Grand Ave.; 945–8988. Huge sandwiches, onion rings, steaks, ribs and chicken. Daily happy hour.

GRANBY

The Longbranch. *Expensive to Moderate.* 185 E. Agate Ave.; 887–2209. Home cooking on main street. Some German dishes. Beer and wine.

GRAND JUNCTION

The Winery. *Expensive.* 642 Main; 242–4100. Full-service restaurant in rustic building. Dinner only. Steak, seafood, salad bar.

The Grill. *Moderate.* 349 W. 8th, Palisade; 464–5792.

Sunflower. *Moderate.* 201 2nd St. (I–70, Exit 37 to Patterson Rd.) Italian and American cuisine in restored post office building. Weekend brunch.

Furr's Cafeteria. *Inexpensive.* 2817 North Ave.; 243–4415. Excellent value. No credit cards.

GRAND LAKE

Red Fox. *Deluxe to Expensive;* 627–3418. Continental-style restaurant. Dinner only.

Chuck Hole Café. *Inexpensive.* 1119 Grand Ave.; 627–3509. Home cooking. Locally popular.

GREELEY

Eat'n Place. *Moderate.* Seven miles north on Hwy. 85 in Eaton; 454–3136. Excellent value. Outstanding Continental and American dishes of seafood, veal, steak, ribs, and French pastries.

Furr's Cafeteria. *Inexpensive.* Hillside Plaza 2638 11th Ave.; 303–356–4097. Clean. Good quality. No credit cards.

LEADVILLE

The Golden Burro. *Moderate.* 701 Harrison Ave.; 486–1239. Victorian setting for family dining. Homemade soup, big breakfasts, fried chicken.

LONGMONT

Old Prague Inn. *Expensive.* 7521 Ute Hwy. 66; 772–6374. Genuine Czech food. Good wine list.

Sebanton French Restaurant. *Expensive.* Closed in August. 424 Main; 776–3686. Small authentic French restaurant. Center of town. Closed Sun. and Mon.

Furr's. *Inexpensive.* 2350 N. Main Street; 303–772–7314. Nice atmosphere. Variety. No credit cards.

LOUISVILLE

Blue Parrot. *Inexpensive.* 640 Main; 666–9994. Spaghetti and beef.

Colacci's. *Inexpensive.* 816 Main St.; 666–9979. This restaurant makes its own pasta and spicy foods. Cocktail lounge. Frequented by people from Boulder and Denver.

LOVELAND

Summit. *Expensive.* 3208 W. Eisenhower; 669–6648. Handsome steak restaurant. Prime rib and king crab specialties. Reservations advised.

Black Steer. *Moderate.* East Fifth and North Lincoln; 667–6679. For meat eaters. Bar.

Bohemian Cottage Restaurant. *Inexpensive.* 8039 West Hwy. 34; 667–3718. Quiet, cozy Czech establishment. Roast duck and dumplings, great schnitzel.

La Cocina. *Inexpensive.* 330 N. Lincoln; 669–0211. Mexican food.

RIFLE

Fireside Inn II. *Moderate.* 0023 Highway 325; 625–2233. Boasting excellent food, salad bar, and cocktails, this relaxing supper club seats 165.

Red River Inn. *Moderate.* At motel with same name; off Interstate Highway, 718 Taughenbaugh; 625–3050. A full-service, family-style restaurant.

SOUTHERN COLORADO

Land of Legends

by
EUGEN A. ARCHULETA

Gene Archuleta, a writer living in Castle Rock, is a native Coloradoan who has written about the people of his state all his life as a reporter in several southern Colorado cities.

Southern Colorado is the land of legends.

It is the awesome mountains that have caused the area to be called the "The Switzerland of America."

It is the mysterious ruins of the prehistoric Anazasi Indians at Mesa Verde and Hovenweep.

It is the spectacular works of nature seen in the Great Sand Dunes National Monument, the Black Canyon of the Gunnison, and three other monuments in seven national forests, a national recreation area, and a national park.

Man has increased the glory of southern Colorado by adding two huge man-made lakes, the Blue Mesa and Navajo, enlarging the natural fisheries of the area, and building the narrow-gauge railroads that still operate in southern Colorado—the Cumbres and Toltec Scenic Railway and the Silverton, which provides a spectacular trip through mountain canyons from Durango, to Silverton, a mining town tucked away in the high San Juan Mountains.

In addition to what the ancients left, and what nature created, modern man has left a tricultural imprint on southern Colorado that gives it its special flavor.

Painted on this tapestry of the magnificent outdoors is the record of the Hispanic colonists, the explorers, the trappers, prospectors and miners, the ranchers, and the Indians who have made southern Colorado what it is today.

The legends of the area mix easily with the presence of agriculture, industry, and four-season resorts that is today's southern Colorado. For information on major ski and summer resorts, see the earlier chapter on the subject.

EXPLORING SOUTHERN COLORADO

Colorado Springs

Colorado Springs is a prosperous city nestled along the Front Range of the Rockies that is leaping past its resort-and-retirement beginnings to become a hotbed for the high-tech military, space, and research industries.

With over 35 museums to match every taste, natural wonders, and a variety of other attractions, Colorado Springs remains one of Colorado's most popular vacation areas.

The military is a strong presence in Colorado Springs. Military retirees account for the largest single income source in the El Paso County (Colorado Springs) area, and the active payroll from the United States Air Force Academy, NORAD (North American Air Defense Command), and army base Fort Carson gives Colorado Springs a special flavor.

NORAD itself, located in the bowels of Cheyenne Mountain, can be visited with advance reservations. Information on the tour is available from the visitors' center, south of U.S. Highway 24 and Petersen Boulevard.

Moreover, Colorado Springs is home to the United States Olympic Training Center. Athletes from all over the country come to train and test at the facilities of the OTC and to compete against each other in some of the finest sports facilities in the country.

Colorado Springs has been host to two National Sports Festivals and, as headquarters for the U.S. Olympics, is always in the center of amateur athletics.

With the new, Colorado Springs retains the attractions that first drew travelers to "the Springs", as it is known in Colorado: the geologic formations that are the red sandstone cliffs of the 940-acre Garden of the Gods, the Cave of the Winds, Seven Falls cascading three hundred feet through a deep canyon, the Cheyenne Mountain Highway, and, of course, Pikes Peak.

Pikes Peak

Pikes Peak is neither the tallest nor the most impressive of Colorado's mountains, but it is the most accessible. A mountain toll road runs from Colorado Springs to the summit, open daily from May to October. From Manitou Springs, the Pikes Peak Incline Railway runs to the summit from May through October.

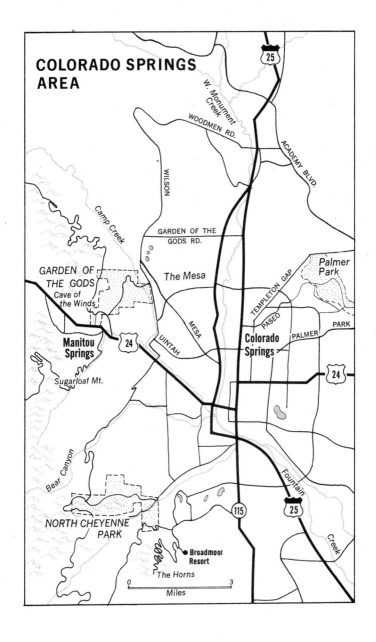

COLORADO SPRINGS
AREA

Every Fourth of July, auto racers from throughout the country challenge the mountain in the annual timed Pikes Peak Hill Climb.

Up the road from the Pikes Peak Incline Railway is Serpentine Drive, and at its summit is the Cave of the Winds, open daily with guided tours every 15 minutes.

Colorado Springs' "other" mountain is Cheyenne Mountain, which towers over the Broadmoor.

The Broadmoor

Under the shadow of Cheyenne Mountain is perhaps Colorado's finest resort, the Broadmoor. World-renowned, it is famous for the many Olympians and world-champion ice skaters who have trained at its ice arena.

The Broadmoor began with a turn-of-the-century hotel building that still retains the old-world charm and service that one expects at a luxury resort. It has three beautiful golf courses, designed by Donald Ross, Robert Trent Jones, and the Arnold Palmer organization. The Broadmoor also boasts 16 tennis courts, 15 elegant shops, and a conference center that brings in world-class entertainment. Eight restaurants and bars cater to every taste.

First and foremost, the Broadmoor is noted for its ambience, and as a resort for all seasons.

Cheyenne Mountain

Up the slopes of Cheyenne Mountain on the Cheyenne Mountain toll road is the Cheyenne Mountain Zoo, which has an excellent collection of animals.

Up the road is the Will Rogers Memorial, with its collections on the life and times of one of America's favorite humorists.

A little farther on is Seven Falls, a 300-yard chasm with picturesque falls. The view from the summit of the Cheyenne Mountain road makes the uphill climb worthwhile.

U.S. Air Force Academy

The United State Air Force Academy is located north of town on I-25 and Academy Boulevard. The 18,000-acre grounds are open to the public daily during daylight hours, and there is an excellent self-guided tour of one of the most-photographed spots in Colorado.

The Air Force Academy Visitor's Center does an excellent job of telling the story of the Academy and the Air Force with exhibits and photographs.

During the Academic year, the noontime parade of cadets on their way to the dining hall is well worth seeing.

More Natural Wonders

On the west side of town, the Garden of the Gods is a park with natural sandstone formations, hiking trails and two roads. The formations are Paleozoic and Mesozoic rocks that have been bent and uplifted by fault and left the towers, pinnacles, and mushroom rocks that compose the Garden of the Gods.

Thirty-five miles west of Colorado Springs, on U.S. Highway 24, the Florrisant Fossil Beds National Monument preserves an ancient lake bed that has yielded some of the finest fossils from layers of shale.

South of the Springs

South of Colorado Springs, Colorado opens up into a land of mountains and plains.

The southern portion of of the state is where people of two cultures met—the Hispanics and the settlers from other states. Today, these two mesh, but each has its own history for the traveler to enjoy.

The southeastern portion of the state is agricultural, with produce, especially Rocky Ford melons, the primary product. This area developed most of the melons bought today as cantelope, as well as the bigger varieties of watermelon.

Along the I-25 Corridor running nearly due south of Colorado Springs, are the towns of Pueblo, Walsenburg, and Trinidad, each very different and offering different attractions.

Pueblo

Pueblo is a highly diversified metropolitan area, with a revitalized downtown, suburban shopping centers, and an enclosed mall providing shopping for all of southern Colorado.

Pueblo boasts a symphony orchestra, chorale, ballet, theatrical groups, and a large arts and conference center. Other cultural activities include the Rosemount Victorian House Museum, El Pueblo Museum, and the Fred W. Weisbrod Aircraft Museum.

The Pueblo Reservoir is the largest body of water in southern Colorado, offering boating, water sports, fishing, and has a shoreline of over 60 miles. The unique Pueblo Plaza Ice Arena, Motorsports Park, and Zoo, complement the 57 parks and 76 tennis courts, eight public swimming pools, two golf courses, and numerous softball and football fields.

Pueblo is host to the annual Colorado State Fair held in late summer with top entertainment and world-class rodeo.

The Walsenburg Area

West of the small town of Walsenburg is the growing resort of Cuchara. A ski area, this is also a popular summer destination.

An 18-hole championship golf course located in the shadow of the Spanish Peaks has been constructed adjacent to the town of La Veta to complement the hiking, fishing, and hunting the area is noted for.

La Veta itself offers the intriguing Francisco Fort Museum, with exhibits on the early days of the Cuchara Valley.

Lathrop State Park, three miles west of Walsenburg on U.S. Highway 160, offers fishing, camping, and other water sports as well as a nine-hole public golf course.

Trinidad

Trinidad is a pretty little city nestled under Fishers Peak. With cobblestone streets, the downtown preserves a 19th-century feel. The Baca and Bloom houses on Main Street provide a glimpse into both the Hispanic and ranching past of the town. The two mansions were built side-by-side by two early residents and are preserved today as examples of both Spanish culture and the 19th-century era of open-range cattle barons. Of special note is the Victorian Rose Garden of the Bloom House.

The Eastern Plains

Out in the plains, northeast of Trinidad, Las Animas's Kit Carson Museum is a memorial to the mountain man, soldier, and governor. Nearby is Bent's Fort, a trading post of the Mountain Man era of Colorado that has been painstakingly restored.

Farther to the northeast, in the town of Burlington, is the Kit Carson Carousel, a national historic site built in 1905 with 45 handcarved animals and 52 original oil paintings. It's located at the town fairgrounds.

Southwest of the Springs

The Sangre De Cristos, named the "blood of Christ" by the early Spanish settlers who first saw the reddish-colored sunset on the peak on Easter, are the southern end of the Front Range of Colorado's mountains.

South and west of Colorado Springs is one of the most legendary of mining camps: the Cripple Creek-Victor area. Cripple Creek, named for the cow that stumbled and kicked up a fortune, still sees sporadic mining activity, but the economy relies on the summer tourist trade.

The Cripple Creek Mining District Museum tells the story of the overnight millionaires and the violent labor struggles that characterized these mining frontier towns. The Cripple Creek–Victor Narrow Gauge Railroad gives riders a four-mile ride through mining country, and the Imperial Hotel, one of Colorado's proud relics of the mining era, offers lodging and Victorian theater, May–Oct. The district has a combination of scenery and history that makes it irresistible.

Tucked away along the Arkansas River is Canon City, situated on U.S. Highway 50, and the location of Colorado's State Prison, but equally famous as the entry of Colorado's Royal Gorge.

The Royal Gorge, south of U.S. 50 west of Canon City, is one of the deepest canyons in Colorado—1,200 feet with the canyon narrowing to 30 feet at some points. Famous as the site of Colorado's railroad wars and as one of Colorado's premier scenic attractions, it is today spanned by one of the world's highest suspension bridges at 1,055 feet over the Arkansas River.

The Royal Gorge offers an incline railway for those who want to descend to the bottom of the chasm, an aerial tramway across the gorge, and a scenic railway along the rim.

The Arkansas River is one of the more popular rivers in Colorado to raft, with a river-running outfit almost every mile along U.S. Highway 50 from Canon City to Salida.

For others, low water means trout fishing in the Arkansas, with many camping and fishing holes right along the highway.

Farther along U.S. 50 is the turn to Westcliffe and the Wet Mountain Valley, the oft-seen backdrop for many of the Westerns filmed in Colorado. Nearby is the Conquistador Ski Area.

The San Luis Valley

South of the area, the San Luis Valley is an Alpine valley the size of Puerto Rico, but with only 60,000 inhabitants spread over 20 or so little towns. The Valley, as it is known in Colorado, is both the poorest in Colorado and one of the richest. Its per capita income is at the bottom of the state, but its cultural heritage and physical beauty are at the top. It has one of the geologic wonders of America in the Great Sand Dunes National Monument, a rich and varied culture, some of the best scenery and outdoor activities the state has to offer, and a historical overlay that has echoes of the old west which are not very faint at all.

The Sand Dunes

The San Luis Valley is a desert, and the prevailing winds blow from the southwest. During the spring, the winds sweep across the valley and funnel into a low pass at the northeast end, dropping the grains of sand and depositing them where the great sand dunes now rise 700 feet over the valley floor.

The sand dunes are located 31 miles northeast of Alamosa on Colorado State Highway 150. Located at this mustn't-miss sight is a visitors' center that interprets the massive formations, camping facilities, and a nature trail.

Fort Garland (1858–1883), on U.S. Highway 160 at the foot of La Veta Pass, holds the restored adobe U.S. military outpost that gave the town its name. It is quite an eye-opener for those who believe the Hollywood image of a frontier fort. Open daily during the summer.

The valley has more to make it a living museum, with the oldest town in Colorado, San Luis, 50 miles south of Fort Garland on Colorado Highway 150. The town is still thriving around its plaza, and the Hispanic adobes of the southern part of the valley give way gradually to the ranching and farming style of the north.

The Monte Vista Wildlife Refuge, 17 miles south of Alamosa on U.S. 285, is a 13,000-acre refuge for migratory birds (whooping cranes) and upland game. There's a self-guided tour daily except in hunting season.

At the south end of the valley, a remnant of a railroad that was to reach Mexico survives in the high mountains between Antonito, Colorado, and Chama, New Mexico. Maintained by a commission put together by the states of New Mexico and Colorado, the "Cumbres and Toltec" narrow-gauge scenic railroad gives a spectacular trip to the summit of Cumbres Pass.

The San Luis Valley is hunting and fishing. From the almost-warm water fishery of Sanchez reservoir in the south to the high mountain lakes and reservoirs that ring the valley to the west, this is fishing country. The Conejos River and the Rio Grande have national reputations, and the gold medal waters of Wagon Wheel gap have produced some record lunkers.

Hunting for elk, deer, antelope, and black bear are popular within season, although the mountains west of the valley saw the last of Colorado's grizzlies die just a few years ago.

Up the Rio Grande, Creede is a mining town with an active present and an historic past. A highlight of the town is the Creede Repertory Theater.

Up the South Fork of the Rio Grande is Wolf Creek Pass, a legendary mountain pass on U.S. Highway 140, the old Navajo Trail.

Gunnison Country

The Gunnison country is Colorado outdoors. It's a big area, composed of counties that are as large as some states, drained by the Gunnison and San Miguel rivers.

The Gunnison River is the more famous, and rightly so. With its tributaries, the Lake Fork, the East, the Cement, the Taylor, the Tomichi, it is Colorado's best fishing.

Each tributary river has its special feel. The Taylor, between Taylor Reservoir and Almont, is noted for its population of German Browns. The Lake Fork is only a flies-and-lures water for much of its length, while the Blue Mesa Reservoir (in the Curecanti National Recreation Area) is Colorado's largest body of water and one of its best-known fisheries.

The reservoir is a good fishery for lake trout, Kokanee salmon (that spawn in the fall up the Gunnison), and other species. Winter ice fishing draws enthusiasts from all over the state, and the numerous small reservoirs, streams, and lakes of the Gunnison high country are everything a fisherman could ask for.

The Curecanti Recreation area offers more than just fishing: camping, boating (with a full-service marina), a visitors' center, and other activities abound. One special trip of note is the National Park Service's boat tours from beneath the Blue Mesa dam on the lake formed by the Morrow Point dam. It is a spectacular journey and shouldn't be missed by geology buffs.

Also well known to avid fishing enthusiasts is the Black Canyon of the Gunnison. The Canyon itself is a National Monument for 12 miles of its length, but for fishermen, the action starts below the series of Bureau of Land Management dams and continues on to the junction with the North Fork. Because of the cold discharge from the bottom of the reservoir, the Canyon is now prime trout water, and no fisherman should ever pass up a chance to try his or her luck here.

The Black Canyon of the Gunnison National Monument is one of the geologic marvels of western Colorado. With dark, almost black walls with swirled layers of gneiss on them, the Black Canyon is narrower and deeper than any other canyon in the country: 2,700 feet down, 1,100 feet across. The combination makes it the most dramatic of canyons.

The south rim is reached by a road 13 miles east of Montrose on U.S. Highway 50, and 10 miles on a paved road from there; there's a visitor's center and camping here. The south rim is open daily; the north rim side is closed in the winter months.

In the fall, the Gunnison country is the home to the deer and elk hunters that come to enjoy Colorado's big game herds.

Gunnison's small museum, the Pioneer, located on U.S. 50 on the eastern edge of town, is open only during the summer and has an excellent collection on local history and railroad history.

Up the valley 27 miles from Gunnison on Colorado Highway 135 is Crested Butte, a four-season resort that is a National Historic District with its Victorian-era gingerbread houses, and a popular ski area in winter months (*see* Ski and Summer Resorts).

South of Gunnison, on Colorado Highway 149, is the town of Lake City. Once a mining center in the heart of the San Juans, Lake City is now a vacationer's paradise with fishing, hiking, and other outdoor activities. It is the county seat and the site of the only trial that convicted a man of cannibalism—the notorious Alfred Packer.

Montrose-Uncompahgre Area

To the west, off U.S. Highway 50 is the Uncompahgre Valley and the town of Montrose. Of note here is the Ute Indian Museum, three miles south of Montrose on U.S. Highway 550. This museum is one of the best in Colorado, with an extensive collection of 19th-century artifacts of the tribe that once called the Uncompahgre home.

Another museum of note is the Montrose County Museum, located in the old depot at 11 N. First, with an extensive collection of farm implements and vehicles.

Highway 550 is called the Million Dollar Highway because of the tremendous cost of building the road through the mountains; but today the name stands for the vistas that can be seen along its route from Montrose to Durango.

South on the highway is the Ridgway dam, which is a water-project dam that may provide limited fishing when completed. It might also clean up the San Miguel River to allow fishing, as it has long been contaminated by mine waste.

Ouray, 37 miles south of Montrose on U.S. Highway 550, grew from a mining camp to Victorian splendor under the towering San Juans. A National Historic District, the town is a popular stop for visitors and summer residents.

Of special interest here is a superb collection of art works in the County Courthouse. The building itself is a Victorian gem. Across the street from the courthouse is the County Museum, located in what was once the local hospital (420 Sixth Ave.). It's an outstanding musuem of the mining past of Ouray. The turn-of-the-century Elks Home on Main Street is a historic site that Brother Elks should not miss the opportunity to visit.

Over the Dallas Divide from Ridgway is the ski resort of Telluride (*see* Winter and Summer Resorts), which has achieved fame for its summer festivals, starting with the Bluegrass festival in June and running through the Film Festival of the end of August and the hang-gliding competitions of the fall.

The Four Corners Region: Mesa Verde

If there is one place to see in Colorado, it is Mesa Verde. A National Park, Mesa Verde is ten miles east of Cortez on U.S. Highway 160. It is a collection of the mesa-top and cliff dwellings of the vanished Anazasi Indians built over 700 years ago. This archaeological treasure is one of the must-see sights of America, ranking with the Grand Canyon and Yosemite.

Almost 40,000 Indians once lived in these intricate dwellings before mysteriously departing. The park itself has a museum and museum store, lodging, and some campsites.

The Park Service has done everything it can to provide easy access to several of the sites, particularly Cliff House and Balcony House, where the ruins are open for inspection and guided tours.

Other Attractions of the Four Corners Region

The Four Corners Region has several other sites of archaeological interest, as well as an active Indian Reservation with handcrafts and pottery for sale.

Four Corners is so named because it is the only place in the United States where four states come together: Colorado, Utah, Arizona and New Mexico. There's a monument at the spot, and children particularly delight in standing in all four states.

Outstanding among the other archaeological sites here is the Hovenweep group, in Hovenweep National Monument, 40 miles east of Cortez over gravel roads. Hovenweep is Mesa Verde without the rebuilding, or the crowds, but also with a special type of ruin that haunts the imagination.

The heart of Four Corners country is the town of Durango. A bustling community, it has at once the Victorian charm of its downtown and the vibrance of a growing city.

Durango is the southern terminus of the Silverton, the most famous of Colorado's remaining narrow-gauge lines (the Cumbres and Toltec and the Silverton were once part of one line, the Denver, Rio Grande, and Western). The trip from Durango to Silverton is a highlight of any trip to Colorado.

North of Durango you find Tamarron, a four-season resort 18 miles from town on U.S. Highway 550, with an unparalleled conference center. It has all of the usual amenities of a resort, with athletic facilities and spa, as well as snowmobiling, jeep tours, ice fishing, indoor tennis, rafting, and its crown jewel, the 18-hole championship golf course that is open only to guests of the resort.

Farther north on Highway 550 is the Purgatory Ski Area. (See "Ski and Summer Resorts" chapter for its description.) One item of note: Purgatory has an Alpine slide that is a prime attraction in the summer months.

The San Juan Mountains on the north offer the best in fishing, hiking, and hunting in season.

To the east of Durango, another four-season resort has made the town of Pagosa Springs a destination resort: Fairfield's Pagosa. It is a complete resort, with everything from fishing to golf, with a full-time tennis pro and cross-country skiing in the winter, and a top-notch spa.

To the south of Pagosa Springs on Colorado Highway 550 is one of Colorado's least-known attractions: Navajo Reservoir. This reservoir, which straddles the New Mexico-Colorado border, is one of the best fishing holes in the state, containing everything from catfish to trout. It's not as famous as Lake Powell, but it should be. It's better fishing.

PRACTICAL INFORMATION FOR

SOUTHERN COLORADO

HOW TO GET THERE AND HOW TO GET AROUND. By air. Colorado's southern half is served by several commuter airlines and has airports capable of handling jets in Colorado Springs, Pueblo, Gunnison, Montrose, and Durango, all served by regularly scheduled service. The major carriers are *Continental* and *Continental Express,* and *United Express.*

By bus. *Greyhound-Trailways* services Colorado along the major routes, I-25, U.S. 285, and U.S. 160. Routes converge in Denver.

By car. Auto travel in Colorado is as varied as the Interstate and the jeep trails that cross the state. In general, Colorado roads are excellent, but passes can be frightening for the first-time driver. Hint: To make time in the summer's tourist crunch, travel after sundown.

Colorado's high passes are subject to closure and vehicles should have chains or adequate snow tires. Weather can be stormy at any time of the year. Road information is available from the Colorado State Patrol, east of I-25: 639–1234; west: 639–1111.

For car rentals, the following is a sample of what's available: **Colorado Springs:** *Dollar,* 303–591–6464; *Economy,* 303–630–7398. **Durango:** *National,* 303–259–0064. **Gunnison:** *Budget,* 303–641–4403; *Hertz,* 800–654–3131. **Montrose:** *Budget,* 303–249–6083; *Dollar,* 303–249–3810. **Pueblo:** *Hertz,* 800–654–3131; *Budget,* 303–948–3363.

HOTELS AND MOTELS. With tourism one of Colorado's biggest industries, accommodations from the most luxurious to the inexpensive are available in each area. There are two high seasons—June through Labor Day and, for those areas near the ski slopes, December through March.

Rates are based on double occupancy, European plan. *Deluxe,* $85–$110; *Expensive,* $75–$84; *Moderate,* $40–$74; *Inexpensive,* under $39.

CANON CITY

Best Western Royal Gorge. *Expensive.* 1925 Fremont; 303–275–3377. Heated pool, restaurant, lounge, trout fishing.

COLORADO SPRINGS

The Antlers. *Deluxe.* In Chase Stone Center, Pikes Peak and Cascade; 303–473–5600. Elegant downtown hotel with traditional service, rooftop pool, several restaurants. Managed by the Broadmoor.

The Broadmoor Resort. *Deluxe to Expensive.* Exit 140B from I-25, south on Nevada to Colorado Highway 122; 303–634–7711. The Broadmoor is a world-class resort with all of the service and amenities that the phrase implies. Tennis, pools, three outstanding 18-hole golf courses, all athletic facilities, bicycle and boat rentals, ice rinks, many restaurants, live entertainment and dancing.

The Clarion Hotel. *Expensive.* 2886 South Circle Dr.; 303–576–5900. Full resort-and-conference hotel with spa and athletic facilities, pool, restaurants.

Colorado Springs Hilton. *Expensive.* 505 Popes Bluff Trail; 303–599–4550. Outdoor pool, restaurant.

Imperial 400 Motor Inn. *Moderate.* 714 N. Nevada Blvd.; 303–636–3385. Downtown. Outdoor heated pool, pleasant rooms.

Motel 6. *Inexpensive.* N. Chestnut at Exit 64 from I-25; 303–520–5400. Clean, minimal lodging.

CRIPPLE CREEK

Imperial Hotel. *Expensive to Moderate.* 123 N. Third St.; 303–689–2713. Restored mining camp queen with antique furnishings. Restaurant, lounge.

FOUR CORNERS

Cortez

Turquoise Motor Inn. *Moderate.* 535 East Main St., west on U.S. 160; 303–565–3778. Best Western, AAA, restaurant, heated pool.

Durango

Tamarron. *Expensive.* 18 miles north of Durango; Box 3131, Durango; 303–247–8801. Four-season resort with spa, health club, golf course, ski area, and full slate of outdoor activities. Also a conference center and restaurants.

Best Western Durango Inn. *Moderate.* U.S. 160W; 247–3251. Cable TV, pool, sauna, restaurant; discount for seniors.

Iron Horse Inn. *Moderate to Inexpensive.* Four miles north of town on U.S. 550, Drawer J; 303–259–1010. Full convention facilities, cable TV.

TraveLodge. *Moderate.* 150 5th St.; 247–0955. Cable TV, heated pool, free coffee. Nearby café.

GUNNISON COUNTRY

Gunnison

Harmel's Ranch Resort. *Deluxe to Moderate.* Taylor River Rd. Box 944A; 641–1740. Scenic spot on river. Lodge, cabins, recreation.

Best Western Tomichi Village. *Moderate.* One mile east of Gunnison on U.S. Hwy. 50.; 303–641–1131. Restaurant, lounge, heated pool, color TV.

Comfort Inn Water Wheel. *Moderate.* Box 882, One and a half miles west of town; 303–641–1650. Adjacent to Gunnison River, Dos Rios Golf course, tennis court, cable TV, rooms and townhouses with cooking facilities.

Super 8 Motel. *Inexpensive.* 701 W. Highway 50; 303–641–0608. Air-conditioning and spa. Package rate available. Café nearby.

Montrose

Best Western Red Arrow Motor Inn. *Moderate.* 1702 E. Main (east edge of town); 303–249–9641. Heated pool, pleasant rooms, fitness center, and restaurant.

San Juan Inn. *Moderate.* 1480 Highway 550 South; 303–249–6644. Newer motel, pleasant rooms, next to restaurant. Indoor pool, hot tub.

PAGOSA SPRINGS

Fairfield Pagosa Resort. *Deluxe to Expensive.* West of Pagosa Springs on U.S. 160, Box 4040, Pagosa Springs; 303–731–4141. A four-season resort with cross-country skiing, fishing, tennis, golf and health spa facilities.

Best Western Oak Ridge Motor Inn. *Moderate.* Downtown near bridge (Box 1799); 303–264–4173. Pool, laundry, restaurant. Nearby mineral baths. Ski packages.

PUEBLO

Holiday Inn. *Moderate.* 4001 N. Elizabeth; 303–543–8050. Enclosed pool. Newly remodeled. Restaurant.

Pueblo West Inn. *Moderate.* 201 S. McCulloch Blvd., Pueblo West; 303–547–2111. First-class Best Western motor inn that is part of a resort complex which includes an 18-hole golf course of tournament quality, two tennis courts, heated pool, restaurant, lounge.

SAN LUIS VALLEY

Alamosa

Alamosa Inn (Best Western). *Moderate.* 1919 Main St., west edge of town; 303–589–2567. Restaurant, indoor pool.

Holiday Inn. *Moderate.* 333 Santa Fe Ave., U.S. Highway 160, east edge of town; 303–589–5833. Restaurant, lounge, and domed indoor recreation center.

Walsh Hotel. *Inexpensive.* 617 6th St.; 303–589–6641. Small hotel. Friendly.

Monte Vista

Kelloff's Movie Manor. *Moderate.* 2830 W. U.S. 160 (west of town); 303–852–5921. Best Western. Restaurant and lounge. Nearby drive-in theater. Private air strip.

South Fork

Wolf Creek Ski Lodge. *Moderate.* Box 283, South Fork, west edge of town on U.S. Highway 160; 303–873–5547. Hot tubs, cable TV, ski lockers.

TRINIDAD

Best Western Country Club Inn. *Moderate.* I–25, Exit 13A; 303–846–2215. Restaurant, pool, horse corral, laundry, tennis, and golf. Near historic district.

Trinidad Motor Inn. *Moderate.* 702 W. Main St.; 303–846–2271. Restaurant, heated pool, cable TV, lounge, 60 units.

GUEST RANCHES. For information on the guest and dude ranches in southern Colorado, write *Colorado Guest and Dude Ranch Association,* Box 300, Tabernash, CO 80478. In particular, you might want to look into the *Don K Ranch,* 2677 S. Siloam Rd., Pueblo, CO 81004; 303–784–6600. Here you can visit a small ghost town and explore the San Isabel Forest and the Sangre de Cristo Range while enjoying good food, a heated pool, and cocktail lounge. Children's counselors available. *Lost Valley Guest Ranch* is 54 miles northwest of Colorado Springs; Rte. 2, Sedalia; 647–2311.

CAMPING. The great outdoors lures the visitor to camp out, and the national forests are the place to do it. Each of the forests in the region has numerous camping facilities, usually consisting of around 20 camping sites, with a picnic table and firepit at each site. Each area has pump water and outhouses. No electricity. All on a first-come, first-serve basis. (See also "National Parklands and Monuments," below.)

For more developed sites, the KOA chain offers the best choice with campgrounds in Gunnison, Pagosa Springs, Del Norte, Ouray, Montrose, Durango, Canon City, Alamosa, Cortez, Castle Rock, and two in Pueblo. Most have hookups and showers and several have pools and game rooms.

TOURIST INFORMATION. *Southern Colorado Tourism Council,* Box 697, Pueblo, CO 81002. Very helpful chambers of commerce can be found in *Alamosa:* Cole Park, Alamosa, CO 81101, 303–589–6531; *Durango:*

2301 N. Main, Durango, CO 81301, 303–247–0312; *Gunnison:* 500 E. Tomichi Ave., Gunnison, CO 81230, 303–641–1501.

SPECIAL-INTEREST TOURS AND SIGHTSEEING. In Ouray, the *Bachelor Syracuse Mine* offers tours 3,350 feet into Gold Hill: 325–4500.

The *Cripple Creek and Victor Railroad* gives riders a four-mile trip through the mining country of the area. Catch the train at the Cripple Creek depot, Memorial Day–Labor Day; 689–2640.

The *Cumbres and Toltec Scenic Railway.* A narrow-gauge line at the south end of the San Luis Valley, once designed to reach Mexico. It takes riders on a spectacular trip to the summit of Cumbres Pass. Catch it at the Antonito depot, one mile south of town, Hwy. 285. Call 376–5483 for reservations.

Of no less a spectacular nature is the National Park Service's *boat tours of the Gunnison Gorge.* These trips take a half-day, and leave from the western end of Blue Mesa Reservoir. Trip reservations are obtained by calling the Elk Creek Marina: 642–0707.

At the 1,200-foot-deep chasm, *Royal Gorge,* visitors can ride an *incline railway* into the gorge, a *narrow-gauge train* around the rim, or an *aerial tram* across the canyon. Royal Gorge is 50 miles southwest of Colorado Springs on Highway 115 and U.S. 50. For information call 275–7507.

One of the most scenic tours in the region is the guide-driven *San Juan Jeep Tours* out of Ouray. Leaving from the center of town, these all-day or half-day tours take passengers up the legendary jeep roads and around the mines of the high San Juans. 325–4444.

Silverton Railway. A breathtaking trip through mountain canyons from Durango to the mining town of Silverton, set in the high San Juan Mountains. Catch it at the Durango depot, 479 Main St. Call for reservations, 247–2733.

A cable car climbs a 1¼-mile incline to the summit of *Pikes Peak* from 518 Ruxton, Manitou Springs. Call 685–9086.

The *United States Air Force Academy,* 10 miles north of Colorado Springs on I-25, welcomes tourists all year (303–472–2555). The Visitors' Center provides details on exhibits, films, parades, and activities (all gratis). The roads through the 18,000-acre academy grounds are open during daylight hours. Just before noon, the cadets assemble outdoors and march in formation to the dining hall for lunch. This military parade is a worthwhile sight. At the end of May, you may see the academy's graduating ceremonies.

SEASONAL EVENTS. January is the month for the *Pagosa Snowmobile Classic* race. Pueblo's *Mozart Festival,* and Durango's *Snowdown Winter Carnival.* **February** brings *Winter Fest* to Pagosa Springs. During **March,** the *U.S. National Men's Curling Championships* are held at the World Arena, Colorado Springs. In **May,** Canon City holds its *Blossom Festival.* Durango celebrates *Narrow-Gauge Days* with a festival and bike race from Durango to Silverton. **June** begins *melodrama* productions in Cripple Creek and Durango. It's also the time of the *Colorado Renaissance Festival,* Larkspur, where the Middle Ages are revived in a mountain setting. Alamosa holds its *Sunshine Festival* and *Roundup Rodeo;* between Creede and South Fork are the *Rio Grande River Raft Races; Donkey Derby Days* in Cripple Creek. **July** Fourth is time for the *Pikes Peak Hill Climb.* The *Broadmoor International Theater* season begins (running through August) at the Broadmoor Hotel in Colorado Springs; name entertainers appear. The *Pikes Peak or Bust Rodeo* is held in **August** in Colorado Springs. Durango hosts the *Navajo Trail Fiesta*. Late August is time for the *Colorado State Fair* in Pueblo: top entertainment, including rodeo; many say this is the best fair in the state. Gunnison holds *windsurfing championships* at Blue Mesa Reservoir. *Ice skating* competitions at the Broadmoor World Ice Arena. **October** and *big-game hunting season* begins; Alamosa holds the *Valley Rally* balloon races. In **December,** the *Hockey Season* opens at the World Arena, Colorado Springs. **December** 31 is the date of the Ad-a-Man Club's *climb to the summit of Pikes Peak;* from here they set off a spectacular *fireworks display* to ring in the new year.

NATIONAL PARKLANDS AND MONUMENTS. We list national forests here for your general information, but be advised that these are actually just administrative units. Recreation such as hunting, fishing, and hiking are available, but unlike activities at national monuments and recreation areas, few are planned. Camping is all on a first-come, first-serve basis.

If you follow the Gunnison River for about 30 miles east of Montrose, you will reach the **Curecanti National Recreation Area,** comprised of three reservoirs—Blue Mesa, Morrow Point, and Crystal. Blue Mesa Lake, 20 miles long, offers three campgrounds (no reservations), boat ramps, and water sports. A marina has rental boats and equipment for fishing and waterskiing. Shore fishing for rainbow trout is best in early spring and late fall. Fishing is regulated by state laws. Be sure you have a current license. Call 303–641–0707 for information. The National Park Service offers boat tours of Gunnison Gorge; see "Special-Interest Tours and Sightseeing," above.

Florissant Fossil Beds National Monument, 35 miles west of Colorado Springs on U.S. 24, is a 6,000-acre site once covered by a prehistoric lake. A museum and interpretive center are on the grounds—some of the finest fossils have been found here. Open daily; 748–3253.

Great Sand Dunes National Monument, located on State 150, 31 miles northeast of Alamosa, contains the highest naturally formed sand piles in the United States, some exceeding a height of 800 feet above the valley floor. The constant pressure of the wind sculpts the finely pulverized sand into a wonderland of hills, valleys, and plains. During the day the dunes can be visible for 70 miles, radiating a rosy warmth of sun on hot sand. The color and mood shift with the angle of the sun, as lengthening shadows change the dunes to violet and mauve. The dunes also produce some of the greatest lightning displays in America: the combination of wind and heat rising from the 55 square miles of sand creates titanic thunderstorms accompanied by extraordinary lightning bolts. The Visitors' Center contains history and information on the area (call 378–2312); campsites (no reservations; closed Dec.–March) and picnic grounds are available, and a nature trail is marked for hikers.

Gunnison National Forest. 1.7 million acres. Facilities are rare, though there are around 60 campsites. Hunting, fishing, and hiking are all popular. Write to Supervisor; 2250 Highway 50, Delta, CO 81416.

The Black Canyon of the **Gunnison National Monument** is 13,672 acres of the deepest, darkest, wildest, and rockiest piece of real estate you will probably ever see. The Gunnison River has cut a narrow gorge, at times only 40 feet wide, through nearly solid granite, to depths ranging from 1,730 feet to 2,725 feet. From the higher elevations it is possible to see the frothing white water below against a background of sunlight reflected from pink mica in the otherwise black walls. Legend has it that the canyon is so dark and narrow at the bottom that it is possible in broad daylight to see the stars by looking straight up. Well-organized boat trips down the river and descents on Indian trails may be taken (see "Sports," below), but only experienced climbers should attempt any other route down the canyon. Some of the best fishing in Colorado is to be found on the Gunnison. The North Rim of the canyon is reached by a gravel road east of Crawford on State 92. The South Rim is reached by US 50 to Montrose and then State Road 347 six miles east. Park rangers have nightly programs during the summer. Campsites and picnic areas are available. South Rim is open daily; North Rim is closed in winter by snow. Campsites on a first-come, first-serve basis. For information call 240–6522.

Hovenweep National Monument is reached by a gravel park road 18 miles north of Cortez, off State 666. The monument is a series of long-abandoned Pueblo settlements that punctuate the barren land and extend into southern Utah. The prehistoric buildings, evidently built by a people similar to those who built Mesa Verde, are open for inspection. A ranger is on duty at Square Tower. Campsites and picnic areas are available, first-come, first-serve. In rainy or snowy weather, check in Cortez before attempting the dirt road. Call 529–4461.

Mesa Verde National Park will doubtlessly impress the traveler. The ruins of these cliff dwellings tell us of a prehistoric civilization from nearly 1,000 years before the American Revolution.

It is believed that about 800 years ago, land overuse, timber depletion, and overhunting forced the tribes that built Mesa Verde to leave their plateau for an area more favorable to them. Archaeologists and national park experts speculate that Mesa Verde's early inhabitants—now known as the *Anasazi*—were pueblo people. *Mesa Verde* ("Green Tabletop") describes the general topography of the surface of the park, not the caves and canyons below. There are three general types of ruins open for inspection. The *pithouses* are shallow holes in the ground, usually covered with straw or grass roofs, which were inhabited by one family. The pueblos form a village around the *kiva,* which was used for religious ceremonies. The *cliff dwellings* were built much later and offered excellent protection to their inhabitants. The *Cliff Palace* was built 200 feet off the canyon floor and contains some 200 rooms. The *Spruce Tree House* is relatively easy to enter and remains one of the best preserved. It has 114 rooms and eight *kivas* and is not unlike today's apartment houses. No one may enter the fragile cliff dwellings unless accompanied by a park ranger.

The museum at Park Headquarters (529–4465) will add to the visitor's understanding of Mesa Verde and its people. The park may be reached by car on US 160, 10 miles east of Cortez. Bus service from Spruce Tree Lodge is available for those who do not wish to drive their cars into the park. The Park includes a restaurant, service station, AAA road service, and tire agency. Evening campfire talks are given by park rangers and archeologists.

The park is open daily, although the Wetherill Ruins, a separate group, and Far View Visitor Center, are open summers only.

Pike National Forest. 77 camping sites, and picnic areas. Write: 3417 N. Elizabeth St., Pueblo, CO 81002; 542–1742.

Rio Grande National Forest. 1.8 million acres with campsites available. Write headquarters at 1803 W. Hwy. 160, Monte Vista, CO 81144. Within is the **Wheeler Geologic Area,** soon to be a national monument. Unique geologic formations nestled in the San Juans; accessible by four-wheel drive or on foot.

San Miquel National Forest. For information write Box 210, Dolores, CO 81323; 882–7296.

Uncompahgre National Forest. One million acres. Headquarters at Gunnison (see above).

San Isabel National Forest. 1,107,000 acres. 3417 N. Elizabeth St., Pueblo, CO 81002.

San Juan National Forest. Contact Supervisor, Federal Bldg., 701 Camino del Rio, Durango, CO 81301; 247–4847.

OTHER NATURAL WONDERS Cave of the Winds. Past Manitou Springs off U.S. 24, atop Serpentine Drive. Breathtakingly beautiful natural cave formations. Forty-five-minute guided tours four times each hour, every day. For information call, 685–5444.

The Garden of the Gods is a world-renowned area consisting of more than two miles of paved roads that meander among towering red sandstone cliffs, balanced rocks, and other dramatic formations. Once sacred ground to natives, the 940-acre park was donated to the city in 1918 by private owners. There are hiking trails. The trading post offers refreshments and telescopes. Three miles northwest of Colorado Springs on Garden of the Gods Rd., off US 24.

14,110-foot-high **Pikes Peak** towers above Colorado Springs. You have several options to reach the summit: you can drive; just follow US 24 west on Colorado Avenue. It takes about four hours to make the mountaintop that way. (A toll gate will exact a fee from you.) For nondrivers, a Swiss cog railway climbs the summit in about three hours from a depot in Manitou Springs, 515 Ruxton. Season is May through early October. (High tariff for adults, reasonable fares for children. Call 685–5401.) The winter snows usually close down part of the famous mountain highway.

Near Colorado Springs, **Seven Falls** cascade 300 feet through a deep canyon. The entire area is beautifully lit at night and at Christmas; to find the Seven Falls, simply follow the South Cheyenne Canyon Road.

ZOOS. *Cheyenne Mountain Zoo.* Above the Broadmoor on Cheyenne Mountain Road, Colorado Springs; 475–9555. Open daily 9 A.M.–4:30 P.M.; adults $4, children $2. There are over 800 animals here: giraffes, bears, elk, deer, penguins, among others. *Pueblo Zoological Park,* on Thatcher Blvd., Pueblo City park; 561–8686. Birds, mammals, reptiles, and a miniature ranch with baby animals. Open daily.

PARTICIPANT SPORTS. Southern Colorado is the home of getting-out-and-doing, with everything from some of the best fishing, hunting, and hiking available to golf, tennis, rafting, and other outdoor sports.

Fishing. Colorado's streams and lakes are open to fishing year-round, with only some local closures for spawning purposes. Year-round fishing can be inexpensively enjoyed by vistors by obtaining one of several types of fishing licenses available to an out-of-state resident. (See "Facts at Your Fingertips.") Fishing on private property requires no license, and many of the resorts maintain lakes and streams for their guests.

Colorado is mostly known for its high mountain trout fishing, but the lakes in the southern part of the state have many warm-water varieties of fish as well, notably bass and catfish at Navajo Reservoir and walleye at Sanchez Reservoir.

In the winter, the Blue Mesa Reservoir is the mecca of ice fishermen, with the Pinnacles and Iola Basin areas the most popular spots for the cold-footers.

Trout fishing on the Conejos, South Fork, Las Animas, Gunnison, or any of the other rivers is famous worldwide; and the popularity of fishing has led to a "Gold Medal" waters concept for several streams. The Wild Life Commission sets bags and size limits, or restricts fishing on these waters to lures and artificial flies only, to encourage growth of the trophy-fish that is the goal of most fishermen.

One of the truly special experiences in Colorado fishing is the fishing-float trips on the Gunnison River. With an experienced outfit, such as *Double Haul Float Trips* out of Montrose (719 South Sixth St., 303–249–3323), a sightseeing and fishing journey through the Gunnison Gorge is an experience that fishermen usually only dream of. Double Haul takes the fly-fisherman down to the bottom of the Gunnison gorge for a 13-mile raft excursion for fishing and guide-prepared meals little short of gourmet.

Trips are available by reservation only, though limited day excursions are available. The season runs from June through September, depending on water conditions.

Local Colorado newspapers publish the Division of Wildlife "Fishing Report" in the Wednesday or Thursday editions, and these reports run down the current conditions on every stream and lake in the region.

Golf. Although Colorado has been known more for rodeo than golf in the past, it's becoming a mecca for the championship-class golf courses located in the mountains. The winter resorts are finding that the summer tourists bring their clubs and want to tee off into the Alpine sunset.

Leading the pack are the fabulous resort courses of the *Broadmoor* (Colorado Springs), *Tamarron* (Durango), *Pueblo West* and *Fairfield-Pagosa Resort*.

The Broadmoor is rightly the most famous with three championship courses. Open to guests of the Broadmoor and the Antlers Hotel, the three courses that comprise the Broodmoor, are a blend of the great "old" feeling of the 1918 Donald Ross course and the new challenge of the Arnold Palmer organization south course. Stay at the Broadmoor just to play these courses; 634–7711.

At Tamarron, 18 miles north of Durango, the feeling is that of a manicured haven surrounded by the mountainous San Juans. The 6,400-yard course has a bit of everything in an almost-wild setting. Open to guests of the Tamarron Resort; 247–8801.

Pueblo West at the Best Western is a long, 6,975-yard 18-hole challenge tucked away off the beaten track in Pueblo West. Full of interesting and sneaky traps, the course is well worth a detour for a day of play; 547–2280. Open to the public.

Pagosa Pines at the Pagosa-Fairfield resort has one of the best views in the state of Colorado along the southern rim of the San Juans. It's a challenging and enjoyable course, with many high tee boxes that make your ball seem to fly forever. Now open only to guests of the Pagosa-Fairfield, it is well worth a trip to Pagosa Springs to play the 6,124-yard course; 731–4141.

Try the new *Cuchara Valley Course,* an 18-hole gem designed by Tom Weiskopf. It promises to be another jewel in the expanding diadem of the Cuchara Valley.

Yet not to be forgotten are the municipals of the area, such as Colorado Springs' *Patty Jewett,* the oldest-surviving golf course in Colorado, 578–6825, or Alamosa's beautiful little nine-hole course, 589–2260. Other gems are Pueblo's *Municipal,* 561–4946, Gunnison's sensational *Dos Rios,* 641–1482, and courses in Salida, 539–6373, La Junta, 384–7133, Cortez, 565–9208, Durango, 247–1499, Monte Vista, 852–4906, Montrose, 249–2176, Walsenburg, 738–2730, Grandote (near South La Veta, Highway 12), 742–3123, and Trinidad, 846–9954.

Hikers and climbers are blessed with thousands of square miles of national forest and park to chose from. The best advice is to inquire locally and consult the U.S. Geologic survey topographic series maps for trails and conditions.

Hunting. Colorado's big game herds are famous and draw nimrods from around the west for the annual harvest of deer, elk, and antelope. All big-game hunting in Colorado, whether on private land or national forest, is governed by the Colorado Wildlife Comission, and all hunting season and other regulations are set by that body. (See "Facts at Your Fingertips.")

Colorado's big game season is the fall. Starting in late August with special limited seasons for archery and black powder, Colorado seasons climax with the late October "separate" seasons for elk and deer, usually separated by a few days. Then they finish off with a "combined season" in early November. Exact season dates vary from year to year and are usually set by the Wildlife Commission in its June meeting.

Skiing. Southern Colorado has several of the famous destination-class skiing resorts that are nationally known, such as Crested Butte, Telluride, and Purgatory (*see* Ski and Summer Resorts section), but it also has several smaller areas that offer some of the best of Colorado's skiing.

Wolf Creek, near the summit of the pass of the same name on U.S. Highway 160, is the powder hound's heaven. It receives, by far, the most snow of any Colorado area, with an annual average of 415 inches.

You can always expect great conditions, small crowds, five lifts (three chairs, two pomas) and a 8,000-square-foot base lodge at the area. Open from November to May. 303–731–5605.

Monarch is located on U.S. Highway 50 near the summit of Monarch Pass. It is a small four-season resort with horseback riding, rafting, hiking, tennis, and raquetball nearby. The ski area has four double chair lifts spread over a wide-variety of terrain and a lounge, rentals, and food service is at the base.

Monarch also offers a full cross-country area at the Madonna Mine, just east of the area, with rentals, pre-set trail, and instruction. Open Thankgiving to April. In state 800–332–3668; out-state 800–525–9390.

A favorite of locals is *Conquistador;* located in the Wet Mountain Valley near Westcliffe on Colorado Highway 96.

With a triple chair and one double and two pony lifts, Conquistador has a blend of 25 percent expert, 55 percent intermediate, and 20 percent beginner that make it a nice family place to ski. Open late November to April. 303–783–9206.

Cross-country skiing. With the good snow fall in Southern Colorado (the local joke is nine months snow, three months poor sledding), cross-country skiers are everywhere.

Of particular note for the traveler are the several cross-country areas that have set and maintained trails, rentals, and instruction: *Purgatory, Telluride,* (see "Ski and Summer Resorts") *Pagosa Springs-Fairfield, Monarch,* (see above) and *Cumbres Pass.*

Pagosa Springs-Fairfield offers trails, instruction, and rental, but in a broad valley near Pagosa Springs.

Cumbres Pass, which is Colorado Highway 17 west of Antonito, is the least developed of the areas. With rentals and some set track at the Conejos Ranch (303–376–5457), Cumbres Pass is nothing more than a state highway that's closed in the winter—which makes it an ideal trail for snowmobiling, cross-country skiing, and snowshoeing. An annual citizen's race in March highlights the ski-touring year.

Other popular areas for ski-touring include Florissant National Monument near Colorado Springs (see "National Parklands and Monuments"), Crested Butte, Vista Valley Ski Ranch near Steamboat (303–879–3858), Vail Cross Country Ski Center (303–476–3239), Frisco Nordic Center (303–668–0866), and C Lazy U Ranch near Granby (303–887–3344).

Tennis is available everywhere, with two resort centers with professional instruction at Tamarron and Pagosa-Fairfield. Numerous municipal courts abound. Check phone books.

One more unusual sport is **sailplaning**—with the *Black Forest Glider Port* north of Colorado Springs a center. For reservations call 495–2436.

SPECTATOR SPORTS. Colorado is **rodeo** country, and every month of the summer offers a good one. See "Seasonal Events."

For **football** fans, the *United States Air Force Academy* plays a major-college slate as a member of the Western Athletic Conference, while *Adams State College,* Alamosa, and *Ft. Lewis College* in Durango play tough small-college ball as members of the Rocky Mountain Athletic Conference. *Colorado College* **Hockey** *and Football* in Colorado Springs.

Other attractions for the fan are the pari-mutuel **dog races** at *Pueblo Greyhound Park,* 556–0370.

HISTORIC SITES. (Also see "Museums," below.) The *Baca and Bloom Houses* on Main Street, Trinidad, invoke memories of the past. Felipe Baca was a Spanish rancher, who built his home here in 1869. Pioneer Frank Bloom was a rancher, cattleman, and banker. Of particular interest is the Victorian Rose Garden of the Bloom mansion. Call 846–7217; open 10 A.M.–4 P.M. Memorial Day to Labor Day.

Bent's Fort. The old trading post built on this site (8 miles east of La Junta on Hwy. 194) in the 1850s has been restored. Builders used sketches made by early travelers when Bent's Fort was a place for Indians and trappers to exchange furs and pelts for supplies, tools, cloth, and other goods. Shops, refreshments, and tourist information available. 8 A.M.–6 P.M. daily; 384–2596.

Fort Garland. On U.S. Highway 160, west of La Veta, at foot of La Veta Pass. This is a restored adobe military outpost built in 1859 and once commanded by Kit Carson. Open daily during summer daylight.

Imperial Hotel. 123 North Third St., Cripple Creek; 689–2713. Built in 1896 when this mining town was the "promised land." The decor is authentic 1890s elegance. Rooms are available; see "Hotels and Motels," above.

MUSEUMS. (See also "Historic Sites," above.) The museums in **Colorado Springs** are numerous:

Begin with the *Pro Rodeo Hall of Champions* honoring the history of rodeo and its stars. Located off of I-25 in northern Colorado Springs (exit 147; 101 Pro Rodeo Dr.). Open daily in the summer; 9 A.M.–5 P.M. 593–8840.

The *Wildlife World Museum,* with an extensive collection of taxidermy, sculpture, and paintings of rare and trophy wildlife displayed. Located 14 miles north of town, exit 161 from I-15. Open daily; 9:30 A.M.–5 P.M. weekdays; from 10 A.M. weekends. 488–2460.

The *Hall of President's Living Wax Studio,* U.S. Highway 24 and 21st St., is akin to Madam Tussaud's. Open daily 10 A.M.–5 P.M. 635–3553.

The *National Carvers Museum,* I-25 at exit 158, exhibits over 3,000 woodcarvings from across the United States. Open Daily 9 A.M.–5 P.M. 481–2656.

The *May Natural History Museum,* nine miles south of town on Nevada Avenue, offers rare specimens from the jungles of the world. Open daily, mid-May to Labor Day. 576–0450.

The *Pioneers' Museum,* 215 S. Tejon St., features local history displays and assorted memorabilia from the early days of Colorado Springs. Open daily except Monday and holidays. 10 A.M.–5 P.M., Tues.–Sat.; Sun. 2–5 P.M. 578–6650.

The *Colorado Springs Fine Arts Center,* 30 West Dale St., shows contemporary painting and special exhibits. Open daily except Monday. Tues.–Sat. 10 A.M.–5 P.M., Sun. 1:30–5 P.M. 634–5581.

The *Western Museum of Mining and Industry,* I-25 at exit 156A, is dedicated to the hard rock miners. Ore samples, demonstrations. Open daily 9 A.M.–4:30 P.M. 598–8850.

Will Rogers Shrine, Cheyenne Mountain Highway. A 100-foot granite tower built by a friend of the famed American humorist. Photos, murals, and other memorabilia. This is a popular scenic overlook. Toll road. 475–9555.

BEYOND COLORADO SPRINGS

County Courthouse, Ouray. A suberb collection of art housed in a classic Victorian building. Mon.–Fri. 8 A.M.–5 P.M. 325–4405.

County Museum. 420 Sixth Ave., Ouray. Once the local hospital, this is now an excellent museum of Ouray's mining history. Open summers.

Cripple Creek Mining District Museum, Cripple Creek. Housed in the once-busy railroad terminal, this museum features displays of the past of the frontier towns of the regions: the overnight millionaires, those who lost everything, the violent labor struggles. 9 A.M.–5 P.M., summers. 689–2634.

Francisco Fort Museum. La Veta. Exhibits on the early days of the Cuchara Valley. Open daily summers.

Kit Carson Museum. Las Animas. Here are displayed mementoes of the famous mountain man, soldier, and governor. Opens Memorial Day. 456–2005.

Montrose County Museum. 11 N. First, Montrose. Located in the old depot this museum tells of this area's past with an extensive collection of farm implements and vehicles. Open summer months only. 249–1915.

El Pueblo Museum. 905 S. Prairie, Pueblo. An excellent museum on local history. Open summers. 564–5274.

Ute Indian Museum. 17253 Chipeta Rd., south of Montrose on U.S. Highway 550. This is considered one of the best museums in Colorado with a large collection of artifacts of the Ute tribe. Open summers only. 249–3098.

CULTURAL ACTIVITIES. *Creede Repertory Theater.* Creede. Five plays every summer—comedy, drama, revivals of the Victorian era in revolving repertory. 658–2540. *Sangre de Cristo Fine Arts and Conference Center,* Third St. and Santa Fe, Pueblo. The cultural center of southern Colorado. Theatrical performances, concerts, and exhibits year-round. 543–0130.

DINING OUT. Traveling and eating in southern Colorado can be a treat. With its special mixed heritage, good Mexican food is found almost everywhere, and good restaurants abound.

Most of the lodgings listed under "Hotels and Motels" have restaurants attached to them or nearby. A full meal at a *Deluxe* establishment costs $20 and up; an *Expensive* restaurant (exclusive of drinks, tax, tip) will run $16–$19; *Moderate,* $10–$15; *Inexpensive,* under $10. Most establishments accept major credit cards, but it's wise to double-check in advance.

CANON CITY

Salis. *Expensive.* 807 Cyanide Ave. 275–7221. Nouvelle cuisine; patio dining.

Mr. Ed's Family Restaurant. *Moderate.* 1201 Royal Gorge Blvd.; 275–5833. Standard fare in a relaxed atmosphere.

COLORADO SPRINGS

Broadmoor Hotel Dining Rooms. *Deluxe to Moderate.* In the Broadmoor Hotel; 634–7711. There are a number of fine restaurants in this complex: the Broadmoor Tavern; the Main Dining Room; the elegant Charles Court; the Penrose Dining Room and the Golden Bee, an English Pub of the 19th century that was brought over and rebuilt. The Penrose Room is a superbly managed gourmet restaurant with elegant appointments, view of the Cheyenne Mountain. International cuisine: noisettes of veal with chanterelles, osso bucco Milanese, Wiener schnitzel, filet mignon, fresh poached salmon, rack of lamb. Delicious appetizers and desserts. Nightly dancing to old-fashioned music.

The London Grill. *Expensive.* Pikes Peak and Cascade at the Antlers Hotel; 473–5600. Well-known gourmet outpost. Excellent meats and fresh fish. Tableside cooking, elegant atmosphere, Sunday brunch.

The Three Thieves Steakhouse. *Moderate.* 3835 N. Academy; 596–3513. Steak and seafood in a casual setting, good value. Open seven days a week.

Flying W Ranch. *Inexpensive.* 3330 Chuckwagon Rd.; 598–4000. Winter steak house and summer chuckwagon suppers. Western entertainment. Reservations necessary.

GUNNISON COUNTRY

Glenn Eyrie. *Expensive.* Highway 50 South, Montrose; 249–9263. Noted restaurant with superb staff and menu. Chef's choice always a winner.

The Trough. *Moderate.* 1½ miles west of Gunnison, Highway 50; 303–641–0019. Steak, seafood, and libations.

Mario's. *Inexpensive.* 213 W. Tomichi Ave., Gunnison; 641–1374. Italian specialties and sandwiches.

PUEBLO

La Renaissance. *Moderate.* 217 E. Routt Ave.; 543–6367. Casual and relaxed dining in the unique atmosphere of an old church.

Furr's Cafeteria. *Inexpensive.* 1101 Bonforte Blvd.; 303–544–9473. Convenient dining and over 100 dishes prepared daily. No credit cards.

SAN LUIS VALLEY

Lara's Soft-Spoken Restaurant. *Moderate.* 801 State Ave., Alamosa; 589–6769. Family-run restaurant with varied menu.

Monte Villa Inn. *Moderate.* 921 1st Ave., Monte Vista; 852–5166. Salad bar, shrimp specialties, Mexican-American food, baked goods. Early American decor.

TRINIDAD

Country Club Inn. *Moderate.* Exit 13A, I–25; 303–846–2215. Luncheon buffet. American dinners.

El Capitan. *Inexpensive.* 321 State St.; Trinidad; 846–9903. Mexican-American fare and sandwiches. Full bar.

Index

General Information and Facts at Your Fingertips

Geographical and Practical Information

(The letter H indicates hotels, motels, and other accommodations. The letter R indicates restaurants.)

Fodor's Travel Guides

U.S. Guides

Alaska
American Cities
The American South
Arizona
Atlantic City & the
  New Jersey Shore
Boston
California
Cape Cod
Carolinas & the
  Georgia Coast
Chesapeake
Chicago
Colorado
Dallas & Fort Worth
Disney World & the
  Orlando Area

The Far West
Florida
Greater Miami,
  Fort Lauderdale,
  Palm Beach
Hawaii
Hawaii (Great Travel
  Values)
Houston & Galveston
I-10: California to
  Florida
I-55: Chicago to New
  Orleans
I-75: Michigan to
  Florida
I-80: San Francisco to
  New York

I-95: Maine to Miami
Las Vegas
Los Angeles, Orange
  County, Palm Springs
Maui
New England
New Mexico
New Orleans
New Orleans (Pocket
  Guide)
New York City
New York City (Pocket
  Guide)
New York State
Pacific North Coast
Philadelphia
Puerto Rico (Fun in)

Rockies
San Diego
San Francisco
San Francisco (Pocket
  Guide)
Texas
United States of
  America
Virgin Islands
  (U.S. & British)
Virginia
Waikiki
Washington, DC
Williamsburg,
  Jamestown &
  Yorktown

Foreign Guides

Acapulco
Amsterdam
Australia, New Zealand
  & the South Pacific
Austria
The Bahamas
The Bahamas (Pocket
  Guide)
Barbados (Fun in)
Beijing, Guangzhou &
  Shanghai
Belgium & Luxembourg
Bermuda
Brazil
Britain (Great Travel
  Values)
Canada
Canada (Great Travel
  Values)
Canada's Maritime
  Provinces
Cancún, Cozumel,
  Mérida, The
  Yucatán
Caribbean
Caribbean (Great
  Travel Values)

Central America
Copenhagen,
  Stockholm, Oslo,
  Helsinki, Reykjavik
Eastern Europe
Egypt
Europe
Europe (Budget)
Florence & Venice
France
France (Great Travel
  Values)
Germany
Germany (Great Travel
  Values)
Great Britain
Greece
Holland
Hong Kong & Macau
Hungary
India
Ireland
Israel
Italy
Italy (Great Travel
  Values)
Jamaica (Fun in)

Japan
Japan (Great Travel
  Values)
Jordan & the Holy Land
Kenya
Korea
Lisbon
Loire Valley
London
London (Pocket Guide)
London (Great Travel
  Values)
Madrid
Mexico
Mexico (Great Travel
  Values)
Mexico City & Acapulco
Mexico's Baja & Puerto
  Vallarta, Mazatlán,
  Manzanillo, Copper
  Canyon
Montreal
Munich
New Zealand
North Africa
Paris
Paris (Pocket Guide)

People's Republic of
  China
Portugal
Province of Quebec
Rio de Janeiro
The Riviera (Fun on)
Rome
St. Martin/St. Maarten
Scandinavia
Scotland
Singapore
South America
South Pacific
Southeast Asia
Soviet Union
Spain
Spain (Great Travel
  Values)
Sweden
Switzerland
Sydney
Tokyo
Toronto
Turkey
Vienna
Yugoslavia

Special-Interest Guides

Bed & Breakfast
  Guide: North America
1936...On the
  Continent

Royalty Watching
Selected Hotels of
  Europe

Selected Resorts
  and Hotels of the U.S.
Ski Resorts of North
  America

Views to Dine by
  around the World